THE DEVELOPMENT
OF MEDICAL LIABILITY

The way the law responds to death or personal injury resulting from medical treatment has changed over time. Expectations of success in medical interventions have risen. Hospitals have become more complex and use more advanced technology. This has had an impact on the liability of medical practitioners, both in generating new problems and in raising standards of expected care. While the focus is civil liability, typically either through contract or tort, this volume of essays also examines compensation systems outside private law. This topic has grown in significance since 1945. The problems encountered by the law are similar across the different jurisdictions, even if the health service arrangements are different. The legal changes are also set against changes in the institutional background, such as the role of the state, the availability of insurance and the professionalisation of medical practitioners.

EWOUD HONDIUS is Professor of Law at the University of Utrecht, the Netherlands.

COMPARATIVE STUDIES IN THE DEVELOPMENT
OF THE LAW OF TORTS IN EUROPE

Series editors
John Bell and David Ibbetson

THE DEVELOPMENT OF MEDICAL LIABILITY

Volume 3

Edited by

EWOUD HONDIUS

CAMBRIDGE
UNIVERSITY PRESS

CAMBRIDGE
UNIVERSITY PRESS

University Printing House, Cambridge CB2 8BS, United Kingdom

Cambridge University Press is part of the University of Cambridge.

It furthers the University's mission by disseminating knowledge in the pursuit of
education, learning and research at the highest international levels of excellence.

www.cambridge.org
Information on this title: www.cambridge.org/9781107475823

© Cambridge University Press 2010

First published 2010

A catalogue record for this publication is available from the British Library

ISBN 978-0-521-11143-0 Hardback
ISBN 978-1-107-47582-3 Paperback

Hardback only available as:
ISBN 978-0-521-19953-7 6-volume set

CONTENTS

Series Editors' Preface　　*page* vii
List of Abbreviations　　ix

1　General introduction　　1
EWOUD HONDIUS

2　The development of medical liability in England and Wales　　27
WARREN SWAIN

3　The development of medical liability in Scotland　　54
NIALL R. WHITTY

4　The development of medical liability and accident compensation in France　　70
SIMON TAYLOR

5　The development of medical liability in Austria　　108
BERNHARD A. KOCH

6　The development of medical liability in the Netherlands　　132
EWOUD HONDIUS

7　The development of medical liability in Spain　　160
MARÍA PAZ GARCÍA RUBIO AND BELÉN TRIGO GARCÍA

Appendix: code provisions　　188
Index　　205

v

PREFACE BY SERIES EDITORS

The European Legal Development series has arisen from a project funded by the AHRC from January 2005 until February 2008.

The aim of the project as a whole was to examine the nature of legal development in Western Europe since 1850, focusing sharply on liability for fault. Behind this there is a more abstract purpose, to attempt to cast some light on the factors which have influenced the way in which the law has changed over this period. Legal historians have looked at the general question, usually focusing on the rather facile distinction between the English common law and continental European legal systems. Though rooted in the sources, these works have been marred by a somewhat unsophisticated methodology and an inevitably selective use of evidence. Comparative lawyers have developed far more sophisticated methodologies, but their theoretical perspectives have too often borne little relation to empirical data. Over the last twenty years, tort lawyers have looked at the same types of question; but their analysis has invariably been at a high level of generality and has rarely looked at the historical component. By bringing together experts with different disciplinary backgrounds – comparative lawyers and legal historians, all with an understanding of modern tort law in their own systems – and getting them to work collaboratively, we have aimed to produce a more nuanced comparative legal history, and one which is theoretically better informed.

The topic of legal development is broad and, to make it manageable, we have undertaken a programme of work which has built up from a number of case studies and has moved towards a more general analysis and conclusions. Although we have been concerned with the development of the law, and although many of those involved in the project have been lawyers, we have also been concerned to include and benefit from the insights of historians and scholars in other disciplines.

Liability for fault between 1850 to 2000 has been our major area of study. Around 1850, there were many similarities in approaches to liability for fault across the legal systems of Western Europe. But since then, there has been significant divergence. Our method has been first to chart the changes and then to seek the explanations for what happened. Although there have been many changes in tort and delict laws over the period, the idea of liability for fault remains central to private law approaches to the compensation of victims of harms caused by the actions of others.

As a first stage, the project worked on six Case Studies which illustrate the general theme of liability for fault and its development within the period:

Product Liability
Legal Doctrine
Medical Liability
Relations between Neighbours
Technological Change
Traffic and Railways

This research involved scholars from a range of countries, in particular, England and Scotland, Spain, the Netherlands, Germany, France, Sweden, Austria and Italy. Each working group drew on the expertise of both senior and more junior scholars familiar with different European legal systems, and contained a mixture of comparative lawyers and legal historians.

A second stage has involved further groups examining a number of salient factors in legal development. The topics covered in this stage are:

Institutions and Professions
Social and Political Ideas
The Economy (including the impact of insurance)
A final strand to the work is an overview book.

This book, edited by Ewoud Hondius, provides us with a good example of the benefits of this approach. We gain a clear insight into the way in which a relatively new area of tort liability arose, and the interactions between legal systems in a period of greater professionalisation in medicine and increase in technical sophistication as well as the complexity of the bodies delivering medical care. The factors for legal development identified in this book are ones which will be developed in later volumes.

Particularly in relation to this book, the editors are grateful to the contribution of Colm McGrath, PhD student on the AHRC project, who made a significant contribution to the formulation, discussion and execution of this part of the project. His own work on this topic in relation to German law will be published separately and will complement significantly the understanding of this area presented in this book.

John Bell
David Ibbetson

ABBREVIATIONS

ABGB	*Allgemeines Bürgerliches Gesetzbuch*
ADEPA	*Asociación El Defensor del Paciente*
ADR	Alternative Dispute Resolution
AJDA	*Actualité Juridique – Droit Administratif*
ANAES	*Agence nationale d'accréditation et d'évaluation en santé*
AnwBl	*Anwaltsblatt*
ÄrzteG	*Ärztegesetz*
Asp	Act of the Scottish Parliament
AVMA	Action for Victims of Medical Accidents
BGBl	*Bundesgesetzblatt*
BGH	Bundesgerichtshof
BMA	British Medical Association
BMJ	*British Medical Journal*
BOE	*Boletín Oficial del Estado*
Bull. civ.	*Bulletin de la Cour de cassation, civil*
BW	*Burgerlijk Wetboek*
CAA	*Cour administrative d'appel*
Cass. Ass. Plén.	*Cour de cassation, Assemblée plénière*
Cass. civ.	*Cour de cassation, chambre civile*
Cass. crim.	*Cour de cassation, chambre criminelle*
Cass. req.	*Cour de cassation, chambre des requêtes*
CC	*Codigo Civil*
CE	*Conseil d'Etat*
CE Ass.	*Conseil d'Etat Assemblée*
chr.	*Chronique*
CLJ	*Cambridge Law Journal*
CLO	Central Legal Office
Cmnd.	Command Paper
concl.	Conclusions
Cr. App. R.	*Criminal Appeal Reports*
CSOH	Court of Session, Outer House Reports
D	*Digest of Justinian*
D	*Recueil Dalloz*

ix

DH	*Recueil Dalloz Hébdomadaire*
DP	*Recueil Dalloz Périodique*
ECHR	European Convention on Human Rights
Edin. LR	*Edinburgh Law Review*
ER	*English Reports*
EvBl	*Evidenzblatt*
F	*Findlay Reports*
GAMM	*Le groupe des assurances mutuelles médicales*
Gaz. Pal.	*Gazette du Palais*
GlUNF	J.A. Glaser and J. Unger *et al.* (eds.), *Sammlung von zivilrechtlichen Entscheidungen des k.k. Obersten Gerichtshofes, Neue Folge* (Vienna: Manz, 1900–1919)
GMC	General Medical Council
GWD	*Green's Weekly Digest*
IR	*Informations rapides*
JBl	*Juristische Blätter*
JCP	*Juris-Classeur Périodique, la Semaine Juridique*
JO	*Journal Officiel*
JR	*Juridical Review*
KAG	*Krankenanstaltengesetz*
KAKuG	*Bundesgesetz über Krankenanstalten und Kuranstalten*
Leb.	*Recueil Lebon*
LGDJ	*Librairie Générale de Droit et de la Jurisprudence*
Lloyd's Rep. Med.	Lloyd's Reports Medical Cases
LRJAP	*Ley de Régimen Jurídico de las Administraciones Públicas y del Procedimiento Administrativo Común*
LS	*Legal Studies*
Maurès	A. Maurès, *Etude sur la responsabilité professionnelle et légale du médecin* (Paris: 1900, doctoral thesis)
MDDUS	Medical and Dental Defence Union of Scotland
MDU	Medical Defence Union
Med. LR	*Medico-Legal Reports*
Med. Law Rev.	*Medical Law Review*
MLR	*Modern Law Review*
NHS	National Health Service
NHS(S)A	National Health Service (Scotland) Act
NHSiS	National Health Service in Scotland
NHSNSS	NHS National Services Scotland
NICE	National Institute for Clinical Excellence
NILQ	*Northern Ireland Law Quarterly*
NJW	*Neue Juristische Wochenschrift*
NLJ	*New Law Journal*

obs.	Observations
OGH	*Oberster Gerichtshof*
OH	Outer House
OJLS	*Oxford Journal of Legal Studies*
ONIAM	*Office National d'indemnisation des accidents médicaux, des affections iathrogènes et des infections nosocomiaux*
ÖRZ	*Österreichische Richterzeitung*
PALS	Patient Advocacy Liaison Services
Penneau doctoral thesis	J. Penneau, *Faute et erreur en responsabilité médicale* (Paris: 1972, doctoral thesis)
Penneau, *Faute et erreur*	J. Penneau, *Faute et erreur en matière de responsabilité médicale* (Paris: LGDJ, 1973)
PIQR	*Personal Injuries Quarterly Review*
PL	*Public Law*
PN	*Professional Negligence*
PUF	*Presses Universitaires de France*
QIS	Quality Improvement Scotland
RabelsZ	*Rabels Zeitschrift für Ausländisches und Internationales Privatrecht*
rapp.	Rapport
RD	*Real Decreto*
RdM	*Recht der Medizin*
RDSS	*Revue de droit sanitaire et social*
RdW	*Rechtspraak van de Week*
Resp. civile et assur.	*Responsabilité civile et assurance*
RJ	*Repertorio de Jurisprudencia*
RRJ	*Revue de la recherche juridique*
S.	*Recueil Sirey*
SC	Session Cases
SEHD	Scottish Executive Health Department
SLPQ	*Scottish Law & Practice Quarterly*
SLT	*Scottish Law Times*
somm.	*Sommaires*
StGB	*Strafgesetzbuch*
STS	*Tribunal Supremo*
SZ	*Entscheidungen des Obersten Gerichtshofes in Zivil- und Justizverwaltungssachen*
TC	*Tribunal des Conflits*
VersR	*Versicherungsrecht*
VersVG	*Versicherungsvertragsgesetz*
ZBl	*Zentralblatt für die juristische Praxis*

1

General introduction

EWOUD HONDIUS

1 Introduction

Medical liability is one of the core issues analysed in the European Legal Development project undertaken by the University of Cambridge. This chapter explores some of the developments in medical liability and the backgrounds thereof, which are further analysed in the national reports. The legal systems which have been selected for this purpose are Austria, England and Wales, France, the Netherlands, Scotland and Spain. Occasionally references to other jurisdictions will be provided. This will particularly be the case with regard to Finland, which is one of the Nordic countries having introduced a patient insurance scheme. Another jurisdiction[1] which will in some instances be referred to is that of the United States, where medical negligence law has developed earlier than in Europe as a distinct legal category.

Many liability questions are solved the same way all over Europe. But there are also differences. These differences are perhaps of a temporary nature. The law with regard to medical services has been developing fast; what in one jurisdiction has just been settled may soon become the law in other legal systems. Yet there are differences, and in this introduction to the book, some of the main differences will be set out. These relate to the question how medical malpractice should be dealt with: by public or private law (Section 2), in contract or tort (Section 3), what role codes of conduct play (Section 4), the history of liability in private law (Section 5), the role of patients' rights (Section 6), the standard of care (Section 7), proof and causation (Section 8), who is liable (Section 9), damages (Section 10), exemption clauses (Section 11) and patient insurance systems (Section 12). An intriguing question is the extent to which harmonisation of medical negligence law is to be expected at the

---

[1] Or to be more precise: a number of jurisdictions, each state having its own law.

European level (Section 13). Finally, some general conclusions will be reached (Section 14).

This chapter relies principally on the national reports published in this volume. Useful information could also be extracted from two projects with aims which are similar to those of the European Legal Development project: the Project on Medical Liability in Pennsylvania[2] and the Netherlands-based 'Shifts in Compensation project'.[3] The latter project, like the European Legal Development project, is looking for events which caused the regime to change. The Shifts in Compensation project distinguishes between major and minor shifts. Major shifts are considered to be those changes to the law that involve a significant reform of the compensation system, where the rules on entitlement, the claims procedure and compensation methods are significantly changed,[4] such as the introduction of the patient insurance scheme in the Nordic nations, the *loi* of 4 March 2002 in France and the case of *Chester v. Afshar*[5] in England. Minor changes introduce limited changes to the entitlement criteria, the claims procedure or the compensation method.[6]

The Shifts in Compensation project includes mass medical catastrophes, such as those involving Thalidomide and HIV. The present study has a smaller scope: it only covers the individual liability of hospitals and health care providers. The latter may include nurses and other personnel, but in fact the law focuses almost exclusively on medical doctors. Like the Shifts in Compensation project, this project focuses on the medical adverse event, which according to the Harvard Medical Practice Study consists of an injury caused by medical management rather than the underlying condition of the patient.[7]

Two other publications which will be referred to occasionally are two comparative casebooks, compiled by Faure and Koziol,[8] viz. by Winiger, Koziol, Koch and Zimmermann.[9]

---

[2] See William M. Sage and Rogan Kersh (eds.), *Medical Malpractice and the U.S. Health Care System* (Cambridge: Cambridge University Press, 2006). A useful overview of the American situation is also given in '2006 Medical Malpractice Symposium' (2006) 59 *Vanderbilt Law Review* 1015–381, 1457–98.

[3] Contact shifts@rip.nl.

[4] Rui Cascao and Ruud Hendrickx, 'Shifts in the Compensation of Medical Adverse Events', unpublished paper for the Shifts in Compensation conference, Rotterdam, 2006.

[5] [2004] UKHL 41. See also the Dutch and Spanish annotations in (2007) 15 *European Review of Private Law* 433–50.

[6] Cascao and Hendrickx, above n. 4.   [7] *Ibid.*, para. 1.2.

[8] Michael Faure and Helmut Koziol (eds.), *Cases on Medical Malpractice in a Comparative Perspective* (Vienna: Springer, 2001).

[9] B. Winiger, H. Koziol, B. A. Koch and R. Zimmermann (eds.), *Digest of European Tort Law, Vol. 1: Essential Cases on Natural Causation* (Vienna: Springer, 2007).

This chapter does not present an overall picture of relevant data. In some of the reviewed jurisdictions, data are collected by national agencies, such as the National Health Service Litigation Office (NHSLO) in England and Wales and the *Office National d'indemnisation des accidents médicaux, des affections iathrogènes et des infections nosocomiaux* (ONIAM) in France. The Shifts in Compensation project tries to compare the available data for the jurisdictions covered. Although the researchers do admit that such comparison is difficult because the data collected do not always present all medical negligence claims. Taking this into account, they found the following claim rate per 10,000 hospital discharges:[10]

Sweden 63
Finland 55
Denmark 40
Germany 24
England 5
France 2

In assessing these data one must be cautious. Thus, under the Nordic patient insurance schemes, claims may not only be filed where liability arises, as in the other European jurisdictions, but also in case of other adverse medical developments. Second, the data are about claims and a claim is not always well founded. Moreover, even where it is well founded, financial compensation may also be quite variable. Thus, under the Nordic insurance schemes, non-material loss is not compensated and material losses, because of the well-developed social insurance, are often compensated to a much lower amount than in other European jurisdictions.

In the following paragraphs, the order in which the national reports will be presented will not be the same everywhere. Rather, those jurisdictions will be presented first which either are an example of the mainstream or rather of the most radical departure thereof.

2   Health care system: public or private law

The structure of the health care system has an impact on the branch of law which intervenes with liability issues. An analysis of medical liability in a jurisdiction should therefore start with a brief sketch of this jurisdiction's health system. This may be wholly private, wholly public, or somewhere in between. In the early nineteenth century, there was private medicine for those who could pay (or who belonged to a mutual insurance that

---

[10] Cascao and Hendrickx, above n. 4, para. 6.

could pay), or there was charitable medicine for the poor and a limited amount of publicly funded medical treatment. In more recent times, the state has become a major provider of health care, and this has had an impact on the importance of private law as the mechanism for providing compensation.[11]

At one extreme, the United Kingdom now basically has a public system, the National Health Service, which in 1948 replaced a mixed system of private, voluntary (charitable) and municipal hospitals.[12] Everyone is entitled to free treatment or has to pay a small charge under the NHS cover, though many people do have private health insurance. In Austria, a large majority of 79% of all hospitals are operated by legal persons under public law; only 21% of the hospitals are privately operated.[13] Austria has a long tradition of social security; at present 97.6% of all Austrians are covered by social security.[14] In Spain, 40% of the hospitals are public and 60% private; the public hospitals are larger however, and provide more health care than the private hospitals.[15] France likewise has a mixed system with a public and a private sector, where 78% of secondary care is provided by the public health service.[16] The Netherlands have recently changed their system of financing health care from a predominantly social health insurance to a private one. Dutch citizens outside the upper-income bracket no longer are automatically insured, but all citizens now have to take out private insurance themselves.[17] Everyone now can freely choose an insurance company and the kind of cover one wishes. The drawback of the system is that some 240,000 citizens have failed to acquire insurance.

To the extent that a health care system is public, the question arises whether or not this means that any liability lies in administrative law or in private law. In France, there traditionally exists a dichotomy.[18] Relations of patients with private hospitals are considered to be contractual – or occasionally delictual – and conflicts with such hospitals are dealt with by the ordinary courts. Relations with state hospitals are considered as administrative law and conflicts with the 'users' (*usagers*) are solved by

---

[11] See Nils Jansen and Ralf Michaels, 'Private Law and the State/Comparative Perceptions and Historical Observations' (2007) 71 *RabelsZ* 345–97; Ralf Michaels and Nils Jansen, 'Private Law Beyond the State? Europeanization, Globalization, Privatization' (2006) 54 *American Journal of Comparative Law* 843–90.

[12] See English (Chapter 2) and Scottish (Chapter 3) reports.

[13] Chapter 5, p. 112.   [14] Chapter 5, p. 111.

[15] Chapter 7, p. 168.   [16] Chapter 4, p. 72.

[17] Henriette Roscam Abbing, 'Recent Developments in Health Law in the Netherlands' (2006) 13 *European Journal of Health Law* 133–42.

[18] Chapter 4, p. 70.

the administrative courts.[19] Spain now makes the same division as does France.[20] No such dichotomy exists in Austria[21] and the Netherlands,[22] where all conflicts between doctors and hospitals on the one side and their patients on the other are dealt with by the ordinary courts. This difference is not simply a matter of which court hears a case, but also affects the liability rules that are applied.[23]

Constitutional law may also play a role, for instance in the form of personality rights which are at the basis of patients' rights, especially in Germany.[24] In France, however, personality rights and self-determination are not referred to in judgments on medical liability,[25] and in the Netherlands this is also rare.[26]

Regardless of the organisation of a jurisdiction's health service, criminal prosecution is always possible against doctors who have infringed the law.[27] Civil liability and criminal liability do sometimes mix. In Spain and Germany, criminal law played a predominant role in the nineteenth century, and this continues in Spain, where the principle applies that everyone who is criminally liable is also civilly liable.[28] In terms of substantive law, criminal liability typically arises in the case of serious or gross fault (*faute lourde*). On the other hand, there may be procedural advantages to use criminal liability. In France, victims often join as *partie civile* in a criminal prosecution initiated by the *ministère public* or even oblige the *ministère* to start criminal proceedings.[29] A major advantage of this procedure is that the costs for the victim are minimal, since the public action will be responsible for obtaining the evidence; a disadvantage is that he depends upon the *ministère public*. Reforms to the Penal Code in 2000 have reduced the extent of criminal liability for negligence, and so the overlap between criminal and civil liability has been reduced.

[19] Chapter 4, p. 70, which mentions, however, that the Law of March 2002 on patients' rights and the quality of the health system now provides the same substantive system for administrative and contractual medical services.
[20] Chapter 7, p. 169.   [21] Chapter 5, p. 112.
[22] Chapter 6, p. 137.   [23] Chapters 4 and 7.
[24] See Olha Cherednychenko, *Fundamental Rights, Contract Law and the Protection of the Weaker Party/A Comparative Analysis of the Constitutionalisation of Contract Law, with Emphasis on Risky Financial Transactions*, PhD Utrecht (Munich: Sellier, 2007) and Chantal Mak, *Fundamental Rights in European Contract Law*, PhD Amsterdam (Alphen aan den Rijn: Kluwer, 2007).
[25] Chapter 4, p. 87.   [26] Chapter 6, p. 140.
[27] Chapter 2 mentions a criminal case from the Mayor's Court of London from as early as 1321: see p. 70.
[28] Chapter 7, p. 170.   [29] Chapter 4, p. 74.

3   Contract or tort

Where the law does create medical liability, this may be under the heading of either tort or contract. In the case of tort, the underlying idea is that an infringement of the patient's physical integrity entitles that person to protection by the law. In the case of contract, the idea rather is that there is a breach of the consensual relationship between doctor and patient. In the United Kingdom, contract law is of minimal importance (except in private medical treatment) because as the English report puts it,[30] there is no contract between NHS patients and the doctor or hospital. The one way then is to sue doctors and hospitals in negligence.[31] Only private patients can sue in contract. Likewise in Scotland negligence and not breach of contract is the ground for medical liability.[32] A jurisdiction where contract law was developed at an early stage is France, where the *Mercier* case in 1936 was pivotal in making medical liability a specific type of civil liability and recognised for the first time a contractual relationship between the patient and the doctor or hospital.[33] In some jurisdictions patients have a choice between contract and tort. In others, the whole dichotomy has lost some of its interest. This is especially the case in the Netherlands. In France, Geneviève Viney has observed a similar tendency.[34]

When required to choose between liability in contract or tort, the main argument in favour of the contract option is that it is based on self-determination, which is considered to be of fundamental importance in the relation between doctor and patient. But it has to be admitted that the contract model does have some disadvantages.[35] First, contract presupposes a capacity to consent, a capacity that is not necessarily present in, for example, psychiatric patients and even absent in comatose patients. Second, the contracting party and the patient are not always one and the same person. Children and persons required to undergo examination by a public official are two groups where the qualities are usually spread over different persons. Third, a contract usually embodies rights

---

[30] Below p. 35.

[31] Historically, other torts, such as trespass on the case, have also been used: below p. 36.

[32] Chapter 3, p. 57.

[33] Cass. civ. 20 May 1936, D. 1936.1.88, as reported in Chapter 4, p. 000. This case was important because it took medical activities such as surgery out of delictual strict liability for things (created in 1930) and maintained liability for fault, albeit now within contract, rather than within delict.

[34] Chapter 4, p. 71.

[35] See Pauline Allen, 'Contracts in the National Health Service Internal Market' (1995) 58 *Modern Law Review* 321–42.

and obligations for both parties. Instead, the medical services contract seems a very one-sided affair, with only two obligations on the side of the patient, one of which – the obligation to provide the physician with the necessary information and cooperation – can hardly qualify as an obligation, but rather as an 'Obliegenheit'.

The project, of which this volume is a part, is basically only concerned with the development of tort law. However, under the functional analysis of comparative law,[36] it is recognised that what in one jurisdiction, viz. that of England and Wales, may be qualified as tort, may well be deemed to be contract in other jurisdictions.[37] Therefore, relevant parts of contract law are included. In any case, the development of contract law does fit into the main research question of the European Legal Development project which is: 'How do Western legal systems develop?'

4 Codes of conduct, disciplinary boards

The conduct of medical doctors is not only governed by liability rules, but also by codes of conduct, codes of ethics, etc., which are established by the profession and where the maintenance of rules is left to disciplinary boards. An example is the *Ordre des médecins* (Organisation of medical doctors), which was set up in France in 1940 and in 1941 produced the first professional code of ethics. The 2002 Act now states that it is the task of the *Ordre* to ensure the competence of medical professionals and that the ethical principles of the medical profession are respected.[38] In other countries, professional bodies were created in the nineteenth century in order to certify medical competence and effectively create a profession. As in the French example, the existence of a profession helped to identify a standard of professionalism which could be applied to medical acts, whether they were conducted by recognised members of a profession or by 'quacks'. As experts appointed by the courts or, in the common law, as expert witnesses called by the parties, members of the professions would have an authoritative status in influencing the standards applied by the courts. As the national reports demonstrate, there is a relationship between decisions of disciplinary boards and medical liability.

---

[36] Konrad Zweigert and Hein Kötz, *Einführung in die Rechtsvergleichung auf dem Gebiete des Privatrechts* (3rd edn., Tübingen: Mohr, 1996), pp. 31–47 (also available in English translation).

[37] Chapters 6 and 4, p. 134 and p. 71.   [38] Chapter 4, p. 75.

5   A history of liability in private law

Medical liability is a rather new phenomenon. Although not wholly unknown in the nineteenth century,[39] until fifty years ago it was rarely invoked in England and Wales.[40] There were, however, cases of liability which caused medical insurance to rise, e.g. in 1927 the jury's award of damages in *Harnett v. Fisher* was so far beyond the previous awards that the medical profession had to immediately raise its insurance cover substantially. Again, as the English reporter describes, the cost of compensation to the National Health System rose from £6.33 million in 1974/1975 to £446 million in 2001/2002. In other liberal professions, one finds similar developments.[41] In Austria, medical malpractice cases – although previously not unknown – only emerged as a hot topic in the last two decades of the twentieth century.[42] The same happened in Spain.[43] In France, the modern rise of medical liability cases had begun earlier, with the *Mercier* case of 1936 usually being taken as the starting point,[44] although liability cases do go back to 1835.[45] In recent years, the number of reported cases of medical liability has increased rapidly also in the Netherlands.[46] This has raised fears that soon liability will no longer be insurable[47] and that the costs of health care will grow beyond what society is willing to pay. On the other hand, it has also been pointed out that, until recently, the number of reported cases in the Netherlands has been consistently extremely low[48] and that even now many cases are not taken to court because this is too expensive or too cumbersome for the patients concerned.

Why did medical liability take off? Was this prompted by the American experience? The leading idea which is suggested in the various national

---

[39] Chapter 2 even mentions two cases decided in the fourteenth century: see p. 35.

[40] As the English reporter observes, as late as fifty years ago, an English author could remark that 'actions against medical men and hospitals [have] until recently been altogether unusual': see p. 28.

[41] Chapter 2, p. 29.   [42] Chapter 5, p. 108. The same is true for Germany.

[43] Chapter 7, p. 164.   [44] Chapter 4, p. 80.   [45] Chapter 4, p. 78.

[46] A. T. Bolt and J. Spier, 'De Uitdijende Reikwijdte van de Aansprakelijkheid uit Onrechtmatige Daad' *Handelingen (Nederlandse Juristen-Vereniging*, 1996), pp. 19–22.

[47] The number of insurance companies willing to insure medical liability in the Netherlands has dropped from twenty to three within twelve years. The companies no longer take on the risk themselves, but rather serve as administrators for insurance mutuals – Bolt and Spier, n. 46. See also J. Spier and O. A. Haazen, *Aansprakelijkheidsverzekeringen op Claims Made-Grondslag* (Deventer: Kluwer, 1996). The same fears were expressed when the first medical liability cases were being brought in the US in the 1860s.

[48] In the first edition of *Beroepsfouten* (Zwolle: Tjeenk Willink, 1976), I. P. Michiels van Kessenich-Hoogendam refers to the fact that over the century preceding publication of her book only twenty medical liability cases have been reported.

reports is that the American experience has rather – perhaps undeservedly so – served as a disincentive. Two elements instead seem to have played a major role: the general development of tort – and contract – law in this area, including a growth of legal aid, and the movement towards patients' rights. The movement towards patients' rights will be dealt with in Section 6 below. Here the growth of tort law will briefly be described.

There is no doubt that tort law generally has increased in legal importance. As Jaap Spier recalls in one of the first volumes published by the Spier/Koziol group, when in 1853 Joel Bishop proposed to write a book on the law of torts, no publisher was interested in a work on such a subject.[49] Ever since, the scope of tort law has rapidly expanded, now covering seemingly every domain of society. The heads of damages to be recovered have also expanded. To an increasing extent, the question is now raised as to what instruments may be used to keep medical liability manageable.[50] One practical reason is that otherwise insurance may become too expensive or even unavailable. Two non-European areas have recently had insurance crises. In Australia, this, according to some authors, alleged[51] crisis has led to some new legislation and in the United States to proposals for new legislation.[52] In England, there has been an Act on compensation that aimed to reduce the amount of litigation in the field of medical liability.[53]

Although the development of medical liability looks spectacular, it should not be exaggerated. As the English reporter observes, the cost of compensation still amounts to only 1% of total NHS expenditures[54] and in relation to the number of medical errors, the number of complaints remains modest.[55] The large amounts of money recovered by some individuals should not blind us to the infrequency of medical claims relative to the number of medical procedures. People now expect to be cured by doctors, and medical services are more numerous and more sophisticated than in the past. As will be seen in Section 7, this change in the application and social importance of tort law should not necessarily be seen as a *change* in the actual rules.

---

[49] J. Spier (ed.), *The Limits of Liability/Keeping the Floodgates Shut* (The Hague: Kluwer Law International, 1996), p. v.

[50] See *ibid.*

[51] Peter Cane, *Atiyah's Accidents, Compensation and the Law* (7th edn., Cambridge: Cambridge University Press, 2006).

[52] '2006 Medical Malpractice Symposium' (2006) 59 *Vanderbilt Law Review* 1015–381, 1457–98.

[53] Chapter 2, p. 52, at n. 244.   [54] Chapter 2, p. 29.   [55] Chapter 2, p. 29.

Strange as it may seem, the aim of liability in tort or contract is not wholly without controversy. That the tort system serves to compensate victims is mostly beyond doubt, but whether it should also serve prevention and satisfaction is less certain. The preventative function may in some instances even clash with the compensation function, viz. when health care providers out of fear for liability claims 'cover up' rather than report accidents or near accidents. In the United States, several states have introduced schemes for safe reporting. The publication of the report 'To Err is Human: Building a Safer Health System' in 2000 led to the adoption in 2005 of the federal Patient Safety and Quality Improvement Act (2004), which aims at protecting the reporter of accidents. A similar statute in Europe is the Act on Patient Safety in the Danish Health Care System.[56] A non-statutory equivalent is the National Reporting and Learning System set up by the English National Patient Safety Agency.[57] A distinction can be drawn between the function of the law in providing compensation, and its function in setting standards or assigning risks, or simply in identifying how a harm (often fatal) happened to a patient. If standards are, by and large, benchmarked against those of the professions, and other mechanisms are developed to assign the responsibility for unsuccesful medical procedures, then that leaves tort/delict with the primary role of compensation and assigning risk, though it is not a major player for most patients in these areas.

6   The patients' rights movement

As in product liability, the growth of medical liability needs to be located in a change of social attitudes. At much the same time as consumers' associations were being established in the product area, in 1963 the charitable Patients' Association was founded in the United Kingdom. In 1982 it was joined by another pressure group.[58] These groups succesfully lobbied for government support. As the English reporter puts it: 'Modern politicians have been quick to recognise the political capital that can be gained by responding to patient concerns.'[59] In 2000, this led to the adoption in the government's five year plan for improving the NHS, and the recognition that the lack of concern for patients was at the heart of the NHS of today.[60] Following this, the NHS has been involved in issuing

---

[56] J. Legemaate *et al.*, *Melden van Incidenten in de Gezondheidszorg* (Utrecht: KNMG, 2006), p. 22. The authors propose a similar system for the Netherlands.
[57] Legemaate, *ibid.*   [58] Chapter 2, p. 33.
[59] Chapter 2, p. 32.   [60] Chapter 2, p. 52.

good clinical standards, providing complaints procedures and setting up disciplinary procedures to deal with doctors whose performance is seriously deficient.[61] In the Netherlands, patients' rights were first advocated by two academics, Jaap Rang and Henk Leenen. Their pleas for legislation were listened to and resulted in the adoption of both substantive law and of a number of complaints systems.

The current development of medical negligence is not appreciated in the same way. The two most extreme views are those presented by the English and the Dutch reporters. Whereas the Dutch reporter considers the development of medical negligence basically very positive, inducing doctors and hospitals to change their attitude towards their patients, the English reporter speaks of 'rampant consumerism' and even of judges who are now prepared to embrace the role of patients' champions.[62] All the same, it would be true to say that in 1850, the patient was grateful for anything the doctor could do to improve his or her health, but he or she had low expectations. By 1960, advances in medicine meant that the patient had a reasonable expectation of success even in serious illnesses. Good health was not a bonus, but became a right, for example in the Preamble to the French Constitution of 1946.

7 Standard of care

Over the past century there have been shifts in the standard of care required from professionals in medical cases. In Germany and Spain, the criminal liability imposed in the nineteenth-century legislation turned on gross fault. Similarly, this was the standard applied in French administrative law to mechanical procedures involving any kind of complexity. French criminal law was the same. But in the course of the 1920s, civil law in France and Germany came to play a more important role and the standard of ordinary fault came to be applied to standard medical procedures, which were becoming more common.

Should doctors inform their patients as to the risks of the treatment they propose? It nowadays seems a truism to state that they are. And yet, there is one jurisdiction in the European Union, where the law is – or at least until recently was – less settled than in other member states, and that, to the surprise of many a student, is English law. In *Sidaway v. Board of Governors of the Bethlem Royal Hospital*,[63] it was held (per Lord Bridge of Harwich) that 'the risk of damage to the spinal cord of such severity

[61] Chapter 2, pp. 32–5   [62] Chapter 2, p. 27.   [63] [1985] 1 All ER 643.

as the appellant in fact suffered was, it would appear, certainly less than one per cent. (…) In these circumstances, the appellant's expert witness's agreement that the non-disclosure complained of accorded with a practice accepted as proper by a responsible body of neuro-surgical opinion afforded the respondents a complete defence to the appellant's claim.' It is, then, left to the doctors to set their own standards as to the question whether or not they should inform their patients of certain risks. Or, as Lord Scarman observed in the same case: 'the law imposes the duty of care; but the standard of care is a matter of medical judgment'. This is also called the Bolam principle, after the case of *Bolam v. Friern Hospital Management Committee*,[64] where it was held 'that in the case of a medical man negligence means failure to act in accordance with the standards of reasonably competent medical men at the time'. A similar test is applied in Scotland under the *Hunter v. Hanley* doctrine.[65]

The test is quite distinct from that applied in most continental jurisdictions. According to Article 7:453 of the Dutch Civil Code, a health care provider shall exercise the level of care expected from a conscientious health care provider. At first sight, the two tests are virtually identical. In fact, there is a gulf between them. The 'standards of reasonably competent medical men at the time' are radically different from 'conscientious health care providers', because in the latter case it is the court which decides, not the medical community as in the first case. The impact of informed consent is but one of the examples to show the difference.

Informing the patient is not the only point on which jurisdictions may differ where the standard of care is concerned. Diagnosis, advice and treatment are the three traditional medical functions. Here we find that Europe's small jurisdictions are sometimes running behind. The reason for this may be precisely the fact that they are small: as two authors have observed, 'where a legal system by its size tends to engender less litigation there are fewer occasions on which courts are presented with facts suitable to test or to clarify the application of existing legal rules'.[66] However, when precedents from the ordinary courts are lacking, there are other means of finding the law. One common solution in such cases is to take into consideration the awards of disciplinary bodies. One must of course always

---

[64] [1957] 2 All ER 118.

[65] *Hunter v. Hanley* 1954 SLT 303, OH; 1955 SC 200, IH; 16 Feb 1956, OH, unreported – see Angus Stewart, ' "Best Interests": Towards a more Patient-Friendly Law?' (2007) 11 *Edin LR* 62–80 and 251–3.

[66] Reinhard Zimmermann and Simon Whittaker (eds.), *Good Faith in European Contract Law* (Cambridge: Cambridge University Press, 2000), p. 655.

bear in mind that disciplinary bodies and liability law serve different functions. But often, the fact situations are very similar and practitioners may therefore profit from the body of disciplinary awards. It is therefore of interest that such awards are reported.

Another way of filling the gap is that of having recourse to comparative law. French and German case law especially is so all-embracing, that it will not be difficult for researchers from other countries to find precedents which may be useful in their jurisdiction. Once again, these decisions have no decisive authority, but their arguments may have persuasive powers. In fact, small jurisdictions such as the Netherlands often find inspiration from legislation, case law and doctrinal works from other countries. Small jurisdictions seem to have an advantage on this point which emanates from the very fact that they are small. In the larger jurisdictions, courts are less inclined to look abroad for guidance or inspiration, although the experience of Spain shows that even large jurisdictions make use of comparative law to fill in the gaps in their own system.[67] One of the hindrances is that of language. Not all French judges read German and the reverse is probably also true. It is therefore of some importance that case law is made available not only in the country's own language, but in other languages as well.[68] Comparative law was used only to a limited extent in the early twentieth century and has become more significant later.[69]

In discussing the standard of care, only the care of individual providers of health care has so far been referred to. We should also take into account the standard of care shown by institutions, such as hospitals and (social and private) insurance companies. When looking at the statistics of complaints filed in various hospitals, one is sometimes appalled at the fact that in some hospitals much more, up to tenfold, complaints are lodged than in others. This may of course be a matter of complaint consciousness: urban patients may find it easier to complain than those in rural areas. But a better explanation is that the organisation of certain hospitals lags behind. For instance, no protocol has been drawn up for taking over

---

[67] Chapter 7, p. 166.

[68] This is one of the major functions of the wave of European private law reviews such as *Europa i Diritto Privato*, the *European Review of Private Law (Europäische Zeitschrift für Privatrecht)*, the *Zeitschrift für Europäisches Privatrecht* and the *Zeitschrift für Gesamteuropäisches Privatrecht*. See also my paper 'Pro-active Comparative Law: the Case of Nordic Law' (2008) 50 *Scandinavian Studies in Law* 143–55.

[69] Basil Markesinis, *Comparative Law in the Courtroom and Classroom/The Story of the Last Thirty-Five Years* (Oxford: Hart, 2003), p. 273.

of patients by the day shift.[70] It is therefore interesting that in new regulations of tort liability, such as the Swiss draft legislation (which, however, has not been presented to Parliament), liability for faults in the organisation is especially dealt with.

8　Proof and causation

In the common law, the traditional position regarding proof of medical malpractice is stated in *Wilsher v. Essex Health Authority*[71] by Lord Bridge of Harwich: 'whether we like it or not, the law, which only Parliament can change, requires proof of fault causing damages as the basis of liability in tort'. This position, which lies at the basis of a large number of malpractice cases, has increasingly come under attack. The common law does help plaintiffs with the doctrine of *res ipsa loquitur*: the case speaks for itself. There is also the procedural technique of discovery, which has been in use in the United States for some time: the court requires the defendant to make available to the plaintiff all documents pertaining to the question at stake. In the nineteenth century, the patient would have been aware of who caused the problem. In the early twentieth century, the arrival of technologies such as x-rays could help provide evidence of the patient's condition before medical treatment and afterwards, so proof of fault was easier. But with more complex medical interventions, the proof of fault became difficult, especially where there might be multiple actors involved in a person's treatment in hospital.

The most radical solution – apart from strict liability – is a reversal of the burden of proof: the health care provider must prove that the medical misfortune of his patient was not caused by any mistake of his. It is this solution of the 1991 European Draft Directive on Services Liability, which caused much dissatisfaction in the medical profession (and was therefore dropped). Indeed, nowhere in the jurisdictions covered by this volume is there a reversal of the burden of proof. Spain has in fact a general reversal of the burden of proof in tort cases, with the sole exception of medical liability.[72] However, in exceptional cases, when devices or techniques which are especially dangerous are used, the Spanish Supreme Court does presume a fault.[73] Furthermore, in some specific cases, such as plastic surgery, odontological operations and vasectomies, an obligation to obtain

---

[70] On organisational mistakes see E. Deutsch, 'Das Organisationsverschulden des Krankenhausträgers' NJW 2000, 1745–9.
[71] [1988] 1 All ER 871.　　[72] Chapter 7, p. 176.　　[73] Chapter 7, p. 177.

a result is presumed.[74] In the Netherlands, the courts have developed a reversal of the burden of proof as well – the 'omkeringsregel'.[75]

It may be argued that a reversal of the burden of proof is unnecessarily blunt. *Res ipsa loquitur* together with a discretionary power for the court to impose the burden of submitting evidence and of offering proof upon the party who is in the best position to submit or offer this, should deal with the matter.

Another problem is that of causation. Here once again we find major differences between various European jurisdictions. In some jurisdictions, causation is little more than a *conditio sine qua non* test, of a mainly physical nature. In others, causation is the major criterion for deciding whether or not someone will be held liable.[76] The wrongful birth cases mentioned below offer an illustration of this thesis.[77]

9 Who is liable?

The case is known in all jurisdictions:[78] after surgery, a patient complains of unbearable pain. An x-ray shows that a needle has inadvertently been left in his belly before it was stitched up. Health care providers, says the textbook, should always count the number of foreign objects which they put into the belly and the number they take out – and preferably these numbers are equal.[79] Suppose this is not the case, how can the patient prove which member of the surgery team committed the fault? The patient will most probably have been unconscious during the surgery[80] and so will not have been in a position to see who with his own eyes. This was the reason why actions for compensation have been denied in the past.

The problem mainly arises because of the intricate organisational pattern within the hospital. There will be no problem when all members of the team are employed by the hospital. As Lord Denning observed in

---

[74] Chapter 7, p. 176.   [75] Winiger *et al.*, above n. 9, pp. 408–9.

[76] Lara Khoury, *Uncertain Causation in Medical Liability* (Oxford: Hart, 2006).

[77] Another example, not dealt with in the national reports, would have been the loss of a chance theory see Sarah Green, 'Coherence of Medical Negligence Cases/A Game of Doctors and Purses' (2006) 14 *Medical Law Review* 1–21 and Winiger *et al.*, above n. 9, pp. 589–92.

[78] BGH NJW 1989, p. 2943.

[79] Only in cases of life and death is it defensible to willingly leave behind an object in the stomach.

[80] This is not always the case: in *Phelan v. East Cumbria Health Authority* [1991] 2 Med LR 419, a patient complained that during surgery he woke up and suffered unbearable pain – but was unable to communicate this to the doctor involved.

Roe v. Minister of Health, hospital authorities are responsible for the whole of their staff.[81] In those hospitals, where private enterprise is tolerated, or even recommended, the *Roe* approach is not available. One solution is provided by the Dutch Civil Code, which holds the hospital liable for whatever goes on on its premises.[82] This of course leaves open the possibility of redress by the hospital against the doctor concerned. A similar situation has been reached in France in more recent times. Within the hospital, it can be difficult to identify whether the consultant doctor (not employed by the hospital) or the nurse (employed by the hospital) was responsible for the medical intervention that harmed the patient. The solution has been to make the hospital directly liable for a failure in delivering a service, rather than vicariously liable for the acts of its employees. This is the solution adopted in the 1990s in French administrative law. Here liability in contract may be more useful as is the case in Germany.

10   The measure of damages

The case has become a classical one in comparative law. Angela and Bernd have four children. They want to move to a larger house. In order to pay the higher mortgage, Angela takes up her former position. Angela and Bernd do not want any more children. Bernd has himself sterilised by way of vasectomy in the hospital. A year later, Angela is pregnant again. Angela and Bernd decide to keep the baby. They claim compensation from the hospital. Are they entitled to this? First, a factual question has to be solved. What went wrong with the sterilisation? This may be either medical malpractice or nature. But in case of the latter, the hospital may still be liable for misinformation. A second question is what heads of damages Angela and Bernd may claim. There is now little doubt that Angela is entitled to immaterial damages for having to suffer the pain of giving birth. But what about the couple's demand for the costs of upbringing their newborn baby?

A first example is a Dutch case on wrongful birth of 1997.[83] The *Hoge Raad* expresses the opinion that the award of compensation for expenses to raise the child – born normal and healthy – was not in conflict with the human dignity of the child, or with its right to life. In line with the general rules on compensation, no non-material damages were awarded.[84]

---

[81] [1954] 2 All ER 131.   [82] Chapter 6, p. 145.

[83] *Hoge Raad*, 21 February 1997, *Nederlandse Jurisprudentie* 1999, 145 (Note by C. J. H. Brunner).

[84] Non-pecuniary harm as a general remedy is available only in a limited number of legal systems – H. Stoll, 'Chapter 8, Consequences of Liability: Remedies', in A. Tunc (ed.),

Apart from expenses for raising the child, the Dutch court also acknowledges the possibility of compensation for loss of income for the mother. This case has had some influence in other European jurisdictions, among others owing to the fact that it has been translated into other languages. The fact that it is one of very few Dutch cases dealt with in the first volume of Van Gerven's *Ius Commune Casebooks for the Common Law of Europe*, has contributed to its influence on Scottish law.[85] It has in turn been influenced by German law, witness the 'dissenting' conclusions[86] of Advocate-General Vranken.[87]

This brings us to the second example of a wrongful birth case: the Scottish case of *McFarlane v. Tayside Health Board*.[88] Here, comparative law also plays a role, although the House of Lords in the end opts against the German–Dutch approach. A third example is a Norwegian wrongful conception case, in which both Dutch and German precedents are considered – and also rejected.[89]

Now turning to 'wrongful life', two cases are of special interest. The *Kelly* case is dealt with at length in the Dutch report.[90] The *Kelly* case has not been the first one in which compensation was awarded to a baby born disabled after a failure to diagnose this before birth.[91] The earlier *Perruche* case in France[92] has attracted at least as much attention, especially after the legislature intervened by abolishing the child's right to compensation. French authors have attributed this to a strong lobby of the

---

International Encyclopaedia of Comparative Law, Torts, vol. 2 (Tübingen: Mohr/ Dordrecht: Nijhoff, 1986), no. 17.

[85] Walter Van Gerven *et al.*, *Tort Law/Scope of Protection* (Oxford: Hart, 1998), p. 161.

[86] Judgments of the *Hoge Raad*, like those of the French *Cour de Cassation* and of the European Court of Justice, are preceded by a conclusion of the *procureur-generaal* or one of his deputies, the *advocaten-generaal*.

[87] See also Hans Stoll, *Haftungsfolgen im Bürgerlichen Recht/Eine Darstellung auf Rechtsvergleichender Grundlage* (Heidelberg: Müller, 1993), 280–6.

[88] [1999] 4 All ER 963.   [89] Højesteret 1999, *Norsk Retstidende* 2000.

[90] Chapter 6, p. 147.

[91] See Elizabeth Adjin-Tettey, 'Claims of Involuntary Parenthood: Why the Resistance?', in Jason W. Neyers, Erika Chamberlain and Stephen G. A. Pitel (eds.), *Emerging Issues in Tort Law* (Oxford: Hart, 2007), p. 85–111; J. K. Mason, 'Wrongful Life: the Problem of Causation' (2004) 6 *Medical Law International* 149–61; A. Morris and S. Saintier, 'To Be or Not to Be: is That the Question? Wrongful Life and Misconceptions' (2003) 11 *Med LR* 167; H. Nys, 'Wrongful Life: Enkele Beschouwingen Tegen de Achtergrond van de Franse Rechtspraak' (2005) *Gezondheidszorg Jurisprudentie plus* pp. 69–72; T. Weir, 'The Unwanted Child' (2002) 6 *Edin LR* 244, as well as the bibliography given in Chapter 6 below.

[92] Cass. civ., 26 March 1996, D. 1997, 35 and Ass. Plén., 17 November 2000, D. 2001, 332; JCP 2001.II.10 438.

medical industry and law professors, which even succeeded in convincing the associations of handicapped persons to support this legislation.[93]

Actions by disabled children have strongly been resisted in common law jurisdictions. In England, the Congenital Disabilities (Civil Liability) Act 1976 is generally considered to disallow the child an action for damages. In *McKay v. Essex Area Health Authority*, the Court of Appeal brought forward four arguments against allowing compensation to a child, suffering from the congenital rubella syndrome.[94] First, the doctor's duty of care to the fetus does not extend to a duty to terminate its life; second, to admit such an action compromises the value of life and devalues the life of a disabled child to the extent that it was considered not worth preserving; third, it is impossible to compare the damage resulting from a flawed life with non-existence; and fourth, successful actions will encourage doctors to recommend termination of pregnancy in doubtful cases.

11 Exclusion clauses

In health care, clauses excluding liability are not widespread. Unlike lawyers, medical doctors usually do not use stationery with a printed exclusion clause at the bottom. Were they to employ such clause, it is doubtful whether it would be valid. Under the Dutch Civil Code, the exclusion clause is plainly invalid. Where jurisdictions do have no such rule, application of the unfair contract terms legislation will usually lead to the same result.

Perhaps though, not all exclusion clauses should be held invalid. Let's take the example of a famous professional football player, who earns a high salary. Now if this famous football player presents himself to a hospital for a knee operation without disclosing the fact that an incorrect surgery could result in an income loss of €100 million, the hospital will not necessarily be liable to the full extent of this amount, even if the jurisdiction concerned adheres to the maxim 'take your victim as you find him'. With the help of causation or contributory negligence, a court may well settle the damages much lower. If this is the case, why not codify this possibility into the contract? Perhaps this is a clause dealing with liability, but apparently it is not derogating from the law and

---

[93] Philippe Jestaz and Christophe Jamin, *La doctrine* (Paris: Dalloz, 2004), pp. 241–2.

[94] See J.K. Mason, 'Wrongful Life: the Problem of Causation' (2004) 6 *Medical Law International* 149–61.

therefore should not be subjected to unfair contract terms legislation, which only applies to clauses which derogate from the law. This is apparent from statutory provisions such as § 311(3) of the German Civil Code (the former §§ AGB Gesetz): 'Diese Vorschrift sowie die § 312 und 313 gelten nur für Bestimmungen in Allgemeinen Geschäftsbedingungen, durch die von Rechtsvorschriften abweichende oder diese ergänzende Regelungen vereinbart werden.'

12   The Nordic patient insurance scheme

In 1971, Sweden adopted a radically different approach towards medical injuries. The model has also been adopted in the other Nordic countries. Theoretically, the system leaves untouched liability rules, but it provides for an extra insurance cover. Hospitals take out an insurance for their patients. Whenever something happens which in other jurisdictions could lead to liability, the hospital and the patient address themselves, together, to the insurance company. The system has the advantage that hospital and patient are not forced into litigation, which admittedly is not a positive element in their relationship. It has the disadvantage that it is expensive, at least if it were to be transplanted to continental European countries. A matter of doubt is whether the Nordic model is sufficiently open to accommodate new developments both with regard to medical techniques and ideas in society of who should bear the risk.

The patient insurance scheme is not the only such scheme in the Nordic countries. In fact it has become so popular to have specific compensation schemes covered by insurance that the original legislative tort provisions hardly are of interest nowadays. Insurance schemes have broken off the development of tort law. For this reason, it was judged valuable to include a short introduction to this alternative to liability.

Since the patient insurance model is not set out in a national report in this volume, it may be of interest to give some more explanation. I will base this on the most modern patient insurance scheme, the Finnish Patient Injuries Act, which took effect on 1 May 1999.[95] Pursuant to this Act, which revised the Act of 1987[96] and was itself revised in

[95] The following is mainly taken from a brochure 'Finnish Patient Insurance', published by the Finnish Patient Insurance Centre in Helsinki.

[96] See Raimo Lahti, 'Towards a Comprehensive Legislation Governing the Rights of Patients: The Finnish Experience', in Lotta Westerhäll and Charles Phillips (eds.), Patient's Rights (Stockholm: Nerenius and Santerus, 1994), pp. 207–21; Raimo Lahti, 'The Finnish Patient

2005,[97] patient insurance covers bodily injuries sustained by patients in connection with medical treatment and health care given in Finland. Bodily injury refers to illness, injury, or other weakening of health, or death. Donors of blood or organs are also covered by the Act. Under section 2 of the Act, the insurance only covers bodily injuries which are likely to have resulted from treatment and which meet any one of seven conditions: (1) treatment injury, resulting from examination, treatment or similar action: the test is that of the experienced health care professional; (2) equipment-related injury, caused by a defect in medical equipment or instruments; (3) infection, originating from an examination, treatment or similar action, although no compensation will be paid if the patient is expected to tolerate the injury; (4) accident-related injury; (5) fire and burn injury, resulting from an incident affecting either the premises where the patient was being treated or the equipment used for the treatment; (6) pharmaceuticals incorrectly supplied, that is contrary to the prescription or in violation of applicable regulations;[98] (7) unreasonable injury, caused by examination, treatment or similar action, if the action has caused permanent illness or injury or death.

Compensation must be claimed within three years of the date on which the patient became or should have become aware of the injury, and within ten years of the event (section 10). Patient insurance covers medical treatment expenses, loss of income or maintenance, pain and suffering, permanent loss of function and permanent cosmetic injury. The administration of the Act has been entrusted to the Patient Insurance Centre. Any patient who is dissatisfied with a decision of the Centre may ask the Patient Injuries Board to review the case. The Board may also give general recommendations (section 11).

In 2006, the Finnish Patient Insurance Centre received a total of 7,958 claims. The amount paid in claims in 2006 was €21.4 million. Claims handling costs totalled €6.6 million. Twenty-six tort law suits were brought to court in 2006. The volume of premiums written in 2006 was €47 million, of which a part is reserved for future claims.[99]

Injury Compensation System', in Sheila A. M. McLean (ed.), *Law Reform and Medical Injury Litigation* (Aldershot: Dartmouth, 1995), pp. 147–61.

[97] The text is available in English on the website of the Finnish Patient Insurance Centre at www.pvk.fi.

[98] Injuries caused by pharmaceuticals correctly supplied or prescribed are covered by pharmaceutical insurance and handled by the Pharmaceuticals Insurance Pool.

[99] Annual Report 2006. The author is grateful to Professor Raimo Lahti (Helsinki) for providing him with these data.

The Patient Insurance Model has attracted widespread attention in other European countries, such as Austria,[100] Belgium,[101] Germany,[102] the Netherlands[103] and the United Kingdom.[104] Although the Nordic model leaves compensation under general tort – or contract – rules intact, it nevertheless has caused a basic demarcation line in the actual handling of medical claims.

13   Harmonisation at a European level

Medical liability is at present mainly a national affair. But there is also an embryonic body of European law. Here, a distinction should be made between the Council of Europe and its Convention on Human Rights (ECHR), and the European Union and its regulations and directives. As for the Council of Europe, the importance of the ECHR for patients' rights is well known. Among others, the First Protocol of the Convention has played a role in medical matters. The French law of 2002 which retroactively took away a child's right of compensation for being born disabled was considered infringing of the right to property under Article 1 of the First Protocol in relation to its retroactive effect.[105] In 1997, the Council further adopted the Convention on Human Rights and Bio-Medicine. Under Article 24 of this convention, '[t]he person who has suffered undue damage resulting from an intervention is entitled to fair compensation

---

[100] J. W. Pichler, *Rechtsentwicklungen zu Einer Verschuldensunabhängigen Entschädigung im Medizinbereich. 1. Die Patientenversicherungsrechte in Schweden, Finnland und Dänemark* (Vienna, Cologne, Weimar, 1994).

[101] See, e.g., N. Fraselle (ed.), *La Responsabilité du Prestataine de Services et du Prestation de Soins de Santé* (Brussels: Bruylant, 1992); J. L. Fagnart, 'L'assurance de Risque Médical' (2005) *Commission Université-Palais* 301.

[102] Christoph Kranich and Jan Böcken (eds.), *Patientenrechte und Patientenunterstützung in Europa* (Baden-Baden: Nomos, 1997).

[103] W. R. Aerts, 'De Zweedse No-fault Verzekering ter Vergoeding van Medische Schade' (1990) 1 *Jaarboek Konsumentenrecht* 259–73; B. A. J. M. de Mol, *Medisch Letsel in het Ziekenhuis No-fault Verzekering/Een Verkennende Studie*, PhD thesis (Rotterdam, 1988).

[104] See M. Brazier, 'The Case for a No-Fault Compensation Scheme for Medical Accidents', in S. A. M. McLean (ed.) *Compensation for Damage/An International Perspective* (Aldershot: Dartmouth, 1993), pp. 51–74 (*pro*) and S. A. M. McLean, 'Can No-Fault Analysis Ease the Problems of Medical Injury Litigation?', *ibid.*, pp. 75–90, as well as M. A. Jones, *Medical Negligence* (London: Sweet and Maxwell, 1991), pp. 6–9 (*contra*). The Pearson Report (1978) also advised against the adoption of a no-fault system in England and Wales.

[105] European Court of Human Rights, 6 October 2005, *Draon and Maurice* – see also subsequently Cass. civ. (1), 24 January 2006 (three cases), *Petites affiches*, 31 March 2006.

according to the conditions and procedures prescribed by law'. This raises
the question whether the decision of a court in a case such as the Dutch
Kelly case to award compensation to the child is compatible with this provision.[106] A preliminary question is whether the Convention can provide
us with any answers, because it appears to cover only the ethical problems
involved in the application of biology and medicine (Article 1). Even if
the preliminary question is answered in the negative, one may still raise
the question to what extent the provisions of the Convention may play an
auxiliary role in the *Kelly* debate, referred to in section 10.

As for the European Union, the European Commission presented to
the European Council a draft directive on the liability for services in
1991. In the face of heavy criticism, the proposal had to be withdrawn.
But at present, there is a renewed interest in this matter due to the present
Bolkestein directive on services. In the adjoining area of patient safety,
a 2005 conference initiated by the European Union resulted in the
Luxembourg Declaration on Patient Safety.

The question whether or not to harmonise may be subdivided into three
sub-questions: (a) Is the European Union competent? (b) Is harmonisation feasible? (c) Is it desirable? The first question is not difficult to answer:
there is a clear basis for a directive in the Treaty of Amsterdam. As for the
feasibility, this chapter shows that many issues have to be solved before
true harmonisation will succeed. The last question is the most political
one: do we really wish for a liability system, in which doctors and hospitals
may be held liable under exactly the same circumstances in Denmark and
Greece, in Ireland and Portugal? Once again, the answer is positive. The
need for mobility of doctors and patients is no less than that of producers
and consumers of products. The arguments against are somewhat diverse:
there supposedly is no need for harmonisation, witness the scarcity of present cross-border hospitalisations, and law is a part of culture and culture
simply is different in the various European jurisdictions. The first argument is not very impressive. It may indeed be turned around. The present
lack of mobility of patients – doctors seem slightly more adventurous –
may also be caused by the lack of harmonisation. The latter argument is
more difficult to refute. For indeed there are cultural differences between
the various countries. The organisation of health care – private practice
or National Health Service – the division of labour between first line and
second line health care, the acceptance of second opinions, of abortion
and euthanasia, not to think of legal differences, are there to prove this.

---

[106] Chapter 6, p. 147.

And yet, can this not also be said for most other sectors of European society? Freedom of persons appears to be of overriding importance. For that purpose, harmonisation – not complete unification – is essential.

In some areas of health care there is a growing case law of the European Court of Justice which demonstrates the increasing impact of the European Union in health services. A good example is cross-border patient mobility. The basis for the recent activities of the EU in this area is the European Social Agenda for the period 2005 to 2010.[107]

Beyond Europe lies the world at large. Is a global medical liability foreseeable? Let us put it this way: it is not wholly inconceivable. The World Health Organization has published various directives in the adjoining area of patient safety, such as the 2005 draft directives on adverse event reporting and learning systems.[108] On the other hand, questions such as those bearing on euthanasia may not yet be wholly ripe for worldwide harmonisation.

14   Conclusions

In this final section, two sets of conclusions will be arrived at. The first is in line with the main research question of the European Legal Development project: which possible explanations for development can be identified from the existing literature? The second is to what extent European harmonisation is feasible.

As to the first question, the European Legal Development project has initially identified eight possible explanations for legal development, four external to law – technological, economic, insurance, social and political – and four internal to the law – procedural, ideas and values, doctrinal writing, and judicial dynamics. What is the role of these explanations in the development of medical liability? First, the technological changes in the medical profession have been enormous. On the one hand, many diseases and injuries which only fifty years ago were hardly curable now have a large survival rate. On the other hand, this necessitates an enormously improved organisation, where the risks of mishaps equally grow.[109]

---

[107] COM (2005), 33 final. See the Proposal for a Directive of the European Parliament and the Council on the application of patients' rights in cross-border healthcare, COM (2008) 414 final.

[108] See www.who.int/patientsafety/events/05/Reporting_Guidelines.pdf and Legemaate, above n. 56, p. 23.

[109] According to Cascao and Hendrickx, above n. 4, p. 3, the fact that nowadays even simple therapeutic techniques involve the coordinated effort of several health care providers presents specific risks that can affect patients.

For the development of the law, this means that in litigation nowadays medical expert witnesses will often be necessary. The complexity brought about by technology will make it harder for the litigant to identify the wrongdoer. At the same time, the technology will be able to identify more definitively what has happened to the victim. The use of experts in civil procedure has been permitted for some time, so neither this, nor indeed the use of technology to provide better evidence has required a change in the legal rules. On the other hand, complexity has raised issues of the burden of proof and the extent to which an organisation, such as a hospital, should be liable rather than identifying individuals.

On the economic level, the increased access to health care has also increased the number of patients and of complaints. This increased access has often been accompanied by better insurance coverage for patients, as well as for doctors. Newspaper clippings have played a role in making the public aware of medical mistakes.[110] A major political element has been the coming into existence of a countervailing power of patients' associations, occasionally on the bandwagon of the consumer movement. This change of attitude, as well as the numerical increase in the number of incidents of medical malpractice has led to an increase in litigation, but not to many changes in the legal rules in all jurisdictions. The lower tolerance of medical mistakes is shown in particular by the removal of the standard of gross fault as the ground of liability, and the closer alignment of medical law with ordinary delictual (or contractual) liability for fault. The obligation for health care providers to make their documentation accessible to patient-plaintiffs also has been of importance. In two jurisdictions, the shifts have been of major interest. The most radical solution has been the Swedish (Nordic) one, where the tort system has effectively been replaced by an insurance system. Two other

---

[110] A recent Dutch example is the headline 'In Ziekenhuis 1 op 25 Doden Door Fouten Arts' (In hospitals 1 in 25 Deaths by Medical Faults) on the front page of *NRC Handelsblad*, the most respectable Dutch daily newspaper, of 25 April 2007. The number of deaths in 2004 was 1,735 and the number of unnecessary injuries some 30,000, according to research conducted by two independent research institutes. The same newspaper ran the headline 'Bang voor de Dokter' (Scared of the Doctor) on the front page of its Saturday special of 27 January 2007. It deals with the quality of the various specialist health centres, such as those for heart surgery, of which in the 2004–2006 period eight had to stop working upon the indication of the medical inspection (*Medisch Specialisten Registratie Commissie*). For some English examples see Oliver Quick, 'Outing Medical Errors: Questions of Trust and Responsibility' (2006) 14 Med. Law Rev. 22–43, who refers to 'sad and shocking stories of high mortality rates following paediatric heart surgery, the retention of human tissue without consent and the mass murders perpetrated by Harold Shipman'.

jurisdictions, where the law has been subject to a fundamental change are the Dutch system with its adoption of a new regulation of the contract for medical services, which only partially codifies existing case law, and the French law of 2002, which partially was a reaction against the *Perruche* case.

Coming to the explanations which are internal to the law, litigation in medical negligence cases has occasionally caused the law to change. Examples are the cases on 'wrongful birth' and 'wrongful life' and those on reversal of the burden of proof. Although in these cases it is not certain that without them the law would have remained as it stood, they have at least speeded up developments. Also, litigation before courts is now accompanied by quite a number of extrajudicial means of conflict settlement. The ideas and values internal to the law have been subjected to great changes, especially in the last decades. Only recently, medical doctors especially were considered to be more or less unbound by strict rules. Their standard of care was what they usually did, not what they should do. This has changed fundamentally. Medical doctors and hospitals are now seen as ordinary professionals, who should be held liable for their malpractice. The range of the standard of care has also broadened, to include communication with the patient and organisation of health care. This change of ideas and values has been preceded by influential doctrinal writing and judicial dynamics. In the Netherlands, authors such as Leenen and Rang have been instrumental in developing the patients' rights movement which in turn has led to legislation. In all of the jurisdictions covered by this survey, the courts have shown judicial dynamics, at the Supreme Court level often influencing one another – if not in outcome then at least with regard to using arguments.

We now arrive at the second question, that of European harmonisation.[111] Having analysed a number of issues of medical liability, we may arrive at the conclusion that on these issues some of the European jurisdictions are still wide apart. But at least they are growing more interested in one another. Other jurisdictions are still wide apart. Seemingly small differences in formulation of, for instance, the standard of care test do in fact hide a channel of difference between various European jurisdictions. Problems of proof and causation are dealt with in different ways, as is the question who may be held liable and what kind of damages may be

---

[111] It is somewhat incongruous, that while the debate on European harmonisation is going on, there sometimes is no harmonisation at the national level, because the competence to issue regulations has been handed over to local government, as is the case in Austria.

awarded. Only as to exemption clauses does there seem to be widespread consensus.

What is perhaps even more important than these legal differences, is that this analysis has shown that infrastructures also diverge. There is the factual difference between the Nordic countries with their Patient Insurance Schemes and the other jurisdictions with their traditional liability systems. There are the countries where private law is the only part of the law which is relevant and those where administrative and criminal law are of interest (France and Spain). Yet another difference is between those jurisdictions where the general rules of private – or administrative – law apply and those which have adopted specific legislation (Finland, the Netherlands). Where general rules apply, these may be those of tort or – increasingly – contract law. May patients choose between the two regimes or is there no choice (*non-cumul*)? In some countries, doctrine (France) or legislation (the Netherlands) no longer consider the distinction of major importance.

Even where case law is concerned, structural differences may be discerned. Although most continental jurists believe the contrary, the common law may become very inflexible in the hands of the courts. The cases decided in the House of Lords are evidence hereof. Another structural difference is that in the techniques of developing the law (*Rechtsfortbildung*) courts may vary very much. And yet on another point, fundamental rights have quite a diverging impact in various jurisdictions.

So far, only the official law makers, who hold public office, have been discussed. And what about self-regulatory schemes? Here we also find a gulf, this time not between common and civil law, but between those jurisdictions where self-regulation is held in high esteem (England) and those where intervention by non-state bodies is – or rather was – eyed with suspicion.[112]

Where then does this lead us to: is harmonisation of medical liability on a European level to be given up? The recent idea of resuscitating the draft directive on liability for services, albeit for a limited number of domains, demonstrates that this is not a purely academic question.

---

[112] See F. Cafaggi (ed.), *Reframing Self-Regulation in European Private Law* (Alphen aan den Rijn: Kluwer, 2006).

2

The development of medical liability in England and Wales

WARREN SWAIN

Medical practitioners no longer enjoy the high public esteem that they once did.[1] Deference and even respect have collapsed under the weight of rampant consumerism.[2] The medical profession has been buffeted by a series of scandals. The rhetoric of rights has replaced 'doctor knows best'. This change in public attitudes has had an impact on the way that health care is organised. There are more checks and balances than ever before. It has never been easier for a patient to bring a complaint about their treatment. Bureaucracy has flourished and become bloated. After a slow start there are signs that judges too are, at least on occasion, prepared to embrace the role of patients' champions. The contrast between the statements of two former senior judges is stark. First, Lord Denning:

> In a hospital, when a person who was ill and came in for treatment, no matter what care was used there was always a risk, and it would be wrong and bad law to say that simply because a mishap occurred the hospital and doctors were liable. Indeed it would be disastrous to the community. It would mean that a doctor examining a patient or a surgeon operating at the table, instead of getting on with his work would be for ever looking over his shoulder to see if someone was coming with a dagger; for an action for negligence against a doctor was like unto a dagger; his professional reputation was as dear to him as his body – perhaps more so.[3]

---

[1] C. Hawkins, *Mishap or Malpractice?* (Oxford: Oxford University Press, 1985), pp. 13–15.
[2] For the role of consumerism see I. Kennedy, *The Unmasking of Medicine* (London: Granada, 1983), pp. 151–80; H. Teff, *Reasonable Care* (Oxford: Oxford University Press, 1994), pp. 100–2; S. Law, 'A Consumer Perspective on Medical Malpractice' (1986) 49 *Law & Contemporary Problems* 305.
[3] *Hatcher v. Black*, *The Times* 2 July 1954. For a useful summary of the influence of Lord Denning on medical negligence see S. McLean, 'Negligence – a Dagger at the Doctor's back?' in P. Robson (ed.) *Lord Denning and the Constitution* (Farnborough: Gower, 1981), p. 99.

More recently Lord Woolf has said:

> The public's expectations of what the profession should achieve have grown. Like it or not, we have moved from a society which was primarily concerned with the duty individuals owed to society to one which is concerned primarily with the rights of the individual. You may find this difficult to accept, but judges do move with the times, even if more slowly than some would like. The move to a rights-based society has fundamentally changed the behavior of the courts.[4]

As late as 1957, Lord Nathan, in his book *Medical Negligence Being the Law of Negligence in Relation to the Medical Profession and Hospital*, observed that 'actions against medical men and hospitals [have] until recently been altogether unusual'.[5] Claims against doctors are no longer rare. Some observers have even drawn parallels with the United States.[6] The analogy is probably unhelpful,[7] especially given that the jury remains central to civil litigation in America,[8] but the bare figures are startling enough. In the mid-1980s the Medical Defence Union estimated a doubling of medical negligence claims between 1975 and 1985.[9] The cost of compensation to the NHS in 2001/2002 was £446 million compared with just £6.33 million at current prices in 1974/1975.[10] The size of awards has also increased.[11] The impact on a few disciplines is especially

---

[4] Lord Woolf, 'Are the Courts Excessively Deferential to the Medical Profession?' (2001) 9 Med. Law Rev. 1, 3. *Cf.* Lord Irvine, 'The Patient, The Doctors, Their Lawyer and The Judge: Rights and Duties' (1999) 7 Med. Law Rev. 255.

[5] (London: Butterworth, 1957), p. vi.

[6] J. Fleming, *The American Tort Process* (Oxford: Oxford University Press, 1988), p. 16: 'Aside from products liability, no other segment of tort litigation has experienced such rapid growth in the last twenty years.' The literature on the United States is vast. The situation there has generated enormous problems within the insurance industry. For a useful summary see J. Posner, 'Trends in Medical Malpractice Insurance 1970–1985' (1986) 49 *Law & Contemporary Problems* 37. For an empirical analysis across a number of jurisdictions see: D. Dewees, M. Trebilcock and P. Coyte, 'The Medical Malpractice Crisis: A Comparative Empirical Perspective' (1991) 54 *Law & Contemporary Problems* 217.

[7] M. Jones, *Medical Negligence* (London: Sweet & Maxwell, 2003), para. 1–008, n. 40. The malpractice crisis in America is on a wholly different scale in terms of the number of claims and the size of damage awards, see J. Grossen and D. Guillod, 'Medical Malpractice Law: American Influence in Europe?' (1983) 6 *Boston College International & Comparative Law Review* 6, 16–18.

[8] But *cf.* N. Vidmar, *Medical Malpractice and the American Jury* (Ann Arbor: University of Michigan Press, 1997), who argues the role of the jury in precipitating a medical malpractice crisis has been exaggerated.

[9] *Medical Defence Union Annual Report* (London: MDU, 1986).

[10] *Making Amends: A Consultation Paper Setting out Proposals for Reforming the Approach to Clinical Negligence in the NHS – A Report by the Chief Medical Officer* (London: HMSO, 2003), pp. 9, 60 available at www.dh.gov.uk/assetRoot/04/06/09/45/04060945.pdf

[11] *Making Amends*, p. 65 suggests that the average award is close to £260,000.

severe.[12] Nevertheless the extent of the crisis should not be exaggerated. The cost of compensation still only amounts to 1% of total NHS expenditure.[13] Medical negligence may only account for 1.5% of all personal injury claims.[14] The number of medical negligence claims may even be falling.[15] In relation to the number of medical errors the number of complaints remains modest.[16]

If Lord Woolf's observation that Britain has become a rights-based society is accurate[17] then medical negligence is likely to travel in new directions. The balance between claimant and defendant is already beginning to shift. The birth of the NHS, higher expectations of medical care, rapid developments in medical technology, increased press interest and greater enthusiasm for medical negligence litigation amongst solicitors coupled with their right to advertise have also been blamed for the increase in claims.[18] But medical malpractice has not developed in a vacuum. Any increase has to be set against a general rise in litigation.[19] Medical practitioners are not the only professionals who are more likely to be defendants in a negligence suit[20] and the courts are anxious to avoid accusations that the medical profession is afforded special protection.[21]

[12] R. Dingwall, P. Fenn and L. Quam, *Medical Negligence A Review and Biography* (Oxford: Centre for Socio-Legal Studies, 1991), pp. 10–11; L. Mulcahy, 'Threatening Behaviour? The Challenge Posed by Medical Negligence Claims' in M. Freeman and A. D. E. Lewis (eds.), *Law and Medicine Current Legal Issues 2000* (Oxford: Oxford University Press, 2000), pp. 81, 92–6; Jones, *Medical Negligence*, para. 1–016; *Making Amends*, pp. 38–9.

[13] *Making Amends*, p. 26.

[14] *Making Amends*, p. 59 compared with an estimate of 0.2% in the 1970s.

[15] Figures published by the NHS Litigation Authority suggest the number of negligence claims may actually be falling, see *National Health Service Litigation Authority Report and Accounts 2005* (London: HMSO, 2005) p. 13 available at www.nhsla.com/publications.

[16] L. Mulcahy, *Disputing Doctors. The Socio-legal Dynamics of Complaints About Medical Care* (Maidenhead: Open University Press, 2003), ch. 4.

[17] S. Deakin, A. Johnson and B. Markesinis, *Tort Law*, 5th edn. (Oxford: Oxford University Press, 2003), p. 5.

[18] Nathan, *Medical Negligence*, p. 5; Grossen and Guillod, 'Medical Malpractice' 15–16; Dingwall *et al.*, *Medical Negligence*, p. 12; V. Harpwood, 'The Manipulation of Medical Practice' in Freeman and Lewis (eds.), *Law and Medicine*, pp. 47, 48–50.

[19] P. Atiyah, 'Tort Law and the Alternatives: Some Anglo-American Comparisons' (1987) *Duke Law Journal* 1002; B. Markesinis, 'Litigation-Mania in England, Germany and the USA: Are We So Very Different?' [1990] CLJ 233; K. Williams, 'State of Fear: Britain's "Compensation Culture" Reviewed' (2005) 25 LS 499.

[20] As graphically demonstrated by the contrast between *Rondel v. Worsley* [1969] 1 AC 191 and *Arthur JS Hall & Co. v. Simons* [2002] 1 AC 615. On some recent trends outside the context of medical malpractice see H. Evans, 'The Rise and Fall of Professional Negligence: One Practitioner's View' (2005) 21 PN 27.

[21] Woolf, 'Are the Courts Excessively Deferential' 1, 2; Lord Ackner 'The Doctor in Court – Victim or Protected Species' (1992) 8 PN 54, 55.

1   The structure of health care in England[22]

In 1948 Britain's National Health Service[23] replaced a mixture of private practice,[24] voluntary and municipal hospitals.[25] Health care has undergone many structural changes since 1948 but overall responsibility remains with the Secretary of State for Health[26] whose duties are delegated to a combination of Strategic Health Authorities, Primary Care Trusts (PCTs) and Care Trusts through regulations, directions and circulars. Twenty-eight Strategic Health Authorities are responsible for monitoring PCTs and NHS Trusts and for developing a strategy for improving quality of care.[27] The three hundred PCTs act as purchasers of health care for local communities. They are also responsible for improving standards and ensuring that national targets are met.[28] Care Trusts coordinate different health and social services agencies with overlapping functions.[29]

Primary care under the NHS is provided by a combination of NHS Trust Hospitals, Foundation Trusts, General Practitioners (GPs) and non-NHS providers. NHS Trust hospitals are funded through NHS contracts with PCTs.[30] Since 2004 some NHS Trust Hospitals have been granted

---

[22] The discussion of the structure of health care is largely derived from A. Grubb (ed.), *Principles of Medical Law*, 2nd edn. (Oxford: Oxford University Press, 2004), ch. 1 and C. Newdick, *Who Should We Treat? Rights, Rationing, and Resources in the NHS*, 2nd edn. (Oxford: Oxford University Press, 2005), ch. 4. The Department of Health website contains a wealth of legal and factual detail on the operation of the different agencies within the NHS.

[23] For the political background see C. Webster, *The National Health Service A Political History*, 2nd edn. (Oxford: Oxford University Press, 2002).

[24] A. Digby, *The Evolution of British General Practice 1850–1948* (Oxford: Oxford University Press, 1999).

[25] B. Abel-Smith, *The Hospitals 1800–1948* (London: Heinemann, 1964).

[26] National Health Service Act 1977.

[27] For a summary of the functions of the Strategic Health Authorities see NHS factsheets: *Strategic Health Authorities* available on the publications section at www.dh.gov.uk. For individual Strategic Health Authorities see NHS factsheets available at www.info.doh.gov. uk/nhsfactsheets.nsf. Their legal framework is governed by the National Health Service (Functions of Strategic Health Authorities and Primary Care Trusts and Administrative Arrangements) (England) Regulations 2002 (SI 2002/2375).

[28] For a summary of the functions of PCTs see *Corporate Governance Framework Manual for Primary Care Trusts Version Six 2003* (London: HMSO, 2003), pp. 6–18. For information on individual PCTs see NHS factsheets available at www.info.doh.gov.uk/nhsfactsheets. nsf. Their legal framework is governed by National Health Service (Functions of Strategic Health Authorities and Primary Care Trusts and Administrative Arrangements) (England) Regulations 2002 (SI 2002/2375).

[29] Health and Social Care Act 2001, ss. 45–6.

[30] A. Davies, *Accountability – A Public Law Analysis of Government by Contract* (Oxford: Oxford University Press, 2001), pp. 89–184.

foundation status.[31] Foundation Hospitals, which are overseen by an independent regulator,[32] have a greater degree of independence from state control.[33] As part of their remit to provide primary care, PCTs enter into a contract with GPs.[34] Most GPs have a contract of this sort – known as General Medical Service (GMS) agreements. Around a fifth of GPs[35] now work under Personal Medical Services (PMS) agreements.[36] PMS agreements are designed to promote greater flexibility and mean that some GPs are employees of the PCTs rather than independent contractors.

Since the late 1940s private health care has continued to thrive alongside the NHS. Around twelve million people have private health insurance.[37] In recent years the government has been keen to promote greater cooperation between private health care providers and the NHS as a way of relieving pressure on resources and reducing waiting times.[38]

2 The regulation of health care and health care professionals in England

Writing in 1964 one former NHS patient complained that:

> Patients are becoming impatient: of being treated like chipped flower-pots in for repair, of queues; of being kept in ignorance – not through willful design, merely because it's no one's job in a hospital to tell the patient what is happening.[39]

---

[31] Health and Social Care (Community Health and Standards) Act 2003.

[32] For a summary of the role of the Health Care Commission see A. Davis, 'Foundation Hospitals: A New Approach to Accountability and Autonomy in the Public Services' [2004] PL 825–7.

[33] For details of the operation of foundation hospitals see the publications section at www. dh.gov.uk; Davis, 'Foundation Hospitals' argues that the claim that Foundation Hospitals will be at 'arms length' from government is largely illusory.

[34] GPs recently agreed to a new form of contract. For details see www.dhsspsni.gov.uk/ hss/gp_contracts/index.asp. For a summary of these reforms see R. Lewis, 'A Fresh New Contract with General Practitioners' (2002) 324 BMJ 1048–9; R. Lilley, *The New GP Contract* (Oxford: Radcliffe Medical Press, 2003).

[35] R. Lewis and S. Gillam, 'Personal Medical Services' (2002) 325 BMJ 1126–7.

[36] These new arrangements were authorised by the National Health Service (Primary Care) Act 1997 and governed by Personal Medical Services Agreements Regulations 2004 (SI 2004/627). For a discussion of the operation of PMS in practice see J. Shapiro, 'Personal Medical Services: A Barometer for the NHS?' (2000) 321 BMJ 1359–60; Lewis and Gillam, 'Personal Medical Services'.

[37] Y. Doyle and A. Bull, 'Role of Private Sector in United Kingdom Healthcare System' (2000) 321 BMJ 563.

[38] *For the Benefit of Patients* (London: HMSO, 2001) available at www.dh.gov.uk/ assetRoot/04/07/67/81/04076781.pdf.

[39] G. Cohen, *What's Wrong with Hospitals* (Harmondsworth: Penguin, 1964), p. 9.

But the seeds of patient power had already been sown. The charitable Patients' Association was formed the previous year.[40] Modern politicians have been quick to recognise the political capital that can be gained by responding to patient concerns. In the introduction to the government's five-year plan for improving the NHS, the then Secretary of State argued that 'at its heart the problem for today's NHS is that it is not sufficiently designed around the convenience and concerns of the patient'.[41] NHS 'governance' is designed to promote fair allocation of resources, increase public involvement and improve the quality of care.[42] Following the inquiry into Bristol Royal Infirmary,[43] the issue of standards has become bound up with the question of the proper scope of patient and public involvement in health care.

The National Institute for Health and Clinical Excellence (NICE)[44] is responsible for issuing guidance to NHS institutions about the provision of treatments and drawing up National Service Frameworks on clinical practice. Under the Health Act 2001, Strategic Health Authorities, PCTs and the NHS have a duty to consult the public.[45] Public consultation is carried out through Patients' Forums. The forums also provide patients with information on complaints procedure and provide independent advocacy services for patients who wish to proceed with a complaint.[46] The Patient Advocacy Liaison Services (PALS) acts as a conciliation service enabling problems to be resolved without resorting to lengthy formal procedures or litigation.[47] PALS are part of the NHS Trusts or PCTs. The Independent Complaints and Advocacy Service (ICAS) was established in 2003. It provides advice to disgruntled patients, largely through the Citizens Advice

[40] See www.patients-association.com. In 1982 it was joined by another pressure group, Action against Medical Accidents see www.avma.org.uk.

[41] *The NHS Plan: A Plan for Investment A Plan for Reform* (Cm. 4818-I, 2000) available at www.dh.gov.uk/assetRoot/04/05/57/83/04055783.pdf.

[42] Grubb (ed.), *Medical Law*, paras. 1.110–49; C. Newdick 'NHS Governance after Bristol: Holding on or Letting go?' (2002) 10 Med. Law Rev. 111.

[43] *Learning from Bristol: The Report of the Public Inquiry into Children's Heart Surgery at the Bristol Royal Infirmary 1984–1995* (Cm. 5207, 2001). The final report is also available at www.bristol-inquiry.org.uk. On the role of the report in health care reform see J. Bridgeman, ' "Learning from Bristol": Healthcare in the 21st century' (2002) 65 MLR 241.

[44] National Institute for Clinical Excellence (Establishment and Constitution) Order 1991 (SI 1999/220), reg. 3 as amended by SI 1999/2219. For information on the functions of NICE see www.nice.org.uk.

[45] Health and Social Care Act 2001, s. 11.

[46] Grubb (ed.), *Medical Law*, paras. 1.122–6.

[47] For a summary of the function of PALS see the publications section at www.dh.gov.uk.

Bureau. In its first year it dealt with nearly 9,000 complaints.[48] Various bodies including the Commission for Healthcare Audit and Inspection,[49] the National Clinical Assessment Service,[50] the Council for Regulation of Health Care Professionals[51] and the National Patient Safety Agency[52] exist in order to promote good clinical standards.

Self-regulation of the medical profession has a long history.[53] In modern times it largely follows the same format as the General Medical Council (GMC) which was created to regulate doctors in 1858.[54] In the last decade self-regulation has become more intrusive. Doctors will soon be required to possess a licence to practice which, as in the United States, will be subject to periodic revalidation.[55] The GMC has powers to suspend and exclude doctors from its register along with a series of other sanctions[56] where they are guilty of 'serious professional misconduct'. Investigations take place within a legal framework including the Human

[48] Grubb (ed.), *Medical Law*, paras. 2.177–85; *Independent Complaints Advocacy Service (ICAS) The First Year of ICAS: 1 September 2003–31 August 2004* available in the publications section at www.dh.gov.uk.

[49] Grubb (ed.), *Medical Law*, paras. 1.136–40; available in the publications section at www.healthcarecommission.org.uk.

[50] Grubb (ed.), *Medical Law*, paras. 1.140–4; www.ncas.npsa.nhs.uk.

[51] Grubb (ed.), *Medical Law*, paras. 1.145–6. The Council has the power to refer decisions of the GMC to the High Court where it considers that they have been unduly lenient under the National Health Service Reform and Health Care Professionals Act 2002, s. 29 see *Council for the Regulation of Health Care Professionals v. GMC* [2005] 1 WLR 717.

[52] Grubb (ed.), *Medical Law*, paras. 1.147–9; www.npsa.nhs.uk.

[53] (1511) 3 Hen 8 c. 11; *Bonham's Case* (1610) 8 Co. Rept. 113 b, 207 (a); *Goevelt v. Burnell* (1699) Carth. 491; *Grenville v. College of Physicians* (1700) 12 Mod. 386.

[54] Medical Act 1858. Currently the Medical Act 1983. For other health care professionals see the Pharmacy Act 1954; Dentists Act 1984; Opticians Act 1989; Osteopaths Act 1993; Chiropractors Act 1994; Nurses, Midwives and Health Visitors Act 1997; Nursing and Midwifery Order 2001 (SI 2001/253).

[55] The process has been postponed to allow for consultation with the Department of Health following the Shipman Inquiry see www.gmc-uk.org/doctors/licensing/revalidation/index.asp; D. Newble *et al.*, 'GMC's Proposals for Revalidation' (2001) 322 BMJ 358. On the American experience see J. Norcini, 'Recertification in the United States' (1999) 319 BMJ 1183.

[56] For a summary of possible sanctions see www.gmc-uk.org. Some have expressed concerns that the GMC is still too lenient: A. Simanowitz, 'Performance Procedures for Seriously Deficient Professional Performance are Flawed' (1996) 313 BMJ 562; P. Wilmshurst, 'The GMC is too Lenient' (2002) 325 BMJ 397. Dame Janet Smith's report on Shipman considered these matters in detail. *The Fifth Report – Safeguarding Patients: Lessons from the Past – Proposals for the Future* (Cm. 6394, 2004) contains a full discussion and criticism of the GMC's procedures. It is available online at www.the-shipman-inquiry.org.uk/fifthreport.asp. For a summary see C. Dyer, 'Shipman Inquiry Finds GMC has Fundamental Flaws' (2005) 330 BMJ 10.

Rights Act 1998 and judicial review.[57] A doctor has a right of appeal from the GMC to the High Court.[58] The Council for the Regulation of Health Care Professionals also has the power to refer a direction of the GMC to the High Court on the grounds of undue leniency.[59] In the past, findings of 'serious professional misconduct'[60] were usually confined to cases of criminal activity, financial offences, certification, inappropriate sexual relations with patients and alcohol offences.[61] In 1983, the GMC's Blue Book, which provided guidance on conduct, stated that the GMC was 'not ordinarily concerned with errors in diagnosis or treatment, or with the kind of matters which give rise to action in the civil courts for negligence'.[62] Attitudes began to change in the mid-1980s.[63] Proper care and treatment are explicitly included in recent guidelines.[64] In addition to the misconduct procedures, since 1997 the GMC, in the guise of the Committee on Professional Performance, has similar powers in relation to doctors whose performance has been or is 'seriously deficient'.[65]

3   Redress through litigation: standards of care

A victim of medical malpractice has a greater range of options than ever before. A support structure guides complainants at every step. Inevitably some victims still prefer to seek legal redress. Claims against the NHS are handled by the NHS Litigation Authority.[66] In common with the majority of personal injury cases most medical negligence claims will be settled without reaching trial.[67] Litigation is seen by some victims as the best way

---

[57] For a summary of the procedure of the GMC see R. G. Smith, *Medical Discipline: The Professional Conduct Jurisdiction of the General Medical Council 1858–1990* (Oxford: Oxford University Press, 1994), pp. 55–96; Grubb (ed.), *Medical Law*, paras. 2.41–126.

[58] NHS Reform and Health Care Professions Act 2002, s. 30. Previously appeals were heard by the Privy Council.

[59] NHS Reform and Health Care Professions Act 2002, s. 29; *Ruscillo v. Council for Regulation of Health Care Professionals* [2005] 1 WLR 717.

[60] For various attempts to define 'serious professional misconduct' see *Doughty v. General Dental Council* [1987] 3 All ER 843, 847; *Roylance v. GMC (No. 2)* [1999] Lloyd's Rep. Med. 139. Smith, *Safeguarding Patients*, paras. 17.4–53.

[61] Smith, *Medical Discipline*, ch. 4 and Appendix.

[62] Cited in Grubb (ed.), *Medical Law*, para. 2.62.

[63] Smith, *Safeguarding Patients*, para. 17.45.

[64] See www.gmc-uk.org/guidance/good_medical_practice/good_clinical_care.asp.

[65] Medical (Professional Performance) Act 1995; *Sadler v. GMC* [2003] 1 WLR 2259. Smith, *Safeguarding Patients*, para. 27.212 recommended that the GMC's powers be extended to include 'deficient clinical performance'.

[66] Grubb (ed.), *Medical Law*, paras. 8.95–97.

[67] P. Cane, *Atiyah's Accidents Compensation and the Law*, 6th edn. (London: Butterworths, 1999), pp. 213–14; *Making Amends*, p. 60.

of securing an apology and gaining assurances that lessons have been learnt from their experience and not just as a way of securing compensation.[68] Formidable obstacles await potential litigants, not least the cost for those who are not legally aided.[69]

Patients have sued doctors for breach of contract when something has gone wrong with their treatment since the Middle Ages.[70] In the modern law, contract claims are of minimal importance because there is no contract between NHS patients and their doctor or hospital.[71] Private patients can sue in contract[72] – a cause of unease to some judges.[73] Contract is not usually a more attractive avenue than negligence even for private patients because, although the courts are usually willing to imply a term that the doctor will exercise reasonable care,[74] judges are much more reluctant to find a warranty from the doctor that a medical procedure will be a success.[75] Contracts are subject to the Unfair Contract Terms Act 1977.[76]

---

[68] C. Vincent et al., 'Why Do People Sue Doctors? A Study of Patients and Relatives Taking Legal Action' (1994) 343 The Lancet 1609; S. Lloyd-Bostock and L. Mulcahy, 'The Social Psychology of Making and Responding to Hospital Complaints: An Account Model of Complaint Processes' (1994) Law & Policy 123; Making Amends, p. 75 where research for the report showed that a mere 11% of complainants were motivated by the prospect of compensation.

[69] Lord Woolf, Access to Justice – Final Report (London: HMSO, 1996) Sec. IV, ch. 15 notes that 92% of successful claimants in medical negligence were legally aided; Making Amends, p. 70.

[70] Covenant: Anon (1321) 86 Selden Society 353; Warner v. Leech (1330) in A. Kiralfy, A Source Book of English Law (London: Sweet and Maxwell, 1957), pp. 184–5; see D. Ibbetson, 'Words and Deeds: The Action of Covenant in the Reign of Edward I' (1986) 4 Law & History Review 71, 92.

[71] Reynolds v. The Health First Medical Group [2000] Lloyd's Rep. Med. 240. In contrast to the position in Canada for example see Pittman Estate v. Bain (1994) 112 DLR (4th) 257.

[72] Thake v. Maurice [1986] QB 644.

[73] Hotson v. East Berkshire Health Authority [1987] AC 750, 760; Greenfield v. Irwin [2001] 1 WLR 1279, 1288–9 (Buxton LJ); Rees v. Darlington Memorial NHS Trust [2004] 1 AC 309, 351–2 (Lord Scott), cf. McFarlane v. Tayside Health Board [2000] 2 AC 59, 76–7 (Lord Steyn).

[74] On the difference between an obligation to provide reasonable care and warranty see MacFarlane v. Tayside Health Board [2000] 2 AC 59, 76 (Lord Steyn).

[75] There was a disagreement on the facts in Thake v. Maurice. Paine J was willing to make a finding that a doctor had guaranteed the success of a vasectomy. Nourse and Neill LJJ in the Court of Appeal were not. In Eyre v. Measday [1986] 1 All ER 488 the Court of Appeal refused to imply a warranty that a sterilisation procedure would guarantee sterility. In Greaves & Co. (Contractors) Ltd. v. Baynham Meikle & Partners [1975] 3 All ER 99, 103–4 Lord Denning remarked that: 'The surgeon does not warrant that he will cure the patient.'

[76] For an overview of UCTA 1977 in relation to personal injury see G. Treitel, The Law of Contract, 11th edn (London: Sweet & Maxwell, 2003), p. 249.

A   Medical negligence

Where a medical practitioner has been grossly negligent he may face a criminal charge of manslaughter.[77] The number of criminal prosecutions against doctors has steadily increased in recent years.[78] But medical negligence is usually a matter for the civil law. It provides a route to compensation for both NHS and private patients.[79] Medical malpractice claims long pre-date the recognition of a specific tort of negligence.[80] There was litigation involving a surgeon in the Mayor's Court of London in 1300.[81] Actions of trespass on the case against surgeons, alleging that the defendant had caused damage while carrying out an undertaking to the plaintiff, appeared in the Royal Court soon afterwards.[82] Two sixteenth-century cases against surgeons show that, in the absence of a special agreement, liability was based on fault.[83]

By the early nineteenth century the substance of the action of trespass on the case – by this time usually abbreviated to case – was fully exposed. In *Searle v. Prentice* Lord Ellenborough explained that 'an ordinary degree of skill is necessary for a surgeon who undertakes to perform surgical

---

[77] *R v. Adomako* [1995] 1 AC 171; *R v. Misra* [2005] 1 Cr. App. R. 21; C. Barsby and D. C. Ormerod, 'Manslaughter: Manslaughter Through Gross Negligence – Whether Sufficient Certainty as to the Ingredients of Offence' (2005) *Criminal Law Review* 234. On gross negligent manslaughter generally see J. C. Smith, *Smith and Hogan Criminal Law* 10th edn. (London: Butterworths, 2002), pp. 385–8.

[78] G. Slapper, 'Manslaughter, Mens Rea and Medicine' (1994) 144 NLJ 941; R. Ferner, 'Medication Errors that have led to Manslaughter Charges' (2000) 321 BMJ 1212; J. Holbrook, 'The Criminalisation of Fatal Medical Mistakes' (2003) 327 BMJ 1118.

[79] *Thake v. Maurice* [1986] QB 644, 657 (Paine J).

[80] For the history of medical negligence see C. Joseph Stetler, 'The History of Reported Medical Professional Liability Cases' (1956–57) 30 *Temple Law Quarterly* 366, Teff, *Reasonable Care*, pp. 173–80. For the American law in the nineteenth century see K. Allen De Ville, *Medical Malpractice in Nineteenth Century America* (New York: New York University Press, 1990). On the emergence of a tort of negligence see D. Ibbetson, 'The Tort of Negligence in the Common Law in the Nineteenth and Twentieth Centuries' in E. Schrage (ed.), *Negligence the Comparative Legal History of the Law of Torts* (Berlin: Duncker & Humblot, 2001), p. 229.

[81] A. H. Thomas (ed.), *Calendar of Early Mayor's Court Rolls 1298–1307* (Cambridge: Cambridge University Press, 1924), p. 81.

[82] *Stratton v. Swanlord* (1374) *Skyrne v. Butolf* (1388) reproduced in J. H. Baker and S. F. C. Milsom, *Sources of English Legal History Private Law to 1750* (London: Butterworths, 1986), pp. 360–7; R. C. Palmer, *English Law in the Age of the Black Death 1348–1381* (Chapel Hill: University of North Carolina Press, 1993), pp. 185–96. On these claims generally see J. H. Baker, *An Introduction to English Legal History* (London: Butterworths, 2002), pp. 329–31.

[83] J. H. Baker, *The Oxford History of the Laws of England Volume VI 1483–1558* (Oxford: Oxford University Press, 2003), pp. 759–60.

operations'.[84] Unambiguously fault liability emerged just as voices were being raised in favour of reform in medical practice. During the next hundred years the boundary between so called 'quack' practitioners and professional medical men began to harden.[85] In 1830 in his book, *The Laws Relating to the Medical Profession*, John Willcock stressed that membership of the professions carried certain responsibilities.[86] Eight years later Tindal CJ attempted to provide some guidance on how far these responsibilities were governed by the law:

> Every person who enters into a learned profession undertakes to bring to the exercise of it a reasonable degree of care and skill. He does not undertake if he is an attorney, that at all events you shall gain your case, nor does a surgeon undertake that he will perform a cure; nor does he undertake to use the highest possible degree of skill.[87]

The jury remained important at this time. They were charged with deciding whether or not a doctor had exercised the required degree of skill, assisted by the evidence of expert witnesses.[88] Erle CJ admitted that the degree of skill could not be defined but added that 'a medical man was certainly not answerable merely because some other practitioner might possibly have shown greater skill and knowledge'.[89]

By the mid-nineteenth century a tort of negligence had begun to take root. It was broken down into three parts: (i) the defendant must have been under a duty to take care towards the plaintiff; (ii) the defendant must have breached that duty; and (iii) the defendant must have caused a loss to the plaintiff. All three conditions have generated problems in medical negligence but the second and third have been particularly problematic.

Duty of care

Most medical negligence claims are concerned with personal injury and it is not usually difficult to establish that a duty of care is owed.[90] There have been two main problems. Until the 1940s there was a great reluctance to impose vicarious liability on hospitals for the negligence of a

---

[84] (1807) 8 East 348, 355.

[85] R. Porter, *Quacks Fakers & Charlatans in Medicine* (Stroud: Tempus, 1989), ch. 8.

[86] J. W. Willcock, *The Laws Relating to the Medical Profession with an Account of the Rise and Progress of its Various Orders* (London: J. and W. T. Clark, 1830), pp. 89–90.

[87] *Lanphier v. Phipos* (1838) 8 C. & P. 475, 479.

[88] For example in *Rich v. Pierpont* (1862) 1 F. & F. 35.

[89] (1862) 1 F. & F. 35, 40.

[90] *Watson v. British Boxing Board of Control* [2001] QB 1134, 1150 (Lord Phillips); *Gregg v. Scott* [2005] 2 AC 176, 225 (Baroness Hale).

doctor.[91] Judges were concerned about the threat to charitable funds.[92] Employers were vicariously liable for their servants but medical men were professionals. In *Hillyer v. The Governors of St Bartholomew's Hospital*[93] Farwell LJ made the point that:

> they are all professional men, employed by the defendants to exercise their profession to the best of their abilities according to their own discretion; but in exercising it they are in no way under the orders or bound to obey the directions of the defendants.[94]

Growing dissatisfaction with *Hillyer* saw hospitals held liable for the negligence of a radiographer[95] and junior house surgeon.[96] Two Court of Appeal decisions, *Cassidy v. Ministry of Health*[97] and *Roe v. Minister of Health*,[98] confirmed that *Hillyer* should no longer apply. The new approach coincided with the birth of the NHS.[99]

Because the hospitals were vicariously liable for their employees (at least those with a contract of service),[100] it need not be at fault. Denning LJ preferred to impose a non-delegable duty on the hospital to treat a patient with reasonable care.[101] There is some recent support for Denning LJ's analysis[102] but it means that a hospital will not be liable without fault. Where a hospital is totally without fault a claimant is still thrown back onto vicarious liability.[103]

The second problem, whether or not damages can be recovered for the birth of a child born as result of a negligent sterilisation, is not unique to

[91] *Evans v. Liverpool Corporation* [1906] 1 KB 160, 166.
[92] *MacDonald v. Glasgow Western Hospital Board of Management and Another* (1954) SLT 228, 233; *Cassidy v. Ministry of Health* [1951] 2 KB 343, 361 (Denning LJ). In contrast there was no difficulty in holding a local authority liable for a negligent teacher see: *Smith v. Martin and the Corporation of Kingston-upon-Hull* [1911] 2 KB 775.
[93] [1909] 2 KB 820. The decision was followed in *Strangeways-Lesmere v. Clayton* [1936] 2 KB 11; *Marshall v. Lindsey County Council* [1935] 1 KB 516. Scottish law adopted a similar approach *Lavelle v. Glasgow Royal Infirmary* (1932) SLT 179. In *Reidford v. Magistrates of Aberdeen* (1933) SLT 155 Lord Clyde stressed that although the result was the same as in England, the way it was reached depended on specifically Scottish principles.
[94] [1909] 2 KB 820, 824.   [95] *Gold v. Essex County Council* [1942] 2 KB 293.
[96] *Collins v. Hertfordshire County Council* [1947] 1 KB 598.
[97] [1951] 2 KB 343.   [98] [1954] 2 QB 66.
[99] [1951] 2 KB 343, 361 (Denning LJ); J. Fleming, 'Developments in the English Law of Medical Liability' (1958–59) 12 *Vanderbilt Law Review* 633, 636.
[100] In *Cassidy* Somervell and Singleton LJJ and in *Roe* Somervell and Morris LJJ.
[101] [1951] 2 KB 343, 359–60; [1954] 2 QB 66, 82.
[102] *X v. Bedfordshire County Council* [1995] 2 AC 633, 740; *Robertson v. Nottingham Health Authority* [1997] 8 Med. LR 1.
[103] *Bull v. Devon Area Health Authority* [1993] 4 Med. LR 117.

the UK.[104] In *Udale v. Bloomsbury Area Health Authority*[105] Jupp J rejected a claim for the cost of bringing up a healthy child born after a negligent sterilisation on the grounds of public policy.[106] The following year Pain J took the opposite view.[107] The Court of Appeal in *Emeh v. Kensington and Chelsea and Westminster Area Health Authority*[108] confirmed that damages could be recovered for the cost of bringing up a child. The child in *Emeh* suffered from congenital abnormalities but it was later,[109] if reluctantly,[110] assumed that the same principles applied to the birth of a healthy child.[111]

The problem has not gone away. Judges, who have slowly abandoned their traditional hostility to public policy[112] and reluctance to address ethical issues head on,[113] have struggled to follow a consistent line. In *McFarlane v. Tayside Health Board*,[114] the House of Lords were faced with a mother's claim for pain and suffering and the financial costs associated with the pregnancy following a negligent sterilisation along with the cost of bringing up the child. Although it was denied that the outcome had anything to do with public policy,[115] in Lord Millett's opinion: 'There is

---

[104] *McFarlane v. Tayside Health Authority* [2000] 2 AC 56, 68 (Lord Slynn). Lord Slynn provides a useful summary of the law in other jurisdictions at pp. 71–3; A. Stewart, 'Damages for the Birth of a Child' (1995) 40 *Journal of the Law Society of Scotland* 298; H. Teff, 'The Action for "Wrongful Life" in England and the United States' (1985) 34 *International and Comparative Law Quarterly* 423. The High Court of Australia has recently rejected the *McFarlane* approach see *Cottanach v. Melchior* (2003) 199 ALR 131 by a majority of just four to three. For a comparison of England and Australia see: P. Cane, 'Another Failed Sterilisation' (2004) 120 *Law Quarterly Review* 189.

[105] [1983] 1 WLR 1098.

[106] C. R. Symmons, 'Policy Factors in Actions for Wrongful Birth' (1987) 50 MLR 269.

[107] *Thake v. Maurice* [1984] 2 All ER 513.   [108] [1985] QB 1012.

[109] *Thake v. Maurice* [1986] QB 644; *Benarr v. Kettering Health Authority* (1988) 138 NLJ 179; *Allen v. Bloomsbury Health Authority* [1993] 1 All ER 651; *Salih v. Enfield Health Authority* [1991] 3 All ER 651; *Robinson v. Salford Health Authority* [1992] 3 Med. LR 270; *Fish v. Wilcox* [1994] 5 Med. LR 230; *Walkin v. South Manchester Health Authority* [1995] 1 WLR 1543; *Goodwill v. British Pregnancy Advisory Service* [1996] 1 WLR 1397.

[110] *Jones v. Berkshire Area Health Authority* (unreported) 2 July 1986; *Gold v. Haringey Health Authority* [1988] QB 481, 484.

[111] For a discussion of the earlier authority see M. Donnelly, 'The Injury of Parenthood: The Tort of Wrongful Conception' (1997) 43 NILQ 10.

[112] C. R. Symmons, 'The Duty of Care in Negligence: Recently Expressed Policy Elements' (1971) 34 MLR 394, 528. Traditional only in the sense that it dates from the nineteenth century see *Richardson v. Mellish* (1824) 2 Bing. 229, 130 ER 294. Earlier judges were less reluctant to address public policy for example *Jones v. Randall* (1774) 1 Cowp. 37, 39.

[113] Woolf, 'Are the Courts Excessively Deferential', 4; Irvine, 'The Patient', 263.

[114] [2000] 2 AC 59.

[115] [2000] 2 AC 56, 76 (Lord Slynn), 83 (Lord Steyn), 95 (Lord Hope), 100–1 (Lord Clyde), 108 (Lord Millett).

something distasteful, if not morally offensive, in treating the birth of a normal, healthy child as a matter for compensation.'[116] Lord Millett awarded £5,000 to reflect the parents' loss of autonomy because their choice not to have further children had been taken away from them.[117] The majority allowed the first part of the claim, treating it as a straightforward case of physical injury,[118] but disagreed on what precisely was recoverable.[119] Several reasons were advanced for rejecting the second part.[120] Lord Steyn went beyond 'formalistic propositions',[121] preferring to rest his decision on 'distributive justice' founded on 'the just distribution of burdens and losses among members of society'[122] which would appeal to the 'man on the London Underground'.[123] The other members of the majority stayed within the confines of legal doctrine.[124]

Before long Court of Appeal judges began to negate the impact of *McFarlane*. A mother was allowed to recover the costs of bringing up a child with congenital abnormalities.[125] Having abandoned 'formalistic propositions' for vague moral and policy arguments, it was probably inevitable that differences would emerge. Brooke LJ was happy to apply distributive justice.[126] Hale LJ stressed the impact of pregnancy on a woman's autonomy[127] and was reluctant to classify the damage as pure economic loss.[128] Another quasi-philosophical device – 'deemed equilibrium' – was pressed into service.[129] It was said that with a healthy child the costs of

---

[116] [2000] 2 AC 56, 111.   [117] [2000] 2 AC 56, 114.

[118] [2000] 2 AC 56, 76, 74 (Lord Slynn), 84 (Lord Steyn), 87 (Lord Hope).

[119] [2000] 2 AC 56, 89 Lord Hope seemed to accept post pregnancy loss of earnings subject to the rules of remoteness. Lord Clyde rejected these damages on principle at p. 106. The later view was accepted by the Court of Appeal in *Greenfield v. Irwin* [2001] 1 WLR 1279.

[120] For critical comment see L. Hoyano, 'Misconceptions about Wrongful Conception' (2002) 65 MLR 883, 886–8; T. Weir, 'The Unwanted Child' [2000] CLJ 238.

[121] [2000] 2 AC 56, 82.

[122] [2000] 2 AC 56, 82. This rather slippery notion is very much in vogue at the moment. It can be traced to *White v. Chief Constable of South Yorkshire* [1999] 2 AC 455, 503–4 (Lord Hoffmann).

[123] [2000] 2 AC 56, 82.

[124] [2000] 2 AC 56, 75–6 (Lord Slynn), 95–6 (Lord Hope) who said the claim was subject to the restrictions placed on recovery for pure economic loss; [2000] 2 AC 56, 105–6 (Lord Clyde) who said the claim went beyond 'a reasonable restitution for a wrong done'.

[125] *Parkinson v. St James and Seacroft Hospital NHS Trust* [2002] QB 266.

[126] [2002] QB 266, 277, 283.   [127] [2002] QB 266, 285–8.

[128] [2002] QB 266, 288.

[129] [2002] QB 266, 293. She expanded on the meaning of 'deemed equilibrium' in *Rees v. Darlington Memorial NHS Trust* [2003] QB 20, 28–9. The concept was strongly criticised in the House of Lords [2004] 1 AC 309, 322 (Lord Steyn), 330 (Lord Hope).

upkeep are balanced out by the benefits brought by the child. When a child was born disabled, the equilibrium was upset.[130]

The following year in *Rees v. Darlington Memorial NHS Trust*[131] a new distinction, this time between different sorts of parent, was used by the Court of Appeal in order to circumvent *McFarlane*. A visually impaired mother of a healthy child was allowed to recover the costs of upbringing. A majority in the House of Lords suddenly saw the attraction of Lord Millett's speech in *McFarlane*. £15,000 was deemed to be an appropriate award.[132] Significantly Lord Hope and Lord Steyn, who sat in *McFarlane*, found it hard to reconcile the approach of the majority with the general principle that an award of damages should reflect actual loss[133] and were content to draw the same distinction as the Court of Appeal.[134]

Finding a coherent doctrine in these authorities is far from easy.[135] Lord Steyn has described the task of extracting a ratio from *McFarlane* as 'gruesome'.[136] He also expressed concern that *Rees* would bring about a 'backdoor evasion' of *McFarlane*.[137] Some of those who heard *Rees* favoured awarding £15,000 irrespective of the health of mother or child,[138] at least in cases of 'wrongful conception'. The position in cases of wrongful birth, which are concerned either with the negligent non-diagnosis of a foetal defect resulting in a failure to terminate or a negligent termination, remains to be determined.[139] Earlier authority suggests that a parent could recover for the cost of bringing up a disabled child.[140] *Rees* seems to send out a message that health authorities should not be allowed to escape the consequences of negligent practice whilst at the same time recognising the serious resource implications of large damage awards.[141] Nevertheless the conventional award approach runs the risk of

---

[130] [2003] QB 20, 28–9 (Hale LJ).   [131] [2003] QB 20.

[132] [2004] 1 AC 309, 317 (Lord Bingham), 319 (Lord Nicholls), 349–50 (Lord Millett), 356 (Lord Scott).

[133] [2004] 1 AC 309, 327–8 (Lord Steyn), 334 (Lord Hope).

[134] [2004] 1 AC 309, 324–5 (Lord Steyn), 331 (Lord Hope), 338, 342 (Lord Hutton).

[135] J. K. Mason, 'From Dundee to Darlington: An End to the *McFarlane* Line?' (2004) JR 365, 375–8.

[136] [2004] 1 AC 309, 321.   [137] [2004] 1 AC 309, 328.

[138] [2004] 1 AC 309, 317 (Lord Bingham), 318 (Lord Nicholls), 343, 349–50 (Lord Millett), 355 (Lord Scott).

[139] *Parkinson v. St James and Seacroft Hospital NHS Trust* [2002] QB 266, 281–2 Brooke LJ said the two situations were distinct.

[140] *Hardman v. Amin* [2000] Lloyd's Rep. Med. 498; *Rand v. East Dorset Health Authority* [2001] Lloyd's Rep. Med. 181; *Lee v. Taunton and Somerset NHS Trust* [2001] 1 FLR 419.

[141] [2004] 1 AC 309, 316 (Lord Bingham).

becoming a fudge, incurring the wrath of feminist legal theorists[142] and NHS accountants alike.

B   Breach of duty

Erle CJ was reluctant to provide concrete guidance to a jury faced with deciding whether a doctor was in breach of his duty of care. Defendants remain to be judged against the standard of reasonableness[143] – a task that involves a complex balancing exercise.[144] By the 1950s wide jury discretion was a thing of the past. Greater guidance was required. It was provided by McNair J in a classic direction[145] in *Bolam v. Friern Hospital Management Committee*.[146] McNair J made two main points. His first, that 'the test is the standard of the ordinary skilled man exercising and professing to have that special skill',[147] has survived unscathed.[148] McNair J then continued:

> He is not guilty of negligence if he has acted in accordance with a practice accepted as proper by a responsible body of medical men skilled in that particular art ... a man is not negligent, if he is acting in accordance with such a practice merely because there is a body of opinion who would take a contrary view.[149]

In a lecture delivered the year before he handed down judgment in *Bolam* McNair J appeared to suggest that the standard required of doctors was a high one:

> The test of negligence is not to be based on the behaviour of the man on the Clapham omnibus but on a proper standard of behaviour of a person having that professional skill and competence. The surgeon and physician must exercise such skill and competence as accords with the general and approved standards for a person carrying out those functions.[150]

---

[142] N. Priaulx, 'That's one Heck of an "Unruly Horse"! Riding Roughshod over Autonomy in Wrongful Conception' (2004) *Feminist Legal Studies* 317.

[143] *Blyth v. Birmingham Waterworks* (1856) 11 Exch. 781, 784.

[144] R. Wright, 'The Standards of Care in Negligence Law' in D. Owen (ed.), *Philosophical Foundations of Tort Law* (Oxford: Oxford University Press, 1995), ch. 11.

[145] *Bolitho v. City and Hackney Health Authority* [1998] AC 232, 239; Teff, *Reasonable Care*, pp. 51–7. McNair J's judgment mirrors the earlier Scottish case of *Hunter v. Hanley* (1955) SLT 213.

[146] [1957] 1 WLR 582.   [147] [1957] 1 WLR 582, 587.

[148] This limb of *Bolam* makes no allowance for inexperience see: *Wilsher v. Essex Health Authority* [1987] QB 730, 750 (Mustill LJ), *cf.* Browne-Wilkinson V-C at 776–7 who disagreed. It is perfectly in line with general principles see *Nettleship v. Weston* [1971] 2 QB 691.

[149] [1957] 1 WLR 582, 588.

[150] Mr Justice McNair, 'Medical responsibility in hospitals' (1956) 24 Med. Leg. Jour. 129, 131.

Whatever the true meaning[151] and context of McNair J's judgment – as a jury direction at a time when juries were unusual[152] – a view soon took hold that a doctor who was able, by the use of expert witnesses, to demonstrate that his behaviour conformed to a recognised body of professional opinion, was not in breach of his duty of care.[153] This interpretation of *Bolam* fitted neatly with the earlier observation that doctors should not be punished for following customary procedure.[154]

The *Bolam* test is not confined to doctors[155] but judges have been more willing to find other professionals in breach where they behaved in a way which coincides with standard practice, on the grounds that the practice itself is unreasonable.[156] In contrast, one judge has observed that 'the *Bolam* principle provides a defence for those who lag behind the times'.[157] Although *Bolam* was largely seen as uncontroversial at the time,[158] later commentators have tended to regard the decision as unduly lenient towards the medical profession.[159]

---

[151] Woolf, 'Are the Courts Excessively Deferential' 5–6; Teff, *Reasonable Care*, pp. 180–2. Fleming, 'Developments' 642 noted that: 'This ruling does not imply ... that conformity is necessarily conclusive, but suggests that it will be accepted as such, unless the practice is demonstrably fraught with obvious hazards.'

[152] H. Teff, 'The Standard of Care in Medical Negligence – Moving on from Bolam?' (1998) 18 OJLS 473, 473–4.

[153] M. Brazier and J. Miola, 'Bye-bye Bolam: A Medical Litigation Revolution?' (2000) 8 Med. Law Rev. 85, 88–95. For an isolated exception see *Hucks v. Cole* (1993) 4 Med. LR 393. The decision dates from 1968. It is probably no coincidence that it was only widely reported once attitudes had changed. The only abbreviated reports at the time were in *The Times*, 9 May 1968 (which omits the crucial passage of Sachs LJ), the *New Law Journal* (1968) 118 NLJ 469 and *The Solicitors' Journal*: (1968) 112 SJ 483. On *Hucks v. Cole* see *Bolitho v. City and Hackney Health Authority* [1998] AC 232, 241.

[154] *Marshall v. Lindsey County Council* [1935] 1 KB 516, 540.

[155] *Whitehouse v. Jordan* [1981] 1 All ER 267, 276; *Gold v. Haringey Health Authority* [1988] QB 481, 489: 'I can see no possible ground for distinguishing between doctors and any other profession or calling which requires special skill, knowledge or experience' (Lloyd LJ).

[156] *Lloyds Bank v. Savory & Co* [1933] AC 201, 203; *Edward Wong Finance Co. Ltd v. Johnson, Stokes and Masters* [1984] AC 296. On occasions the courts have gone down the *Bolam* route even outside medical negligence, for example *Luxmoore-May v. Messenger May Baverstock* [1990] 1 WLR 1009 see F. Meisel, 'Auctioneers' in R. Hodgin (ed.), *Professional Liability: Law and Insurance* (London: LLP, 1996) 181, 191–2.

[157] *Newell and Newell v. Goldberg* [1995] 6 Med. LR 371, 374 (Mantell J).

[158] R. F. V. Heuston, *Salmond on the Law of Torts* 13th edn. (London: Sweet & Maxwell, 1961), p. 439; J. A. Jolowicz and T. Ellis Lewis *Winfield on Tort* 7th edn. (London: Sweet & Maxwell, 1963), p. 184. For an early criticism see J. L. Montrose, 'Is Negligence an Ethical or Sociological Concept?' (1958) 21 MLR 259.

[159] Brazier and Miola, 'Bye-bye Bolam' 85; *Making Amends*, p. 10: 'This test is a difficult hurdle'.

Until recently judges were usually unwilling to challenge the reasonableness of a body of medical opinion or prefer one body of opinion over
another. In *Maynard v. West Midlands Regional Health Authority*[160] Lord
Scarman explained that:

> I have to say that a judge's 'preference' for one body of distinguished pro-
> fessional opinion to another also professionally distinguished is not suffi-
> cient to establish negligence in a practitioner whose actions have received
> the seal of approval of those whose opinions, truthfully expressed, hon-
> estly held, were not preferred.[161]

A doctor could be exonerated if he behaved in accordance with a body
of medical opinion however small.[162] Once the courts began to go beyond
clinical practice and address a wider variety of ethical issues, including
informed consent, the influence of *Bolam* grew still further.[163]

By the 1980s, the consensus was beginning to crack. Some judges
began to suggest that the substance of evidence could be challenged.[164] In
Sidaway v. Bethlem Royal Hospital Governors,[165] although Lord Scarman
said that 'the standard of care is a matter of medical judgment',[166] Lord
Bridge attempted to bring doctors into line with other professionals –
even where there was no division in medical opinion, it could still be condemned as unreasonable.[167] Cases of informed consent like *Sidaway* may
amount to the most significant inroad into the *Bolam* test.[168] In *Bolitho v.
City and Hackney Health Authority*[169] Lord Browne-Wilkinson went further. He pointed out that McNair J had referred to a 'competent reasonable body of opinion'[170] and continued:

> in cases of diagnosis and treatment there are cases where, despite a body
> of professional opinion sanctioning the defendant's conduct, the defend-
> ant can properly be held liable for negligence. In my judgment, that is
> because, in some cases, it cannot be demonstrated to the judge's satisfac-
> tion that the body of opinion relied upon is reasonable or responsible.[171]

---

[160] [1984] 1 WLR 634.   [161] [1984] 1 WLR 634, 640.
[162] *Freitas v. O'Brien* [1993] 4 Med. LR 281 is a particularly glaring example where the procedure was favoured by four or five out of two hundred and fifty neurosurgeons; *Making
Amends*, p. 52.
[163] M. Jones, 'Informed Consent and Other Fairy Stories' (1999) 7 Med. Law Rev. 103;
Brazier and Miola, 'Bye-bye Bolam' 90–1; *Sidaway v. Board of Governors of the Royal
Bethlem Hospital* [1985] AC 871.
[164] *Hills v. Potter* [1984] 1 WLR 641, 653 (Hirst J).   [165] [1985] AC 871.
[166] [1985] AC 871, 881.   [167] [1985] AC 871, 900.
[168] K. Mason and D. Brodie, 'Bolam, Bolam – Wherefore Art Thou Bolam' (2005) 9 Edin.
LR 298.
[169] [1998] AC 232.   [170] [1998] AC 232, 241.   [171] [1998] AC 232, 243.

At the same time he stressed that:

> in a rare case, it can be demonstrated that the professional opinion is not capable of withstanding logical analysis, the judge is entitled to hold that the body of opinion is not reasonable or responsible. I emphasise that in my view it will very seldom be right for a judge to reach the conclusion that views genuinely held by a competent medical expert are unreasonable.[172]

In Lord Woolf's view, *Bolitho* will 'enable a court to distinguish between two sets of medical opinion. When faced with conflicting expert evidence, what a court regularly does is to select the reasoning of the expert which is most logically persuasive.'[173] Academic writers are divided on the likely impact of *Bolitho*.[174] Some judges are openly sceptical.[175] There are nevertheless some signs that judges may be more willing to challenge expert opinion.[176] In *Marriott v. West Midlands Health Authority*,[177] the Court of Appeal upheld the decision of a trial judge who rejected expert testimony as unreasonable. Where a defendant relies on a body of professional opinion, he is required to convince the judge that the opinion is reasonable and responsible[178] but, at the same time, a judge who chooses to reject such evidence must provide a 'coherent reasoned rebuttal'.[179] In reality it may still be relatively unusual for the courts to make a finding of negligence where a doctor follows a commonly accepted practice[180] but, in truth, there may be no one single approach to the question of breach of duty.[181]

---

[172] [1998] AC 232, 243.

[173] Woolf, 'Are the Courts Excessively Deferential' 11.

[174] Teff, *Reasonable Care*, p. 483; Brazier and Miola, 'Bye-bye Bolam' 100–7; K. Amirthalingam, 'Anglo-Australian Law of Medical Negligence – Towards Convergence?' (2003) 11 *Torts Law Journal* 117, 122–4. For a more pessimistic view see M. Jones, 'The Bolam Test and the Responsible Expert' (1999) 7 *Tort Law Review* 226; Jones, *Medical Negligence*, para. 3–030.

[175] Irvine, 'The Patient' 260; Lord Justice Otton, 'Medical Negligence – Is There Something Wrong?' (2001) 69 *Medico-Legal Journal* 72, 74–75: 'it [Bolitho] may prove to be no more than a false dawn'.

[176] *Hunt v. NHS Litigation Authority* (2000) WL 1480071; *Reynolds v. North Tyneside Health Authority* [2002] Lloyd's Rep. Med. 459; *D v. South Tyneside Health Care NHS Trust* [2004] PIQR P150.

[177] [1999] Lloyd's Rep. Med. 23, M. Jones, 'The Illogical Expert' (1999) 15 PN 117.

[178] *M v. Blackpool Victoria Hospital NHS Trust* [2003] EWHC 1744.

[179] *Knight v. West Kent Health Authority* (1998) BMLR 61, 65.

[180] *Pearce v. United Bristol Healthcare NHS Trust* [1999] PIQR P53, 59: 'very seldom' (Lord Woolf MR); A. MacLean, 'Beyond Bolam and Bolitho' (2002) 5 *Medical Law International* 205.

[181] Newdick, *Who Should We Treat?*, pp. 135–44. Practitioners of alternative medicine are particularly problematic. In *Shakoor v. Situ* [2001] 1 WLR 410 it was held that they were not to be judged solely by the standards of qualified doctors or those of alternative practitioners.

Some academic critics of *Bolam* have detected something sinister in the traditional approach.[182] But there is a simpler explanation. The way that judges have deployed *Bolam* is no more than a reflection of the problem of handling evidence which is frequently technical and contradictory as well as outside the experience of most judges. Lord Denning has admitted that: 'The medical people, the engineers, the chemists – all have their jargon which none of the rest of us understands.'[183] As a result, judges are thrown back on expert witnesses.[184] Handling technical information is not unique to medical negligence but there are other factors which make the problem particularly acute in this context. Medicine is an art as well as a science.[185] Patients are unique – they are not like broken televisions.[186] The number of adverse events may be alarmingly high.[187] Medical errors cover a whole spectrum of different types of mistake, some of which are more morally blameworthy than others.[188] The rapid development of medical technologies and the length of time taken for some cases to reach a final conclusion make an assessment of medical procedures even more difficult.[189] There are dangers in setting the standard too high. The impact of a medical negligence claim on the doctor concerned should not be forgotten.[190] As one judge warned, judges ought to be careful not to award compensation on the basis of 'deserving plaintiffs in individual cases'.[191] Merry and McCall Smith have also made the point that:

---

[182] J. Montgomery, 'Medicine, Accountability, and Professionalism' (1986) 16 *Journal of Law and Society* 319; S. Sheldon, 'A Responsible Body of Medical Men Skilled in that Particular Art: Rethinking the Bolam Test' in S. Sheldon and M. Thomson (eds.), *Feminist Perspectives on Healthcare Law* (London: Routledge Cavendish, 1998), pp. 15–32; J. Conaghan and W. Mansell, *The Wrongs of Tort,* 2nd edn. (London: Pluto Press, 1999), pp. 57–60.

[183] Lord Denning, 'The Freedom of the Individual Today' (1977) 45 *Medico-Legal Journal* 49, 59.

[184] A. Merry and A. McCall Smith, *Errors, Medicine and the Law* (Cambridge: Cambridge University Press, 2001), ch. 7 which deals with some of the problems caused by reliance on expert witnesses.

[185] D. Fish and C. Coles, *Developing Professional Judgement in Health Care* (Oxford: Fish and Coles, 1998); V. Nathanson, 'Medical Mistakes: a View from the British Medical Association' in M. Rosenthal, L. Mulcahy and S. Lloyd-Bostock (eds.), *Medical Mishaps Pieces of the Puzzle* (Buckingham: Open University Press, 1999), pp. 200–1.

[186] *Making Amends*, p. 22.   [187] *Making Amends*, pp. 8, 33–7.

[188] Merry and McCall Smith, *Errors*, chs. 1–5.

[189] For a good example see *Townsend v. Worcester District Health Authority* (1994) 23 BMLR 31, 45 where Harrison J stressed the need to assess doctors by surgical practice at the time of the injury.

[190] *Making Amends*, p. 43; Merry and McCall Smith, *Errors*, pp. 216–19; Mulcahy, *Disputing Doctors*, ch. 6.

[191] *Townsend v. Worcester District Health Authority* (1994) 23 BMLR 31, 45.

> There is a tendency to confuse the reasonable person with the error-free person...Even though the courts have repeatedly said that the reasonable person test is anchored in realistic expectations of people, the reasonable person test has progressively failed to take account of the inherent human limitations of actual reasonable people.[192]

The point was not lost on Lord Fraser in *Whitehouse v. Jordan*.[193]

C   Proof and causation

Several judges have drawn attention to the difficulty facing a claimant who needs to show that a doctor's negligence caused his injury.[194] In *Cassidy v. Ministry of Health*, Denning LJ used the doctrine of *res ipsa loquitur*,[195] which allows a prima facie inference of negligence which can be rebutted if the defendant can show that the injury could have occurred without negligence.[196] Because evidence from medical records and expert testimony is usually available, *res ipsa loquitur* will not usually be evoked in practice.[197]

The traditional 'but for'[198] test of causation means that it is not enough for the claimant to show, on the balance of probabilities, that the defendant's breach was a cause of the harm – he must be more than 50% to blame. *McGhee v. National Coal Board*[199] showed that judges were prepared to depart from the 'but for' test some of the time. Lord Reid even conceded that the 'legal concept of causation is not based on logic or philosophy'.[200] Although judges are able to disregard the 'but for' test of causation, this new-found freedom has rarely been tested until recently. Causation has proved as formidable an obstacle as ever. In *Wilsher v. Essex Area Health Authority*,[201] a premature baby suffered from retrolental fibroplasia (RLF) leaving him blind in one eye and partially sighted in the other. It was alleged that the condition was caused by the defendant's negligent provision of oxygen. The claimant's problem was that RLF could also be caused by various medical conditions common in premature babies. The claim

---

[192] Merry and McCall Smith, *Errors*, pp. 244–5.   [193] [1981] All ER 267, 281.

[194] Ackner, 'The Doctor in Court' 55; *Fairchild v. Glenhaven Funeral Services* [2003] 1 AC 32, 76 (Lord Hoffmann).

[195] [1951] 2 KB 343, 365.

[196] P. Atiyah, 'Res ipsa loquitur in England and Australia' (1972) 35 MLR 337.

[197] *Ratcliffe v. Plymouth and Torbay Health Authority* [1998] Lloyd's Rep. Med. 162. For examples of cases where it has been successfully invoked see Jones, *Medical Negligence*, para. 3–135.

[198] *Barnett v. Chelsea and Kensington Hospital Management Committee* [1969] 1 QB 428.

[199] [1973] 1 WLR 1.   [200] [1973] 1 WLR 1, 6.   [201] [1988] AC 1074.

succeeded in the Court of Appeal[202] but failed in the House of Lords, on the back of a distinction between a case like *McGhee*, where there was a known causal agent and the present case, where there were several such agents.[203] Despite the doubts of Lord Hoffmann,[204] the distinction was upheld, albeit obiter, in *Fairchild v. Glenhaven Funeral Services Ltd.*,[205] where the House of Lords were prepared to relax the strict causal test and allow a claim when it could be shown that the defendant's breach materially increased the risk of a particular outcome, even though he could not prove that the defendant had caused the outcome.[206]

Though not a case of medical negligence, *Fairchild* was at least a reminder that, as Lord Hoffmann would have it, causation involves more than a simple factual inquiry – judges need to take account of the purpose of the law.[207] In *Chester v. Afshar*,[208] a surgeon failed to warn his patient that there was a small risk that a proposed operation on her back could cause neurological damage. The operation was carried out without negligence, but the patient was paralysed. A claim was brought on the basis that the surgeon was negligent in failing to warn. It was argued that if she had been aware of the risks, she would have delayed the operation. A later operation carried the same risk but, given the remoteness of the risk, it was likely that it would have been successful.[209] The difficulty facing the claimant was that the surgeon's failure to warn did not increase the risk – it was already there.[210] A claim of this sort had succeeded in Australia.[211] Despite rigorous dissents from Lords Bingham and Hoffmann, the majority were prepared to break the link between breach and damage. In the eyes of the majority, the duty to warn was so important that it had to be protected at the expense of the 'but for' test.[212] Unfortunately, the majority fail to convincingly explain why the duty to warn required special protection

[202] [1987] QB 730.
[203] [1988] AC 1074, 1090–1 (Lord Bridge). Lords Fraser, Lowry, Griffiths and Ackner agreed. The distinction was originally drawn by Browne-Wilkinson VC in the CA [1987] QB 730, 779–80.
[204] [2003] 1 AC 32, 77.   [205] [2003] 1 AC 32, 57 (Lord Bingham), 95 (Lord Hutton).
[206] [2003] 1 AC 32, 68 (Lord Bingham), 76 (Lord Hoffmann).
[207] Lord Hoffmann, 'Common Sense and Causation' Lecture to the Chancery Bar Association 15 June 1999. For a recent statement of his views see Lord Hoffmann, 'Causation' (2005) 121 LQR 592.
[208] [2005] 1 AC 134.   [209] [2005] 1 AC 134, 141 (Lord Bingham).
[210] [2005] 1 AC 134, 141 (Lord Bingham).
[211] *Chappel v. Hart* (1998) 156 ALR 517; T. Honoré, 'Medical Non-disclosure, Causation and Risk: Chappel v. Hart' (1999) 7 *Torts Law Journal* 1; P. Cane, 'A Warning About Causation' (1999) 115 LQR 21.
[212] [2005] 1 AC 134, 143 (Lord Steyn), 152–3, 162–3 (Lord Hope), 163 (Lord Walker).

beyond, say, the right not to be negligently injured by a medical procedure as in *Wilsher*.[213] Nor is it made clear why special protection should be relevant at the causation, rather than the duty of care, stage of their inquiry. Were Lord Hope's view that, if the rules of causation were not relaxed, then the duty would be devoid of all content, correct, it would, taken to its logical conclusion, mean that the rules of causation must be relaxed for every breach of duty.[214]

Despite *Chester v. Afshar*, pragmatism will not always win out against doctrinal purity in matters of causation. The rule that a claimant, who has been treated negligently, cannot succeed in negligence for the 'loss of chance' of a successful outcome, remains. In *Hotson v. East Berkshire Health Authority*[215] the House of Lords failed to address the argument on its merits but were clearly unsympathetic. Lord Bridge even remarked that there were 'formidable difficulties' in equating the case before him as one that was equivalent to loss of a chance in contract.[216] *Gregg v. Scott*[217] presented the House of Lords with an opportunity to reconsider loss of chance in the light of *Fairchild* and the limited approval of loss of chance claims in negligence in *Allied Marples Group Ltd. v. Simmons & Simmons*.[218] The claimant visited his general practitioner with a lump under his arm. He was told that the lump was benign. A year later he was referred to a specialist by another doctor to be told that he was suffering from non-Hodgkin's lymphoma. Because of the delay, his chance of survival, defined as surviving for ten years, was reduced from 42% to 25%. Lord Nicholls thought that to reject the claim would be 'irrational and indefensible':[219] justice and medical reality were said to compel a successful outcome.[220] The majority preferred to stay faithful to earlier authority;[221] those claims where loss of chance had been allowed were distinguished on the grounds that they involved financial loss rather than personal injury.[222] Members of the majority were also worried that were the claim to succeed, the floodgates would be well and truly opened.[223] Baroness Hale was particularly candid, explaining that were the result to

---

[213] This is not to deny that the duty to warn is not important, rather that it is not uniquely so. On the importance of the duty to warn see Jones, *Medical Negligence*, paras. 4-033-42.

[214] [2005] 1 AC 134, 162-3 (Lord Hope), 166 (Lord Walker).

[215] [1987] AC 750.   [216] [1987] AC 750, 782.

[217] [2005] 2 WLR 268; J. Stapleton, 'Loss of the Chance of Cure from Cancer' (2005) 68 MLR 996.

[218] [1995] 1 WLR 1602.   [219] [2005] 2 WLR 268, 272.

[220] [2005] 2 WLR 268, 276.   [221] [2005] 2 WLR 268, 289 (Lord Hoffmann).

[222] [2005] 2 WLR 268, 288 (Lord Hoffmann), 323-4 (Baroness Hale).

[223] [2005] 2 WLR 268, 289 (Lord Hoffmann).

be otherwise, 'almost any claim for loss of an outcome could be reformu-
lated as a claim for loss of a chance of that outcome'.[224]

4   Medical malpractice in Britain: future directions

Structural coherence in the tort of negligence is as far away as ever.[225]
Although reluctant to embrace public policy too openly, some judges
are at least prepared to concede that legal policy plays a part in decision
making.[226] In the last decade or so, the whole tenor of judgments in negligence cases, at least in the Court of Appeal and House of Lords, has
shifted. The traditional inquiry into whether the imposition of a duty of
care is 'fair, just and reasonable' is increasingly seen as unsophisticated.[227]
Judges are increasingly dining *á la carte* – choosing high-minded but
half-understood philosophical concepts like 'distributive justice', 'corrective justice', 'autonomy' and 'deemed equilibrium' from their menus.[228] *Chester v. Afshar* shows that these inquiries are no longer confined
to the question of the existence of a duty of care. Many of these devices
are particularly well suited to medical malpractice. Autonomy has been
at the forefront of the developing doctrine of informed consent.[229] There
are already some signs that the new approach may allow the courts to be
more responsive to the needs of patient claimants. But doctrinal rigid-
ity has not completely gone away. It allowed the rejection of the claim in
Gregg v. Scott which, although technically distinguishable from the claim
for failure to warn in *Chester v. Afshar*, raised many of the same issues.[230]
The elephant in the corner – the impact of a successful claim on finite

---

[224] [2005] 2 WLR 268, 324.
[225] B. Hepple, 'Negligence: The Search for Coherence' (1997) *Current Legal Problems* 69. For
an attempt by a senior judge to map out some of the ground see Lord Steyn, 'Perspectives
of Corrective and Distributive Justice in Tort Law' (2002) 37 *Irish Jurist* 1.
[226] For references to legal policy see *Rees* [2004] 1 AC 309, 317 (Lord Bingham), 322 (Lord
Steyn). See Cane, 'Another Failed Sterilisation' 191–3.
[227] 'Fair, just and reasonable' forms the third limb of the test for duty of care laid down in
Caparo Industries Plc. v. Dickman [1990] 2 AC 605. A similar idea was used by the House
of Lords in *Anns v. Merton LBC* [1978] AC 728.
[228] For the analogy with menus see J. Stapleton, 'Duty of Care Factors: a Selection from
Judicial Menus' in P. Cane and J. Stapleton (eds.), *The Law of Obligations: Essays in
Honour of John Fleming* (Oxford: Oxford University Press, 1998), pp. 59, 62: 'Over the
past twenty years many British and Commonwealth appellant judges have adopted a
franker style of analysis, packaged less in the formulaic labels common in earlier case
law but more in clearly enunciated considerations for and against recognition of a duty.'
[229] Jones, *Medical Negligence*, para. 6–105.
[230] S. Green, 'A Game of Doctors and Purses' (2006) 14 Med. Law Rev. 1.

resources – has still to be dislodged.[231] The increase in successful public law claims against health care agencies suggests that judges might be
more prepared to address issues of resource allocation head on.[232]

The increase in medical malpractice suits and the growing size of damage awards has already prompted consideration of the continued role of
medical negligence. In the United States, a number of writers have argued
that the law of contract provides a better solution than the law of tort to
the growing medical malpractice crisis.[233] The structure of health care in
Britain would seem to rule out this option. Mediation has been tried but a
pilot scheme has not become permanent.[234] The idea of no-fault compensation for medical malpractice was rejected by the Pearson Committee
in the late 1970s.[235] There remains considerable academic support behind
reform,[236] despite the shortcomings of existing no-fault schemes.[237] The
medical profession is increasingly coming around to the idea[238] and the
question was re-opened in a report of the Chief Medical Officer: *Making
Amends*.[239] A comprehensive no-fault scheme for medical accidents was

[231] The issue was referred to by Lord Bingham in *Rees* [2004] 1 AC 309, 316 and Lord
Hoffmann in *Gregg* [2005] 2 WLR 268, 290.

[232] Newdick, *Who Should We Treat?*, ch. 5.

[233] R. Epstein, 'Medical Malpractice, Imperfect Information, and the Contractual
Foundation for Medical Services' (1986) 49 *Law and Contemporary Problems* 201;
P. Atiyah, 'Medical Malpractice and the Contract/Tort Boundary' (1986) 49 *Law and
Contemporary Problems* 287.

[234] L. Mulcahy, M. Selwood and A. Netten, *Mediating Medical Negligence Claims: An Option
for the Future?* (London: HMSO, 2000).

[235] *Royal Commission on Civil Liability and Compensation for Personal Injury* (Cmnd. 7054,
1978), paras. 1–1348–72. For the background to Pearson see J. Fleming, 'The Pearson
Report: Its "Strategy"' (1979) 42 MLR 249; P. Atiyah, 'No-Fault Compensation: A
Question that will not go Away' (1980) 54 *Tulane Law Review* 271.

[236] M. Brazier, 'The Case for a No-Fault Compensation Scheme for Medical Accidents' in
S. McLean (ed.), *Compensation for Damage: An International Perspective* (Aldershot:
Dartmouth, 1993), p. 51; Newdick, *Who Should we Treat?*, pp. 129–32. For defences of the
tort system in medical negligence see Jones, *Medical Negligence*, paras. 1–040–53 and
generally see A. Burrows, *Understanding the Law of Obligations Essays on Contract, Tort
and Restitution* (Oxford: Hart, 1998), ch. 6.

[237] For a discussion of the New Zealand scheme see K. Oliphant, 'Defining "Medical
Misadventure": Some Lessons from New Zealand' (1996) 4 Med. Law Rev. 1;
R. Mahoney, 'Trouble in Paradise: New Zealand's Accident Compensation Scheme'
in S. McLean (ed.), *Law Reform and Medical Injury Litigation* (Aldershot: Dartmouth,
1995), p. 31.

[238] Contrast the BMA's evidence in the *Pearson Report* at paras. 1–1342–43 with *Report of
BMA No Fault Compensation Working Party* (London: BMA, 1987); *Report of BMA No
Fault Compensation Working Party* (London: BMA, 1991).

[239] Jones, *Medical Negligence*, paras. 1–027–34; Merry and McCall Smith, *Errors*, pp. 223–9;
Newdick, *Who Should We Treat?*, 131–2.

rejected on the grounds of cost.[240] An alternative to negligence – the NHS
Redress Scheme – was recommended in two sorts of case.[241] Patients
would be eligible for payment where, as a result of 'serious shortcomings'
in the standard of care, they suffer avoidable harm which was not caused
by the natural progression of the illness.[242] Claims would be capped at
£30,000.[243] The Report also recommended a separate scheme for com-
pensating those who suffer from severe neurological birth defects. The
impairment must be 'related to or resulting from the birth' but the claimant need not prove fault. A successful claimant could expect to receive
up to £50,000 for pain and suffering, £50,000 for home adaptations and
£100,000 per annum for additional care which cannot be provided by
the NHS. Legislation to implement these reforms is currently before the
House of Lords[244] but the government has watered down some of the proposals in *Making Amends*.[245] Critics argue that the proposed scheme is
insufficiently independent because it will be run by the NHS Litigation
Authority.[246]

There may be some grounds to believe that the reforms may facilitate
a greater culture of openness, thereby allowing lessons to be learnt from
medical mistakes.[247] The costs for claimants may be reduced. Delays may
be a thing of the past. But it has been suggested by one solicitor working in
the area that, if the proposals are implemented, they will greatly increase
the financial burden on the NHS. Those with strong cases will continue
to prefer to pursue a claim in medical negligence in the hope of securing

---

[240] *Making Amends*, p. 112.
[241] *Making Amends*, ch. 8. For criticisms of the recommendations see Jones, *Medical Negligence*, paras. 1–054–74.
[242] *Making Amends*, p. 120.   [243] *Making Amends*, p. 120.
[244] NHS Redress Bill (2005–2006 HL 45). The Bill leaves it to the Secretary of State to lay down the details of the scheme. At the time of writing, in May 2006, the Bill has passed its third reading in the House of Lords and is now before the House of Commons. For a comment on the Bill see M. Mansell, 'NHS Redress – Progress and Problems' (2005) 73 *Medical Legal Journal* 121.
[245] The separate scheme for birth defects is omitted: Earl Howe, Hansard HL (6th series) vol. 675, col. 209 (2nd November 2005).
[246] The group Action against Medical Accidents is currently campaigning for the scheme to be run by a body separate from the NHS. Baroness Neuberger made a similar point during the Bill's second reading see Hansard HL (6th series) vol. 675, col. 213 (2 November 2005).
[247] W. Gaine, 'No Fault Compensation Systems' (2003) 326 BMJ 997; C. Vincent, 'Compensation as a Duty of Care: the Case for "No Fault" ' (2003) 12 *Quality and Safety in Health Care* 240. This was one of the arguments put by Lord Warner the Minister of State at the Department of Health see Hansard HL (6th series) vol. 675, col. 205 (2 November 2005).

a larger award. The scheme may only succeed in adding a new class of claimant.[248]

The presence of the most criticised requirements of medical negligence, namely breach and causation, albeit under different names, in the proposals set out in *Making Amends* is significant. It is difficult, short of introducing a system of genuine no-fault compensation and abandoning the requirement of causation, to see how it could be any other way. Some of the criticism levelled at medical negligence is premised on the assumption that judges and doctors are engaged in a joint enterprise designed to prevent patients from receiving due compensation when something goes wrong. But, given the nature of medical science which, even in a highly technological age is still fraught with uncertainties, the complexities and contradictions of scientific evidence, combined with the adversarial trial process, it is perfectly reasonable for judges to err on the side of caution. There is a danger that, in the clamour for patients' rights, the line between a negligent error and a mere error will become blurred. If this temptation is not resisted, the impact on the health care system and health care professionals could be catastrophic. There is some evidence that increasing levels of litigiousness amongst patients has led more doctors to practise defensive medicine which may not always be in patients' best interests.[249]

---

[248] B. Capstick, 'The Future of Clinical Negligence Litigation?' (2004) 328 BMJ 457.

[249] M. Ennis and C. Vincent, 'The Effect of Medical Accidents and Litigation on Doctors and Patients' (1994) 16 *Law and Policy* 97, 99–101; N. Summerton, 'Positive and Negative Factors in Defensive Medicine: a Questionnaire Study of General Practitioners' (1995) 310 BMJ 27. In *Barker v. Nugent* (1987) LEXIS (unreported) Rougier J rejected the argument that defensive medicine should be taken into account in deciding whether there was a duty of care.

3

The development of medical liability in Scotland

NIALL R. WHITTY

I. Introduction: the structure of health care in Scotland

The Scotland Act 1998 established a Scottish Parliament which has exercised legislative power since 1 July 1999 over all matters not expressly reserved[1] to the United Kingdom Parliament. The National Health Service in Scotland (NHSiS) was established on 5 July 1948.[2] Previously 'Scottish healthcare combined elements of voluntary, municipal, provident, private and government provision at both hospital and community levels. Afterwards over [400] hospitals with accommodation for around [60,000] patients, became Crown property.'[3]

The establishment, regulation and operation of the NHSiS is devolved to the Scottish Parliament, together with residual legislative competence over Scots private law including medical negligence. The provision of health care is carried out almost entirely by the NHSiS. The current Act requires the Scottish Ministers 'to promote in Scotland a comprehensive and integrated health service designed to secure improvement in the physical and mental health of the people of Scotland, and the prevention, diagnosis and treatment of illness'.[4] The services so provided are to be free of charge.[5]

---

[1] By Part II of Sch. 5 to the Act. See especially 'Head J – Health and Medicine'. The reserved subjects relating to 'medical law' include abortion; xenotransplantation; embryology, surrogacy and genetics; medicines, medical supplies and poisons.

[2] Under the National Health Service (Scotland) Act 1947. See now National Health Service (Scotland) Act 1978.

[3] Lothian Health Service Archive, 'History of Health': www.lhsa.lib.ed.ac.uk/histheal/nhs/index.html.

[4] National Health Service (Scotland) Act 1978, s. 1. It is also the duty of the Scottish Ministers themselves to promote the improvement of the physical and mental health of the people of Scotland: National Health Service (Scotland) Act 1978, s. 1A(1) (added by the National Health Service Reform (Scotland) Act 2004 (asp. 7), s. 9(1)).

[5] NHS(S)A 1978, s. 1(2): except in so far as the making and recovery of charges is expressly provided for by or under any enactment whenever passed.

Traditionally the private medical sector is much smaller in Scotland than in England and Wales.[6]

The NHSiS is organised in two tiers. The higher tier consists of the Scottish Executive Health Department (SEHD) which is responsible for national policy and reports to the Scottish Ministers who in turn are accountable to the Scottish Parliament. The lower tier consists of fifteen NHS boards classified by geographical area and eight special health boards classified by administrative function.[7] The NHS boards are responsible for local health planning and improvement and for the delivery of hospital, community and primary care services. The health boards enter into contracts with general medical practitioners for the provision of general or primary medical services.[8] The special health boards provide common services on a national (all-Scotland) basis. They include the NHSiS Common Services Agency,[9] one of whose operating divisions is the Central Legal Office (NHSSCLO) which is broadly equivalent in function to the National Litigation Authority in England and Wales in so far as it acts for NHSiS bodies in defending actions for medical negligence in the Scottish courts.[10]

Medical practitioners in private practice are represented by the three medical defence unions, especially the Medical and Dental Defence Union of Scotland (MDDUS) which acts for graduates of Scottish university medical faculties wherever resident.

At one time NHS Trusts formed another legally distinct tier. An NHS Trust is responsible for providing certain health care services for the local population. An Acute Hospital Trust provides hospital services. A Primary Care Trust provides primary care and community health services. In Scotland since 2001, NHS Trusts have operated within an overall framework drawn up by the NHS Board for their area. Trusts as separate

[6] J. W. G. Blackie, 'Scotland' in E. Deutsch and H.-L. Schreiber (eds.) *Medical Responsibility in Western Europe* (Berlin: Springer, 1985).

[7] I.e. NHS Quality Improvement Scotland; NHS Health Scotland; NHS Education for Scotland; NHS National Services Scotland (NHSNSS) (formerly known as the Common Services Agency); Golden Jubilee National Hospital; Scottish Ambulance Service; State Hospital; and NHS 24.

[8] The functions of the GPs are regulated in great detail: see National Health Service (General Medical Services Contracts) (Scotland) Regulations 2004, SSI 2004/115; National Health Service (Primary Medical Services Section 17C Agreements) (Scotland) Regulations 2004, SSI 2004/116.

[9] See above n. 7.

[10] For further details, see the NHSSCLO website: www.clo.scot.nhs.uk/litigation.htm.

legal entities were dissolved by April 2004, and became operating divisions of the NHS Board which is the single employer for the local system.

II. The regulation of health care and health care professionals in Scotland

(1)   The regulation of health care and aspects of its infrastructure

The regulation of health care professions is reserved to the UK Parliament.[11] The infrastructure of the National Health Service is different in Scotland from that in England and Wales.[12] So, for example, the guidance of the National Institute for Clinical Excellence (NICE) does not apply directly in Scotland. Instead a body called NHS Quality Improvement Scotland (NHS QIS) considers the suitability of the guidance for Scotland in the light of any contextual differences.[13] The NHS QIS and other bodies are responsible for improving clinical standards.[14] The fact that pressure groups such as Action for Victims of Medical Accidents (AVMA) and the Patients Association have no presence, or strong presence, in Scotland may help to explain the lower level of litigation in medical negligence.[15]

The NHSiS and private health care providers operate complaints procedures which, despite differences in terminology, both comprise three stages, namely: local resolution; independent review or appeal; and intervention by an external adjudicator.[16] The Health Service Commissioner for Scotland[17] is the adjudicator for NHSiS complaints. The Royal Society of

[11] Scotland Act 1998, Sch. 5, Head G2.
[12] The Patients Forums, the Independent Complaints and Advisory Service (ICAS), the Commission for Healthcare Audit and Inspection, the National Clinical Assessment Authority, and the National Patient Safety Agency have no jurisdiction in Scotland.
[13] E.g. the principles and values of NHSS; epidemiology (frequency, distribution and stage at presentation); the structure and provision of services in Scotland; and other implications for NHSS, e.g. rural issues, predicted uptake, and existing advice from the Scottish Medicines Consortium.
[14] Including NHS Health Scotland and NHS Education for Scotland.
[15] AVMA have been instrumental in setting up a panel of medical expert witnesses for litigation in England and Wales. See the *Report of the Expert Group on Financial and Other Support* (the Ross Report) (Scottish Executive, March 2003), paras. 7.20–7.21 recommending that the Scottish Executive make initial funding available for establishing a Scottish branch of AVMA. There is a Scottish branch of the Patients Association.
[16] See Royal Society of Edinburgh (RSE), *Encouraging Resolution; mediating patient/health service disputes in Scotland* (2002), para. 4.21. In the three years 1997/1998–1999/2000, the total complaints numbered 11,170; 11,519; and 11,129 respectively.
[17] Health Commissioners Act 1993.

Edinburgh Report on *Encouraging Resolution* said that in Scotland it was not possible to trace the proportion of complaints attributable to medical negligence or which move on to litigation for medical malpractice.[18] These should be few since the Commissioner is not empowered to investigate a matter in respect of which the person aggrieved has a civil judicial remedy.[19] Most private health care complaints are governed by procedures set up by a UK body, the Independent Healthcare Association.[20]

In Scotland the use of mediation to resolve medical negligence disputes has so far been negligible.[21] The NHSiS complaints procedures do offer conciliation as a voluntary option for patients and health care providers if both agree to that course but the take-up is very low.[22]

(2)   *The regulation of health care professionals*

Unified cross-border arrangements for self-regulation of the medical profession have existed since at least the establishment of the General Medical Council (GMC) by the Medical Act 1858. The GMC for Regulation of Health Care Professionals has jurisdiction in Scotland.[23] A doctor's appeal against the GMC may lie to the Court of Session in Edinburgh.[24]

III.   Redress through litigation: medical negligence

(1)   *The historical development to the 1950s, with particular reference to the standard of care*

Scots law was not influenced by the English forms of action. In the seventeenth and eighteenth centuries the Scots law of negligence developed from *ius commune* notions of *culpa*. At one time the principle *spondet*

---

[18] RSE, *Encouraging Resolution*, para. 4.23.   [19] 1993 Act, s. 4(1)(b).

[20] Independent Healthcare Association, Code of Practice for Handling Patients' Complaints; see RSE, *Encouraging Resolution*, para. 4.24. Separate figures for Scotland are not available.

[21] RSE, *Encouraging Resolution*, para. 4.28. The RSE group were aware of only one case of medical negligence in which mediation had been used. This reflects the minimal use of ADR in Scotland generally: ibid., para. 4.34. There is no body equivalent to the Patient Advocacy Liaison Services (PALS) in England and Wales, other than Citizens Advice Bureaux.

[22] RSE, *Encouraging Resolution*, para. 4.29.

[23] *Stair Memorial Encyclopaedia Reissue* 'Medical Law' (Edinburgh: Green, 2006 by M. Earle and N. R. Whitty), paras. 14 and 15.

[24] In the case of a person whose address in the register of practitioners in question is in Scotland: NHS Reform and Healthcare Professions Act 2002, ss. 29(5), 30.

peritiam artis, et imperitia culpae adnumeratur[25] was of pivotal importance. Justinian's *Institutes* had stated: 'Lack of skill also counts as fault,
as where a doctor kills your slave by operating on him badly or by giving
him the wrong medicine.'[26] The principle *imperitia culpae adnumeratur*
became a *regula iuris*[27] and was mediated through the *ius commune*[28] to
the Scottish institutional writers.[29] Roman law had allowed an Aquilian
action for bodily injury inflicted on a slave but not on a free man. It was
only after the European Reception, and in Scotland as late as the 1790s,
that the modern delictual action of damages for personal injuries was recognised.[30] In the *ius commune* it appears that 'in discussions concerning
imperitia, liability for medical malpractice played a particularly prominent
role'.[31] The maxim '*imperitia culpae adnumeratur*' was applicable in contracts of hire of services so that an action based on contract lay against a
doctor. In 1914 the general rule was established that a contract for medical

[25] 'He is responsible for skill in his profession, and want of such skill is regarded as a fault':
J. Trayner, *Latin Maxims* (reprint of 4th edn., Edinburgh: Green, 1998), p. 584. See
D.19,2,9,5: 'Celsus, in the eighth book of his Digest, wrote that inexperience [*imperitia*]
should also be counted as fault.' Cited most recently in *Gerrard v. Royal Infirmary of
Edinburgh NHS Trust* 2005 SC 192 referring to G. J. Bell, *Commentaries on the Law of
Scotland* (6th edn., Edinburgh: Clark, 1858, edited by P. Shaw), I,4,7. See also G. J. Bell,
Commentaries (7th edn., Edinburgh: Clark, 1870, edited by J. McLaren), I,489,490.

[26] Justinian *Institutes* 4,3,7,8 (trans. P. Birks and G. MacLeod). '*Imperitia quoque culpae
adnumeratur, veluti medicus ideo servum tuum occiderit, quod eum male secuerit aut
perperam ei medicamentum dederit.*' In D.9,2,7,8 Ulpian cites Proculus as stating that
if a doctor operates unskilfully on a slave an action lies either *ex locato* or under the *lex
Aquilia*. See also (Gaius) D.9,2,8. For comment on the maxim from a Scottish standpoint,
see A. Stewart, 'New Wine in Old Barrels: Medical Negligence and Reasonable Care'
(2007) 11 Edin. LR 251.

[27] D.50,17,132.

[28] R. Zimmermann, *The Law of Obligations, Roman Foundations of the Civilian Tradition*
(1990), pp. 386 ff.; 397 ff.; 464 ff.; 1009; 1028, especially note 198; 1126, note 230.

[29] Lord Bankton, *Institute of the Laws of Scotland in Civil Right* (Edinburgh: Stair Society,
1993–5, reprint of 1751 edn.) I,20,4; J. Erskine, *Institute* (Edinburgh: Law Society of
Scotland, 1999, reprint of 8th edn.) III,1,21; G. J. Bell *Principles of the Law of Scotland*
(10th edn., Edinburgh: Clark, 1899, edited by W. Guthrie), sect. 153; Bell *Commentaries*
(7th edn.) I,489,490.

[30] *Gardner v. Ferguson* (18 November 1795, unreported), Advocates Library Session Papers,
Hume Collection, vol. 87, No. 97: see K. Campbell 'The Session Papers in Four Early
Cases of Damages for Personal Injuries' (Stair Soc., vol. 49, 2002, *Miscellany Four*, ed.
H. L. MacQueen), p. 225. The literature is now considerable.

[31] Zimmermann, *Law of Obligations*, p. 1028, note 198. He continues: 'What the lawyers of
the *usus modernus* had to say about the medical profession, in this context, was not particularly flattering. For Stryk the medical profession was full of sycophants ... Lauterbach
regretfully reported that negligent doctors were only rarely brought before a court of law
and that they were therefore the only people who might kill with impunity.'

treatment raises a duty to take reasonable care, the breach of which is negligence founding an action based not on contract but on delict.[32]

Until the late twentieth century, however, very few reparation actions
for medical negligence were raised in Scotland.[33] The first two reported
actions of damages for personal injury arising from medical negligence
occurred in 1894[34] and 1901.[35] In 1910 it was held that where a person professes to have a high skill as a dentist, then in carrying out dental treatment
under contract he must display at least the same standard of skill as other
members of the dental profession notwithstanding that in fact he is not
qualified as a dentist.[36] The orthodox view was that the liability of professional persons generally,[37] and doctors in particular,[38] depended on a high
degree of negligence.[39] In 1948[40] Lord Blades approved the test of gross
negligence which had been adopted in 1901.[41] In 1955 Lord Sorn said that:

> until recent times, the general impression has been that gross negligence
> must be proved in order to render a doctor liable. This impression has
> been derived from decisions and dicta pronounced in cases relating to
> solicitors' including a dictum by Lord Brougham in 1845 (obiter so far as
> applicable to surgeons) to the effect 'that there should be a negligence of
> a crass description, which we call *crassa negligentia*, that there should be
> gross ignorance …'.[42]

A requirement of gross negligence contrasted with the modern trend in
delict away from the varying degrees of fault (*culpa lata*; *levis*; *levissima*)
of the Institutional writers[43] which were abandoned about 1900.[44] Glegg
on *Reparation*, however, denied that professional men were only liable for

---

[32] *Edgar v. Lamont* 1914 SC 277.
[33] In 1864 it was held that a medical man who gave a medical certificate after careless and
      insufficient investigation would incur serious liability: *Urquhart v. Grigor* (1864) 3 M 283
      at 289 (an action against a medical man for defamation contained in a medical report).
[34] *Simpson v. Allan* (1894) 1 SLT 526 (adjustment of issue; case scantily reported).
[35] *Farquhar v. Murray* (1901) 3 F 859.
[36] *Dickson v. Hygienic Institute* 1910 SC 352.
[37] *Purves v. Landell* (1845) 17 Sc Jur 308, 4 Bell's App 46.
[38] *Farquhar v. Murray* (1901) 3 F 859.
[39] Called variously 'gross negligence' or *crassa negligentia* or *culpa lata*. On the law before
      1955, see H. McKechnie, 'Negligence' in *Encyclopaedia of the Laws of Scotland* vol. 10
      (1930), para. 558; R. H. Dickson, *Medical and Dental Negligence* (London: Lexis Nexis,
      2000), pp. 2, 3; A.T. Glegg, *The Law of Reparation* (4th edn.), by J. L. Duncan, Edinburgh:
      Green, 1995 pp. 467, 468.
[40] *Crawford v. Campbell* 1948 SLT (Notes) 91.
[41] *Farquhar v. Murray* (1901) 3 F 859.
[42] *Hunter v. Hanley* 1955 SC 200 at 207, citing *Purves v. Landell* (1845) 4 Bell's App 46.
[43] E.g. Erskine, *Institute*, III,1,21.
[44] *Farquhar v. Murray* (1901) 3 F 859.

gross negligence.[45] Moreover, in 1953 Lord Guthrie allowed a proof before answer on the allegation that the defender doctor 'had failed to exercise reasonable care and professional skill'.[46]

(2)   The watershed: Hunter v. Hanley (1955)

By the 1950s there was 'an overwhelming need for clarity'[47] which was fairly well provided in 1955 by the leading case of *Hunter v. Hanley*[48] in a formulation which was recently commended as having 'stood the test of time'[49] and still dominates the Scots law of medical negligence.

Mrs Jemima Hunter was being given a series of intra-muscular penicillin injections by her doctor, a general medical practitioner, Doctor Hanley.[50] While the last injection was being given the hypodermic needle broke and its end remained embedded in her hip. A further operation failed to remove it. Mrs Hunter sued for damages of £2,500 for personal injury. The pursuer alleged that the type of needle employed on this occasion was not strong enough and that any doctor possessing a fair and average knowledge of his profession would have known this and used the correct needle. A question then arose as to what was the normal and usual practice in regard to the type of needle required. At the trial by jury, the Lord Ordinary, Lord Patrick, had directed the jury that the test for liability was: 'Did [the defender] depart to a serious degree from the usual and proper practice of doctors so that his departure could be characterised as gross negligence?' The jury returned a verdict for the pursuer. On the defender's motion the First Division ordered a new trial on the ground of misdirection.

In a classic judgment, Lord President Clyde observed that:

> The true test for establishing negligence in diagnosis or treatment on the part of a doctor is whether he has been proved to be guilty of such failure as no doctor of ordinary skill would be guilty of if acting with ordinary care.[51]

---

[45]   A.T. Glegg, *Reparation* (2nd edn., Edinburgh: Green, 1905), pp. 590 ff.; (3rd edn., 1939), p. 509.

[46]   *Kenyon v. Bell* 1953 SC 125.   [47]   Dickson, *Medical and Dental Negligence*, p. 3.

[48]   1955 SC 200.

[49]   *Gerrard v. Royal Infirmary of Edinburgh NHS Trust* 2005 SC 192, per Lord Osborne (delivering the opinion of the court).

[50]   For the background to this famous case, see N. Muir and D. Bell (eds.), *A Century of Care – A History of the Medical and Dental Defence Union of Scotland* (Edinburgh: MDDU, 2002), pp. 77–9; G. Stott, *QC's Diary 1954–1960* (Edinburgh: Murcat, 1998), pp. 19, 20, 39–42, 82, 83.

[51]   1955 SC 200 at 206.

Turning to liability for deviation from normal practice, the Lord President remarked that:

> three facts require to be established. First of all it must be proved that there is a usual and normal practice. Secondly it must be proved that the defender has not adopted that practice, and thirdly (and this is of crucial importance) it must be established that the course the doctor adopted is one which no professional man of ordinary skill would have taken if he had been acting with ordinary care.[52]

The third leg of the tripartite 'deviation test' says the same thing as the 'true test' in slightly different words.

(3)   Cross-border assimilation on breach of duty (standard of care) after Hunter v. Hanley and Bolam

In English law, two years later, McNair J in the famous *Bolam* case[53] purported to apply the test in *Hunter v. Hanley* but modified it by stating that a doctor escaped liability if he acted in accordance with a practice accepted by 'a responsible body of medical opinion' rather than a practice accepted by *one* other doctor (which was one interpretation of the test in *Hunter v. Hanley*). The approach was similar yet sufficiently different to lead to speculation that a different test for medical negligence had been formulated for English law. That has long been a matter of debate in Scotland. One view is that *Hunter v. Hanley* has remained solid and unchanged over the decades, while the English *Bolam* test has been subjected more to modification or elaboration.[54] In Scotland *Hunter v. Hanley* is often cited without reference to *Bolam*. Others state that such English authorities as *Bolam* and *Bolitho* have not affected the continued applicability of the *Hunter v. Hanley* test,[55] or that the *Bolam* test, with its encrustations of later English case law, is the same as the test in *Hunter v. Hanley*;[56] or that it has 'amplified' *Hunter v. Hanley* so as to refer to a standard 'accepted by a responsible body of medical men'.[57] Frequently reference is made to the

---

[52] Ibid.   [53] *Bolam v. Friern Hospital Management Committee* [1957] 2 All ER 118.

[54] R. B. M. Howie, 'The Standard of Care in Medical Negligence' (1983) JR 193; Anon, 'Medical Negligence: *Hunter v. Hanley* 35 Years On' (1990) SLT (News) 325; Dickson, *Medical and Dental Negligence*, p. 31.

[55] *Dougan v. Lanarkshire Acute Hospitals NHS Trust* 2001 GWD 13–516, OH, (3 April 2001, unreported), paras. 23–25 per Lord Nimmo Smith.

[56] See e.g. *Muir v. Grampian Health Board* 2000 GWD 12–442, OH (10 October 2001, unreported), para. 19 per Lord Abernethy.

[57] *Moyes v. Lothian Health Board* 1990 SLT 444 at 449, OH, per Lord Caplan.

approval by the House of Lords in the *Maynard* case[58] of Lord President Clyde's test in *Hunter v. Hanley*.[59]

The preponderant view seems to be that the Scots law and the English law on the standard of care in medical negligence are very similar: medical practice weighs heavily in the scale but is not conclusive.[60]

(4)   The effect of medical expert evidence

The important role played by medical expert evidence and 'normal and usual' medical practice as a consequence of these developments entails a standard of reasonable care in medical negligence that differs from that applicable in most other types of personal injury action. Normally the standard of care in negligence actions involves a balancing test (the calculus of risk) in which the foreseeability of the injury; the degree of likelihood of the injury occurring (the magnitude of the risk); and the seriousness of the probable consequences, are weighed by the court against the difficulty, expense and other disadvantages of refraining from doing the act in question.[61] By reason of the layperson's ignorance of medical science and his or her clinical inexperience, however, the balancing of medical benefits and medical risks in diagnosis and treatment, and perhaps also in other matters such as the disclosure to patients of medical risks, cannot be undertaken by judges, or judges and juries, alone without the aid of medical expert evidence. Moreover, the very ignorance and inexperience which requires the intervention of medical experts also prevents the courts from preferring one body of medical expert opinion over another. The result is that pursuers are normally defeated by the defender's expert evidence and medical negligence actions have a greater failure rate than any other category of personal injury litigation,[62] and in Scotland the great majority fail.

The judicial reliance on professional medical expertise creates a tension between the role of the courts and that of medical experts. For a long time,

[58]   *Maynard v. West Midlands Regional Health Authority* [1985] 1 All ER 635, HL.

[59]   *Moyes v. Lothian Health Board* 1990 SLT 444 at 449, OH; *Phillips v. Grampian Health Board* [1991] 3 Med LR 16, OH; *Goorkani v. Tayside Health Board* 1991 SLT 94, OH; *Muir v. Grampian Health Board* 2000 GWD 12–442, OH, per Lord Abernethy; *Gerrard v. Royal Infirmary of Edinburgh NHS Trust* 2005 SC 192 at para. 77.

[60]   *Honisz v. Lothian Health Board* 2008 SC 235 at para. 39 per Lord Hodge; K. McK. Norrie, 'Common Practice and the Standard of Care in Medical Negligence' (1985) JR 145 at 150–7; K. Feenan, 'Medical Negligence: *Hunter v. Hanley* 35 years on: a reply' (1991) SLT (News) 321; J. R. Griffiths, 'Medical Negligence: An Update of the Law' (1995) 1 SLPQ 25 at 26–31.

[61]   *Morris v. West Hartlepool Steam Navigation Co* [1956] AC 552 at 574, HL, per Lord Reid.

[62]   *Report of the Royal Commission on Civil Liability and Compensation for Personal Injury* (1978) vol. 1 (Cmnd 7054) para. 1326.

the orthodox UK view was that 'the law imposes the duty of care: but the standard of care is a matter of medical judgment'.[63] This was criticised, especially by Commonwealth courts in information disclosure cases,[64] as an unjustifiable surrender by the courts to the medical profession of the judicial function of determining the standard of care and its breach. This critique, however, was not accepted in Scots law as a reason for excluding the role of medical practice from the scope of the duty of disclosure to patients of medical risks.[65] In England in the *Bolitho* case,[66] which has been accepted by a line of Scots cases,[67] the House of Lords affirmed the court's power to reject any professional body of opinion which does not withstand logical analysis, as not being reasonable or responsible. This judicial power to override medical opinion is more important in principle than in practice since it is designed merely as a longstop, to be used only rarely.

(5)   *The standard of care*

The standard of care of a medical or other health care professional must meet the standard of the reasonable professional doing his job, and the standard must be neither too low[68] nor too high.[69] In particular the standard of proficiency to be expected in a district general hospital dealing with patients with all types of illness is not so high as that to be found in a specialist unit in a university teaching hospital or comparable centre of excellence dealing exclusively with special types of illness.[70]

(6)   *Cross-border assimilation of the laws on other aspects of negligence (duty of care; proof and causation)*

With the assimilation of the law on the standard of care there is very little difference between English law and Scots law on medical negligence. As regards the duty of care, Scots law has tracked the trends of English

---

[63] *Sidaway v. Bethlem Royal Hospital Board of Governors* [1985] AC 871, HL, at 881 per Lord Scarman.

[64] *Reibl v. Hughes* (1980) 114 DLR (3d) 1, Can SC (cited in *Gordon v. Wilson* 1992 SLT 849 at 852, OH); *Rogers v. Whittaker* (1992) 179 CLR 479, Aust. HC; *Castell v. De Greef* 1994 4 SA 408 (C).

[65] *Gordon v. Wilson* 1992 SLT 849, OH.

[66] *Bolitho v. City and Hackney Health Authority* [1998] AC 232, HL.

[67] In a line of cases from *Duffy v. Lanarkshire Health Board* 2001 GWD 10–368 to *Gerrard v. Royal Infirmary of Edinburgh NHS Trust* 2005 SC 192 and *Honisz v. Lothian Health Board* [2006] CSOH 24; 2008 SC 235.

[68] See *Dickson v. Hygienic Institute* 1910 SC 352 (n. 36 above).

[69] *Beasley v. Fife Health Board* 2001 GWD 32–1300, OH: see Stewart (n. 26 above).

[70] *Dougan v. Lanarkshire Acute Hospitals NHS Trust* 2001 GWD 13–516, OH.

law,[71] leaning first away from[72] and then towards[73] the vicarious liability of hospitals. In actions for wrongful pregnancy or wrongful birth,[74] it is accepted that the duty of care is the same on both sides of the border, with the controversial Scottish House of Lords case of *McFarlane v. Tayside Health Board*[75] being applied in English law. So, too, a series of English and Scottish appeals to the House of Lords[76] on causation in medical cases are inextricably entwined.

The systems of pleading and procedure were, and are, different both before and after recent reforms.[77] Civil jury trials which were current on both sides of the border at the time of *Hunter v. Hanley*[78] and *Bolam*[79] in the 1950s subsequently declined and are now unknown in English practice. In Scotland civil jury trials, which almost vanished in the 1980s, subsequently experienced a mild revival[80] and have been allowed in the occasional recent medical malpractice case.[81] The trend has not (or not yet) influenced the development of the substantive law on medical negligence.

(7)   Attempts to reverse onus of proof normally unsuccessful

There are some areas of medical negligence practice where it has been suggested that the onus of proof may be reversed. First, the idea arose

[71] See W. Swain, above pp. 37–8.
[72] *Hillyer v. Governors of St Bartholomew's Hospital* [1909] 2 KB 820, CA followed in e.g. *Foote v. Greenock Hospital* 1912 SC 69; *Lavelle v. Glasgow Royal Infirmary* 1931 SC (HL) 34; *Morris v. Caithness Hospitals* 1950 SC 390.
[73] *Cassidy v. Ministry of Health* [1951] 2 KB 343, CA; *Roe v. Minister of Health* [1954] 2 QB 66, CA, followed in *Macdonald v. Glasgow Western Hospitals Board of Management* and *Hayward v. Edinburgh Royal Infirmary Board of Management* 1954 SC 453; *Fox v. Glasgow South Western Hospitals Board* 1955 SLT 337 at 339, OH. See P. Simpson, 'Vicarious Liability' in K. Reid and R. Zimmermann (eds.), *A History of Private Law in Scotland* (Oxford: Oxford University Press, 2000), vol. II, p. 607.
[74] See W. Swain, above p. 39.   [75] *McFarlane v. Tayside Health Board* 2000 SC (HL) 1.
[76] For leading Scottish cases on causation see e.g. *Wardlaw v. Bonnington Castings Ltd* 1956 SC (HL) 26; *McGhee v. National Coal Board* 1973 SC (HL) 37; *Kay's Tutor v. Ayrshire and Arran Health Board* 1987 SC (HL) 145. See also *Kenyon v. Bell* 1953 SC 125, OH approved in *Gregg v. Scott* [2005] UKHL 2 at para. 69, [2005] AC 176 per Lord Hoffmann.
[77] The Woolf reforms in England and the Cousfield reforms in Scotland.
[78] 1955 SC 200 (motion for new jury trial).
[79] *Bolam v. Friern Hospital Management Committee* [1957] 2 All ER 118 (direction to jury).
[80] A.M. Hajducki, *Civil Jury Trials* (2nd edn., Edinburgh: Avizandum, 2006), paras. 2.18–19.
[81] Hajducki, *Civil Jury Trials*, paras. 6.12–14; *Murray v. Lanarkshire Acute Hospitals NHS Trust* 2003 GWD 6–135; *Devlin v. Ghosh* 4 May 2005 Lord McEwan; *Toner v. McLeod* [2006] CSOH 96 (dental negligence); cf. *Fallone v. Lanarkshire Acute Hospitals NHS Trust* [2006] CSOH 51.

that the defender's deviation from a rule of medical practice throws the onus of justification of the deviation on the defender.[82] In Scotland such a reversal of the onus of proof was rejected as inconsistent with the normal rules on evidence in civil proceedings.[83] So, for instance, in the *Devaney* case[84] a youth of seventeen underwent an operation to his aorta, later suffered a cardiac arrest and was found to have become paraplegic. The issue was whether the surgeon had used the wrong operative technique. In absolving him, the court held that there was no onus on him to justify the technique used. Since expert medical opinions diverged, it was not proved that, in being influenced by the risk of lung damage, the defender had done something no competent surgeon would do.

Second, the doctrine of *res ipsa loquitur* was at one time seen as a potentially important technique whereby the courts could covertly introduce strict liability under the guise of negligence. In cases of medical negligence, however, the courts, far from seeking to impose strict liability, in practice lean in the opposite direction so as to make it difficult for pursuers to succeed. In Scotland, while the doctrine has occasionally been applied in medical negligence,[85] it has usually been rejected even in cases calling strongly for its application.[86]

Third, in the domain of causation, there was a controversial view that 'where a person has, by breach of duty of care, created a risk, and injury occurs within the area of that risk, the loss should be borne by him unless he shows that it had some other cause'.[87] In medical negligence cases, this dictum was rejected in Scotland[88] and subsequently disapproved by the House of Lords in English cases.[89]

---

[82] *Clark v. McLennan* [1983] 1 All ER 416 doubted in *Littlejohn v. Ayrshire and Arran Health Board* (1 March 1985, unreported), OH, per Lord Davidson.

[83] *Devaney v. Glasgow Health Board* 1987 GWD 6–196, OH applying *Kelly v. Sir Frank Mears and Partners* 1983 SC 97 at 104; K. McK. Norrie, 'Common Practice' at 158–61.

[84] Ibid.

[85] *Gillespie v. Grampian Health Board* 1990 GWD 11–589, Sheriff Court following *Cassidy v. Ministry of Health* [1951] 2 KB 343 discussed in Dickson, *Medical and Dental Negligence*, pp. 111, 112.

[86] *Aird v. Ramsay* (5 December 1984, unreported), Glasgow Sheriff Court discussed in Dickson, *Medical and Dental Negligence*, pp. 36, 112.

[87] *McGhee v. National Coal Board* 1973 SC (HL) 37 at 55 per Lord Wilberforce.

[88] *Craig v. Glasgow Victoria and Leverndale Hospitals Board of Management* (23 March 1976, unreported).

[89] *Wilsher v. Essex Area Health Authority* [1988] AC 1074 at 1087g, HL; *Fairchild v. Glenhaven Funeral Services Ltd* [2002] UKHL 22, [2003] 1 AC 32, at paras. [22], [65] and [143], [144].

IV.   The conundrum: cross-border differences as to the cost of medical negligence

(1)   Preliminary

The general picture, then, is that the formal substantive law on medical negligence is virtually the same on both sides of the border. Yet there is here a conundrum because in practice, despite the cross-border uniformity of substantive law, there is a wide and as yet unexplained difference in outcomes, that is to say a large difference between the much greater costs of medical negligence in England and Wales and the much smaller costs in Scotland. The Ross Report of 2003[90] pointed to evidence that the cost of medical negligence in Scotland is proportionally much less than in England (indeed only a very small fraction, namely 1.5%, of that in England) but was unable to state with authority why the cost in Scotland was so much less.

(2)   The growth of medical negligence claims in the twentieth century

In Scotland, to a greater extent than in England and Wales, it is difficult to obtain reliable statistical and empirical information as to the number of claims or actions for damages for medical negligence, the success rate of claims, the amounts paid pursuant to settlements, compromises or decrees, the mode of disposal of actions of damages for medical negligence and the rate of change.[91] Work on material held by MDDUS on a sample of 1,000 claims in the ten years to 1983 showed that the annual number of claims had risen from 80 to 300.[92] In 1997 Robert Dickson remarked:

> After *Hunter v. Hanley*[93] the growth in the number of claims made against health boards and the three defence societies was initially slow, and the increase was merely steady until the early 1980s, but there undoubtedly

---

[90] See the Ross Report (n. 15 above) which inquired into the need for financial and other support to victims of HCV (hepatitis C virus) and HIV (human immunodeficiency virus) and other iatrogenic illnesses resulting from NHSiS medical interventions.

[91] J. W. G. Blackie, 'Scotland' in E. Deutsch and H.-L. Schreiber (eds.), *Medical Responsibility in Western Europe* (Berlin: Springer, 1985), pp. 563–5 could give only educated guesses about these matters.

[92] R. Jandoo, *Medical Negligence* (unpublished PhD thesis, University of Glasgow, 1986) quoted by J. W. G. Blackie, 'Medical Negligence in Scotland' (1996) 3 *European Journal of Health Law* 127 at 130. Of the sample, 24% resulted in some payment to the claimant.

[93] 1955 SC 200.

has been a massive rise in the last 10 years. The figures for Scotland show that between 1987 and 1995, there was a fourfold increase in the number of claims made against general practitioners and that the claims against dentists rose by 150%.[94]

In 1948 MDDUS paid out £787 in settlements of medical litigation; in 1996 claim settlements had risen to £2,755,000.[95]

(3)   Levels of medical negligence claims in the secondary sector of the NHSiS: 1997/1998–2001/2002

The empirical information referred to above is random and often speculative, but the Ross Report in March 2003 contains fuller and more systematic statistical information on Scottish medical (or clinical) negligence claims relating to the secondary care sector within the NHSiS,[96] taken from a survey covering the five-year period from 1997/1998 to 2001/2002 and based on cases settled in each year.[97] In summary, over that period the total cost of settlements rose from £3.6 million to £7 million but in an uneven pattern. Adding Central Legal Office (CLO) fees increased the figures from £3.6 million to £4 million and from £7 million to £7.7 million respectively. The apportionment between awards, adverse expenses and CLO fees and outlays was relatively steady at about 79%, 12% and 9% respectively on average. The 'provisions' of NHSiS trusts and boards for clinical negligence[98] continued to rise but the rate of increase over the three years from 1999/2000 to 2001/2002 fell from 53% to 6%.[99] The number of claims lodged against NHS trusts and submitted to CLO had remained level at approximately 500 per year. On average about 70% would have been dismissed or abandoned by the pursuer, leaving some 150 cases per annum which resulted in a compensation award. Approximately 40% of those claims were settled for less than £5,000. A further 17% were settled for between £5,000 and £10,000. At the other end, just 5% of claims

---

[94] Dickson, *Medical and Dental Negligence*, p. 5 citing 'MDDUS Claims Records 1987–1996'.

[95] Muir and Bell (eds.), *A Century of Care*, p. 249.

[96] Ross Report, paras. 7.20–24.

[97] Where the National Health Service Scotland Central Legal Office deals with all claims for medical negligence and for which data are readily available.

[98] Provisions are estimates of future settlement costs arising from past events. The level of provision is determined by NHS trusts/boards from best estimates of likely settlement values of claims being processed or known (some claims may take more than six years to settle) and the future value of structured settlements.

[99] The 6% figure is based on unaudited figures.

accounted for 65% of expenditure.[100] Of the average 150 cases, legal proceedings will be commenced in approximately 60 (40%) cases, with only
10 actually being heard in court (average 43% in the Sheriff Court and
57% in the Court of Session).[101] More generally, approximately 56% of all
claims for which an award is paid were settled within three years, whilst
17% (mostly birth-injury cases) took more than five years. Finally, to put
the claim numbers and costs into perspective, £10 million is 0.2% of NHSiS
resources and, in 2000/2001, the NHSiS dealt with 785,000 inpatients,
400,000 day cases and 1,500,000 accident and emergency cases, a total of
2.6 million cases.[102]

(4)   A comparison of medical negligence claims in
Scotland and in England and Wales

The Ross Report observed that, generally, NHS costs for Scotland will
be 10% of costs for England.[103] It pointed out, however, that in the case
of medical accidents, taking 1999/2000 as a reasonably typical year, the
comparative figures were:

Number of claims received: England: 10,000;[104] Scotland: 500 (5%).
Number of claims processed: England: 23,000; Scotland: 1,500 (6.5%).
Settlements: England: £386 million; Scotland: £3.7 million (this figure is
    lower than average but has no material effect on comparisons between
    Scotland and England) (1.0%).
Provisions: England: £2.6 billion; Scotland: £38 million (1.5%) (figures
    exclude incidents 'occurred but not reported').

It will be seen that the cost of clinical negligence in Scotland is only a fraction of that in England.

(5)   The Ross Report's conclusions on the Scottish system

The Ross Report said that it was not possible to state with authority why
the cost of clinical negligence in Scotland was proportionally so much less
than in England and other parts of the UK, but suggested that the reasons
might include the following:

---

[100] Ross Report, para. 3.6. On average that was nine cases of a value of £100,000 costing
       £3.3 million in total.
[101] Ross Report, para. 3.7.   [102] Ross Report, para. 3.8.
[103] Ross Report, para. 3.10.
[104] Citing Report on Handling Clinical Negligence Claims in England (National Audit Office,
       May 2001).

- that the CLO is the sole handler of clinical negligence claims and has considerable skill and experience in defending them;
- that the NHS staff-to-patient ratio is different in Scotland;
- that a pursuer's access to legal aid is more limited in Scotland;[105] and
- that there was only a limited number of solicitors in Scotland specialising in clinical negligence.[106]

V.   Medical malpractice in Scotland: future directions

The main issues concerning the reform of the system of clinical or medical negligence (including the substantive law, civil procedure, legal aid, the role of mediation and patients' access to justice), the possible introduction of no-fault compensation or strict liability, and related matters were examined, for the first time wholly or mainly from a Scottish standpoint, by the Ross Report.[107] The Report concluded that, given the data analysed above, there was little or no room to reduce or peg the current levels of settlement of claims for damages or to reduce legal defence costs significantly. Structured settlements would have short-term financial benefits to the NHSiS and offer increased financial security for those receiving the award.[108] While the Report[109] recognised that a no-fault compensation system may have advantages,[110] it found that there were also major difficulties since (i) it ignores the important issues of accountability and quality of care. The Report argued that, whilst no system should focus only on fault, if there is fault, it is essential that it be identified to enable lessons to be learned, quality of care improved and dangerous practices avoided. Moreover, (ii) the test for compensation under such a scheme should be medical causation rather than negligence. A broad range of possible injuries can be causally connected with medical interventions. Thus, it is very difficult to set out the exact parameters of a no-fault scheme. Finally, (iii) no-fault compensation would cost substantially more than the current clinical negligence system. While the Report rejected a general no-fault system in Scotland, it did recommend an ad hoc no-fault scheme to meet particular circumstances.

---

[105] Ross Report, ch. 5.   [106] Ross Report, ch. 7.   [107] Ibid.
[108] Ross Report, para. 3.12.   [109] Ross Report, para. 3.30.
[110] Including speed and reduction in legal costs and stress on complainants and health professionals.

4

The development of medical liability and accident compensation in France

SIMON TAYLOR

1   Introduction

Traditionally, the liability of medical professionals for death and personal injury caused by medical accidents has been based on fault in French law, and, until recent legislation, liability principles were developed by the courts. There has, however, been a steady evolution over the period studied from a rather restrictive interpretation of the fault principle which was very protective of the medical profession to a more flexible approach which first took a wider view of what constituted fault incurring liability, and then showed an increasing tendency to impose liability without fault. This tendency became particularly manifest in the 1990s. The important Law *relative aux droits des malades et à la qualité du système de santé* (on patients' rights and the quality of the health system) enacted on 4 March 2002[1] and incorporated in the *Code de la santé publique* (hereinafter Law of 4 March 2002) further facilitates the compensation of victims of serious medical accidents by introducing a new statutory compensation scheme. However, in some respects the legislation represents a reversal in the process of evolution of liability rules by reaffirming that health professionals and organisations will only be liable for fault.

2   Outline of the French health system

2.1   Public and private provision

The provision of health care in France is shared between the public and private sectors, and the liability rules for the two sectors are governed by separate jurisdictions. Hence, actions for damages against private health

---

[1] Loi n°2002–303 du 4 March 2002. See now arts. L.1142–1 to L.1142–29 of the *Code de la santé publique* for the provisions relating to medical accident compensation and liability.

care providers are brought in the civil courts, whilst actions against public health providers are under the jurisdiction of the administrative courts. Before the Law of 4 March 2002 the legal rules applied by the two jurisdictions diverged on various points. As we shall see later, this was the case with respect to their approach to fault and strict liability. There were also significant differences in limitation periods, from ten (in delict) or thirty years (in contract) in the civil courts, to four years in administrative law. The 2002 Law seeks to ensure the unification of the principles applied by the two jurisdictions, and should go some way to achieving this by imposing fault as the sole basis of liability, and introducing a single ten-year limitation period for all medical liability actions.[2] However, the Law retains the two separate jurisdictions for medical liability cases, and it would consequently still in principle be possible for variations to exist between the two jurisdictions in the interpretation of key concepts such as fault.

Primary health care in France is private. In addition, private clinics offer secondary health care. The relationship between the patient and the primary care doctor or private clinic is contractual.[3] Actions against the doctor or private clinic for damages are therefore based on the breach of a contractual obligation owed by the medical practitioner or clinic to use reasonable care and skill based on article 1147 of the *Code civil*. A clinic will also be liable in contract for faults committed in the functioning or organisation of their health service. Exceptions exist where the action will be brought in tort. Hence, the law will consider that there is no contract between the practitioner or health provider and the patient where urgent medical care is administered to an unconscious patient. Should the action be brought by the family of the patient on their own behalf then their action will be based on an action in tort, based on the fault of the defendant, under article 1382 of the *Code civil*. French law operates a strict rule that once a party has a contractual relationship with the defendant he will not be allowed to opt to bring his action in tort (*non cumul*).

Whether the action is brought in contract or in tort does not make a significant difference to the outcome. Apart from the limited circumstances where a contractual guarantee of performance may apply, the liability of the defendant will normally be subject to the proof of fault by the claimant. It will not be possible for the defendant to exclude his liability in such circumstances, and article 1150 of the *Code civil*, which limits liability to

---

[2] Art. L.1142–28 *Code de la santé publique*.
[3] Cass. civ. 20 May 1936, *Mercier*, D. 1936.1.88.

the damage which was foreseeable at the time of the contract, does not apply to medical liability.[4]

Alongside the private sector operates the national health service hospitals offering secondary care. The public health service represents 78% of secondary care available in France.[5] There is considered to be no contract between the public health provider and the patient. The patient is a 'user' (*usager*) of the public health system, and the liability of the service provider will be based on administrative law principles. As I have already mentioned, any action against a national health hospital will consequently be brought before the administrative law courts.

Any uncertainty as to whether public law or private law applies to any particular relationship will be resolved by an application to the Tribunal des conflits.

2.2   Personal and vicarious liability

Recent case law states that doctors who are employees of a private clinic will not be personally liable to patients for faults committed in the exercise of their employment.[6] The action of the victim will be against the clinic for breach of contract.

Where the doctor practises in a public hospital, he will not normally be personally liable. The action for damages will be against the hospital where the fault committed by the doctor falls within his service duties. There are some limited exceptions to this rule. Hence, in some cases doctors will perform private medical services within a public hospital. In such cases, where the loss is due to a medical act performed by the doctor himself and not to the defective organisation of the service or the negligence of hospital personnel, the victim will have to sue the doctor personally in the civil courts.[7]

In rare cases, the hospital doctor may be personally liable for acts which fall outside the scope of his employment (*faute personnelle détachable du service*). In such cases, the doctor will be personally liable in tort before the civil courts. However, cases of personal liability for *faute détachable* are very infrequent. One example is where a woman, classed as a high risk pregnancy, was admitted to the maternity section of a hospital. The doctor

---

[4] J. Penneau, *La responsabilité du médecin* (3rd edn., Paris: Dalloz, 2004) at 15.

[5] C. Evin, *Les droits des usagers du système de santé* (Paris: Berger-Levrault, 2002) at 147.

[6] Cass. civ. (1), 9 Nov. 2004, D. 2005, 253, note F. Chabas. This is also the case for midwives, *ibid.*

[7] Y. Lambert-Faivre, *Le droit du dommage corporel* (4th edn., Paris: Dalloz, 2000) at 677.

on duty did not see the patient but simply gave her a treatment intended to delay the birth, whereas he should have carried out a Caesarean there and then.[8] Another is where the medical staff abandoned an unconscious patient because the treatment room was in flames![9]

3   An overview of the different liability and compensation regimes

3.1   The 2002 statutory compensation scheme for medical accidents

The Law of 4 March 2002 introduced a statutory compensation scheme for victims of medical accidents into the *Code de la santé publique*. Amendments were made by subsequent legislation in December of the same year.[10] The scheme, which will be considered in more detail later, aims to guarantee compensation for victims of serious medical accidents, whether or not such an accident is caused by negligence. In cases where it is established that the fault of the medical practitioner caused the victim's loss, compensation will be provided by the practitioner's liability insurance. Where the accident is not due to the fault of the practitioner or service, compensation will be paid by the State. The scheme also provides for compensation of victims of bacterial infections contracted in health institutions. Applications are dealt with by regional compensation committees. In an attempt to reduce the number of actions in court, a conciliation service is offered to all victims.

3.2   Liability in contract and tort

The legislative reforms retain the traditional liability action. Since the new statutory regime only guarantees compensation to victims of serious accidents, and since this term is defined restrictively, traditional court actions will inevitably remain frequent.

3.3   Criminal liability

Medical practitioners and health services can potentially be liable for a variety of criminal offences. They may be criminally liable where their

---

[8] Cass. crim. 2 Apr. 1992, JCP 1993.II.22105, note Vallar.
[9] Cass. crim. 2 Oct 1958, JCP 1958.II.10834.
[10] Loi no. 2002–1577 du 30 Dec. 2002, JO 31.12.2002.

fault/carelessness has caused death or serious personal injury.[11] There are also offences of failure to help a person in danger[12] and of putting people in danger as a result of the deliberate non-respect of safety measures.[13] The principal grounds for criminal liability will be where death or injury is caused by fault. The doctor's fault will be based on 'errors of manipulation, imprudence, carelessness, negligence or breach of a duty of safety or care imposed by primary or secondary legislation'.[14] A Law dated 10 July 2000[15] now provides that fault for the purposes of criminal law will be assessed in different ways depending on whether the acts or omissions of the defendant constitute a direct or an indirect cause of the injury.[16] Where the defendant's action or omission is the direct cause of the injury, ordinary negligence (*faute simple*) will be sufficient to engage liability and this fault will be assessed in very similar ways to fault in actions in contract or tort.[17] However, where the causal link between the fault and the damage is indirect,[18] then the defendant will only be criminally liable where he has either 'deliberately flouted safety rules imposed by statute or is guilty of a particularly serious fault which has exposed another person to a particularly serious risk which he should have been aware of'.[19]

Criminal procedure rules allow a victim to become a *partie civile*[20] in the criminal action. The victim can either join a criminal prosecution which

---

[11] Art. 221–6 *Code pénal*: causing death by negligence (*atteintes involontaires à la vie*). Arts. 222–19 and 222–20 *Code pénal*: causing physical injury by negligence (*atteintes involontaires à l'intégrité de la personne*).

[12] Art. 223–6 *Code pénal*.

[13] Arts. 223–1 and 223–2 *Code pénal*.

[14] 'une maladresse, imprudence, inattention, negligence ou manquement à une obligation de sécurité ou de prudence impose par la loi ou les règlements'.

[15] Loi n° 2000–647 du 10 July 2000, JO 11.7.2000.

[16] See P. Mistretta, 'La responsabilité pénale médicale à l'aune de la loi du 10 juillet 2000. Evolution ou révolution?' JCP 2002.I.1285.

[17] Although the defendant's behaviour will tend to be assessed more subjectively (*in concreto*) in criminal law.

[18] That is where the person has not directly caused the damage, but has contributed to a situation which has led to that damage, for example the decisions of a manager or hospital administrator responsible for the organisation of the service.

[19] 'soit violé de façon délibérée une obligation particulière de prudence ou de sécurité prévue par la loi ou le règlement, soit commis une faute caractérisée et qui exposait autrui à un risqué d'une particulière gravité qu'elles ne pouvaient ignorer': D. Papanikolauo 'La responsabilité des membres de l'équipe médicale' [2004] *Revue générale du droit médical* 79.

[20] An individual who has been directly harmed by the commission of a criminal offence and who becomes, in his role as a victim, a party to the criminal prosecution. For further description, see G. Viney, *Traité de droit civil. Introduction à la responsabilité* (3rd edn., Paris: LGDJ, 2007) at 188.

has already been started, or can even oblige the *ministère public*[21] to start criminal proceedings. In such cases the *partie civile* can claim damages against the defendant, and the criminal court will assess the victim's claim based on civil law principles. In principle, tort law rules will be applied even where there is a contract between the doctor or clinic and the patient.

Criminal liability plays a significant role within the French system. Recent figures would seem to indicate that more and more cases are being brought against doctors in the criminal courts by patients. Hence, statistics from the *Groupe des assurances mutuelles médicales* from 2002 show that for 2,413 declarations of personal injury concerning private doctors made to insurers, 224 cases were brought before the criminal courts, compared to 687 claims in the civil courts, and 341 complaints to the disciplinary authorities.[22]

There are a number of explanations for the high number of cases before the criminal courts in France. Whilst a desire for 'revenge' inevitably explains the bringing of some actions, a case before the criminal courts offers other significant advantages: the cost of the action is borne by the State, and criminal procedures permit an increased access to evidence.

3.4   Codes of conduct and disciplinary boards

The practice of medicine was regulated from an early period. Already in 1803, a law regulated the use of the titles of doctor and medical assistant. A clear programme of study was established and the medical faculties were responsible for admissions. Criminal penalties were imposed for practising as a doctor without such authorisation and law reports in the nineteenth century have many instances of litigation related to this. Initial registration was then supplemented by continuing professional regulation.

The *Ordre des médecins* was created in 1940 and the first professional code of ethics was produced in 1941. The Law of 4 March 2002 states that it is the role of the *Ordre des médecins* to ensure the competence of medical professionals and that the ethical principles of the medical profession are respected.[23]

Disciplinary jurisdiction is exercised by first instance specialist disciplinary courts (*chambre disciplinaire de première instance*).[24] Appeals are heard by the disciplinary section of the national medical council.

---

[21] Lawyer representing the State who is responsible for bringing prosecutions before the criminal courts.

[22] J. Penneau, above n. 4, at 106.   [23] Art. L.4121–2 *Code de la santé publique*.

[24] Art. L.4124–1 *Code de la santé publique*.

A patient may submit a complaint to the local medical council (*conseil départemental de l'ordre*). The local medical council will attempt conciliation, and where this fails it will then pass the matter to the disciplinary court. Under the recent legislation, the individual patient has the right to appeal before the national disciplinary chamber against a decision of the court. In such cases the patient has the status of a party, which means that he can have access to court files and he can be represented by a lawyer. The sanctions available against the doctor are a warning, a blame, a temporary ban from practising, or striking off the register.[25]

In addition to the role exercised by the *Ordre des médecins*, the *Haute Autorité de Santé* evaluates medical service provision and draws up professional practice rules and guidelines.[26] The Authority was established at the end of 2004 as a principal element in the government's policy of clinical governance.[27]

To what extent do disciplinary decisions and codes of ethics, together with practice guidelines, influence court decisions on the existence and nature of fault? A decision of the disciplinary court is not binding on the civil or administrative courts and is completely independent from any possible civil liability. However, the courts, when assessing the fault of a defendant in an action for damages will, where appropriate, make reference to the medical code of ethics in assessing the defendant's behaviour. This will clearly also be the case with respect to practice guidelines issued from a reputable source, and the non respect by the defendant of clinical guidelines issued by the *Haute Autorité* will presumably, in the majority of cases, be sufficient proof of fault, just as the respect of the guidelines will permit the practitioner to avoid liability. Even so, this may not always be the case. Indeed, the French courts have shown themselves on occasions willing to define a doctor's behaviour as negligent even though he has complied with standard medical practice and norms.[28] International guidelines and norms could also be relevant in the assessment of fault.[29]

---

[25] Art. L.4124–6 *Code de la santé publique*.

[26] It took over this last role from the *Agence nationale d'accréditation et d'évaluation en santé* (ANAES).

[27] Loi n° 2004–810 du 13 August 2004, JO 17.8.2004.

[28] Paris, 4 July 1932, D. 1933.2.113; Paris, 25 April 1945, S. 1946.2.29; Lyon, 16 April 1956, 692; Cass. civ. (1), 6 June 2000, RDSS 2000, 750, obs. L. Dubouis; JCP 2000.II.10447, obs. Mémeteau. *Rapport Cour de cassation* (Paris: La Documentation française, 2001) at 380.

[29] G. Mémeteau, 'L'unification du droit médical en Europe?' [2002] *Revue générale de droit médical* 105 at 121.

4 Analysis of the development of liability rules 1850 to 2000

Before the introduction of legislation in 2002, liability rules in France had been developed by the courts. Whilst the traditional basis of liability is fault, the courts have been willing to apply this concept in different ways depending on the circumstances. Indeed, a study of French case law from the mid-nineteenth century reveals a steady progression from a restrictive interpretation of fault which was very protective of the medical profession to a far broader interpretation, particularly from the middle of the twentieth century.[30]

4.1 The development of fault liability from the mid-nineteenth century

The early period of medical liability was marked by a deferential attitude by the courts towards the medical profession and by a conception of the doctor/patient relationship which favoured medical paternalism. In the first half of the nineteenth century the medical profession argued for immunity from liability where the medical accident had arisen in any situation where a question of medical science or technique was raised.[31] It was argued that liability should be incurred only where the act or omission in question had no connection with the application of medical science, and the courts embraced this view.[32] The earliest recorded case[33] where a doctor was found liable in a clinical negligence action dates from a decision

---

[30] See J. Penneau, *Faute et erreur en matière de responsabilité médicale* (Paris: LGDJ, 1973) (hereafter 'Penneau, *Faute et erreur*').

[31] L. Guerrier and L. Rotureau, *La pratique de jurisprudence médicale* (Paris: Masson, 1890) at 99, cited in M. Harichaux, 'L'obligation du médecin de respecter les données de la science. (A propos du cinquantenaire de l'arrêt Mercier: bilan d'une jurisprudence)' JCP 1987.I.3306. A minority of doctors during this period even went as far as arguing for total immunity from liability: Bouillaut and Maingault, during a debate at the *Académie des médecins* in 1834, referred to by A. Maurès, *Etude sur la responsabilité professionnelle et légale du médecin* (Paris: 1900, doctoral thesis) (hereafter 'Maurès') at 6.

[32] Cass. civ. 18 June 1835, D. 1835.1.300; Besançon, 18 July 1844, D. 1845.2.317; Colmar, 10 July 1850, D. 1850.2.196; Paris, 7 Nov. 1921, Gaz. Pal. 1922.1.39; Trib. Civ. Oran, 20 Oct. 1921, Gaz. Pal. 1921.2.581; Tribunal civil Lanion, 19 Dec. 1932, Gaz. Pal. 1933.1.339. M. Harichaux, 'L'obligation du médecin de respecter les données de la science. (A propos du cinquantenaire de l'arrêt Mercier: bilan d'une jurisprudence)' JCP 1987.I.3306; for a large number of examples of cases from this early period, see Maurès at 62.

[33] At least in post revolutionary France. For earlier, see J.-C. Careghi, 'Une responsabilité médicale a-t-elle existé dans l'ancien regime français' [2003] RRJ 835.

of a first instance court in 1830,[34] but more significantly, the liability of a doctor was first recognised by the Cour de cassation in 1835.[35] In this case, the doctor was found liable in tort under articles 1382 and 1383 of the *Code civil* for grave negligence and particularly for abandoning a patient without warning during treatment. It was stated in this case that 'a doctor cannot be liable for acts or omissions relating exclusively to questions of medical science … but only for negligence, carelessness or not knowing of things it is obvious he should be aware of'. Cases during this early period applied normal fault principles, but the courts tended only to be willing to impose liability where questions of medical science were not raised. Hence, a doctor was found liable where he provided a medical certificate relating to the internment of a patient solely on the basis of declarations made to him, without checking their veracity,[36] where a doctor failed to warn a wet nurse that the child she was given to look after was syphilitic,[37] and the head of a medical service was found liable for allowing a colleague to perform an operation where that person was not qualified to do so.[38] This approach seems to have met with the approval of doctrinal writers at the time.[39]

More medical negligence cases started being brought before the French courts from the beginning of the twentieth century, but remained relatively rare during the first third of the century.[40] During this period the judges continued to be extremely reluctant to get involved in assessing medical science. This reluctance to assess the behaviour of the medical profession can also be seen in civil courts' insistence that a '*faute cara-ctérisée*' or '*faute lourde*' be shown in order to impose liability on a doctor. The expression '*faute lourde*' here did not have the same meaning as in administrative law.[41] In fact, the judges used both terms again simply to indicate that they were only willing to sanction acts or omissions which were obviously negligent without needing to refer to medical science.[42]

[34] Tribunal civil Domfront, 28 Feb. 1830, F. Dubrac, *Traité de jurisprudence médicale et pharmaceutique* (Paris: Baillière, 1882) at 100.

[35] Cass. req. 16 June 1835, S. 1835.1.402.   [36] Caen, 16 Jan. 1901, DP 1904.2.370.

[37] Tribunal civil Amiens, 12 Aug. 1893, *Journal des arrêts de la cour d'Amiens*, 1894, 194.

[38] Bordeaux, 6 Feb. 1900, D. 1900.2.470.

[39] A. Sourdat, *Traité général de la responsabilité* (Paris: Marchal & Godde, 1887); F. Laurent, *Principes de droit civil français* (Paris: A. Durand, 1869–1878); E. Hu, *Etude historique et juridique de la responsabilité du médecin* (Paris: Chaumont, 1880), cited by Maurès at 63.

[40] According to Maurès at 2, there were only two actions for medical negligence brought in 1876, but this had increased to eight to ten actions per month by 1900.

[41] See below p. 81.

[42] J. Penneau, *Faute et erreur en responsabilité médicale* (Paris: 1972, doctoral thesis) (hereafter 'Penneau, doctoral thesis') at 119, also see Penneau *Faute et erreur*; R. Savatier *et al.*, *Traité de droit médical* (Paris: Librairies techniques, 1956) at 291.

Hence, a doctor would be liable for fault if the court was able to reach its decision without any reference to medical theories or methods.

A case from 1931 provides a clear example of the distinction between medical acts that the courts were and were not prepared to sanction.[43] In this case a surgeon was sued by his patient. The surgeon had operated on the patient's leg (the patient worked as a fashion model) to correct a deformity which was the source of aesthetic rather than physical problems. As a result of complications in the surgery, the leg become gangrenous and had subsequently to be amputated. The patient sued the doctor in the civil courts. The court was unwilling to base liability on any mistake in the exercise of medical science. Hence, the court refused to consider whether the defendant had sufficiently examined the patient prior to the operation which may have allowed him to discover potential risks arising from the particular characteristics of her skin. However, the court did impose liability on the doctor in tort under articles 1382 and 1383 of the *Code civil* since it held that he had given insufficient warning to the patient of the risks inherent in the operation. The patient had thus not been in a position to provide informed consent to the operation. The court defined this as a *faute grave*, which it was able to consider since it concerned a question which did not involve an assessment of medical science.

More medical fault cases are reported in the criminal courts, especially in the nineteenth century. A fault of the doctor could also result in his criminal liability under articles 319 and 320 of the *Code pénal* which impose criminal liability for death or injury caused by fault. The courts initially tended to require a more serious fault here than in civil actions,[44] but this line was abandoned in the early twentieth century and criminal and civil fault began to be defined in the same way.[45] A doctor could therefore be found criminally liable for failing to obtain the consent of the patient before an operation, or for exposing him to a risk which was out of proportion to the expected benefit of the medical act.[46] He could also be liable for technical errors such as leaving a foreign object in the body of the patient after an operation,[47] forgetting to give the patient an anti-tetanus jab,[48] or for defective treatment.[49]

---

[43] Paris, 12 March 1931, D. 1931.2.141 note J. Loup.

[44] Cass civ. 14 Nov. 1898, S. 1902.1.27. R. Savatier, above n. 42, at 312.

[45] Cass. civ. 18 Dec. 1912, D. 1915.1.17, note LS; Cass. req. 15 Jan. 1929, D. 1930.1.41, note R. Savatier.

[46] Lyon, 27 May 1936, DH 1936, 465.

[47] Amiens, 16 July 1931, Gaz. Pal. 1931.2.773; Aix, 12 Jan. 1954, D. 1954, 338.

[48] Paris, 10 Feb. 1954, D. 1954, 257.

[49] Cass. crim. 16 April 1921, D. 1921.1.184.

However, in this early period, successful criminal prosecutions of doctors were rare.[50] To a great extent this was because the courts relied on the judgment of experts, who were members of the profession, and seemed to set very high thresholds for the concept of 'serious fault'.

There was a marked increase in the number of medical negligence actions in civil law from the second third of the twentieth century, in parallel with an increase in the use of radiography and developments in surgical techniques which had as a corollary a substantial increase in the number of accidents and thus of court actions against doctors. This was the context for the *Mercier* case in 1936[51] which was significant since medical liability thereby became identifiable as a specific type of civil liability, and the court established for the first time that the civil liability of the doctor to the patient was based on contract.[52] The case stated that the contract between the patient and the clinic or doctor imposed on the latter an obligation 'not to cure the patient, but to provide him in a conscientious and attentive way with the appropriate care in accordance with the current state of scientific knowledge'.[53] The obligation was therefore one of reasonable care and skill (*obligation de moyens*).[54] Prior to this decision, liability of doctors towards their patients was seen as essentially delictual with contract being confined to the recovery of the honorarium for services. However, the recognition of the contractual nature of liability had no effect on the way that fault was assessed until around 1945. In this period, the civil courts still often referred to '*faute lourde*', meaning simply a requirement that there be no doubt as to the obvious nature of the fault.[55]

4.2   The particular case of fault in administrative law

Before the second half of the nineteenth century, the principal purpose of hospitals had been seen as providing accommodation for the homeless

---

[50] G. Levasseur, 'La responsabilité pénale du médecin' in M. Eck *et al.*, *Le médecin face aux risques et à la responsabilité* (Paris: Fayard, 1968) at 154.

[51] Cass. civ. 20 May 1936, DP 1936.1.88, concl. Matter, rapp. Josserand.

[52] Decisions as early as 1857 had recognised the contractual basis of the relationship between doctor and patient, but only with respect to disputes relating to fees: Amiens, 10 Nov. 1857, *Journal des tribunaux* 5 Dec. 1857.

[53] Cass civ. 20 May 1936, *Mercier*, D. 1936.1.88, concl. Matter, rapp. Josserand, note EP. It is noticeable in the decision that the advocate general relies heavily on the 1923 academic writings of the *rapporteur* in the case.

[54] G. Mémeteau, *Cours de droit médical* (Paris: Les Etudes Hospitalières, 2000) at 262; Y. Lambert-Faivre, above n. 7, at 681; J. Bell, S. Boyron and S. Whittaker, *Principles of French Law* (2nd edn., Oxford: Oxford University Press, 2008) at 242–3.

[55] Penneau, doctoral thesis, at 117.

and dying. Legislation in 1851 distinguished hospitals from hospices, and organised the administration and financing of hospitals, principally in the hands of local authorities.[56] In the case of actions against public health service providers, the administrative courts, like their civil counterparts, adopted a very protective position towards defendants. Hence the hospital would only be liable in the case of a *faute lourde*. The concept of *faute lourde* was not used here in the same way as it was employed in the civil courts.[57] In administrative law, the concept refers to a particularly serious fault, caused by grave negligence or recklessness and was used in a particularly restrictive way by the administrative courts.[58] Hence, the administrative courts refused to impose liability where, for example, an unconscious patient was burned by a hot water bottle,[59] and in another case where a patient's wound became infected with gangrene due to the use of stitches which were not sterile.[60] The concept of *faute lourde* was used by the courts as a way of protecting public services and was not specific to medical services. However, it was argued by doctrinal writers that further justifications existed for a more protective regime for doctors in the public sector. Hence, the doctor was bound by public service rules, he could not refuse to treat a patient on the basis of lack of material or personnel, his role was not limited to caring for patients, he had to also train other medical staff. Added to this was the argument that the salary of a national health doctor tended to be less than in the private sector.[61]

In an attempt to avoid disparities between the bases of liability in the public and the private sector, a line of civil court decisions found doctors personally liable in the civil law of torts for faults as a result of medical acts, notwithstanding that the doctor was employed by and acting for a public hospital.[62] Thus in these cases the civil courts were competing with the administrative courts which also claimed jurisdiction over such cases.[63] In practice, victims therefore often had the option between the two jurisdictions, and the Tribunal des conflits was rarely used. In reality, for the doctor, the financial cost was in both cases borne by the hospital since, following a 1943 decree, public bodies were under an obligation to pay for liability insurance for national health doctors. This uncertain

---

[56] N. Destais, *Le système de santé. Organisation et régulation* (Paris: LGDJ, 2003) at 26.
[57] For a basic introduction to the concept of *faute lourde* in administrative law, see J.-F. Brisson and A. Rouyere, *Droit administratif* (Paris: Montchrestien, 2004) at 579.
[58] Savatier, above n. 42, at 484.   [59] CE 13 July 1934, *Smyth*, Leb. 538.
[60] CE 13 May 1937, *Teyssier* Leb. 307.   [61] Savatier, above n. 42, at 485.
[62] Cass. req. 30 Nov. 1938, D. 1939.1.49, note Savatier.
[63] TC 15 March 1902, D. 1903.3.93; CE 8 Nov. 1935, D. 1936.3.15, note Heilbronner.

position was only resolved by a decision of the Tribunal des conflits in 1957 which confirmed the jurisdiction of the administrative courts for faults of doctors working within public hospitals, and this position was accepted by the Cour de cassation by 1960.[64]

4.3   The shift away from the fault requirement towards the use of strict liability in certain cases

Penneau, in his extensive study of medical fault liability published in the early 1970s,[65] notes a progressive tendency from the second third of the twentieth century to separate liability from the requirement of fault, and this tendency became more pronounced from around 1945.[66] In particular, there was an increased reliance on what the author refers to as 'virtual fault' (faute virtuelle). Surgeons were frequently found liable on this basis where they forgot swabs left inside a patient after an operation,[67] but doctors were also held liable in other situations. For example, in a case from 1962,[68] liability was imposed on a doctor on the basis that the operation would not have failed if the correct procedures had been followed. In the case, according to the correct medical procedure, for a particular type of injection, a needle had to be inserted in a particular way, and once inserted, the injection had to be performed quickly and with particular force. Liability was imposed despite the fact that no actual fault or noncompliance with the required procedure was identified. In another case a patient was injured when he fell from a table where he was due to be examined. The court presumed a fault in supervision by the doctor.[69] Again, in a first instance decision in 1960 a surgeon damaged a facial nerve of a newly born child during a Caesarean section. The court based their finding of fault on the fact that the doctor was not qualified in obstetrics, and on the rarity of the accident, even though all the evidence indicated that the operation had been correctly performed.[70] There was even an attempt by lower civil courts to introduce a guarantee of safety (obligation de sécurité) into the contract linking the doctor and patient to enable strict

---

[64] Y. Lambert-Faivre, above n. 7, at 636.

[65] Penneau, doctoral thesis, esp. at 116–38.

[66] See also Savatier, above n. 42, at 288–311. See, for example CE 12 June 1953, D. 1954, 129; Paris, 5 March 1957, JCP 1957.II.10020; Paris, 16 Jan. 1950, JCP 1950.II.5716.

[67] Paris, 29 Oct. 1934, GP 1934.2.905; Trib. civ. de la Seine, 4 July 1939, GP 1940.1.63; Paris, 17 July 1936, DH 1936, 498.

[68] Cass. civ. (1), 19 June 1962, JCP 1962.IV.110; Bull. civ. 1, n°316, 279.

[69] Paris, 4 Nov. 1963, D. 1964, 13.

[70] Seine, 31 May 1960, Gaz. Pal. 1960.2.106.

liability to be imposed on the doctor,[71] although this technique was consistently rejected by the Cour de cassation.[72]

From very early on the courts also showed that they were willing on occasions to define the defendant's act or omission as a fault even though he had complied with what was recognised as accepted or standard medical practice at the time.[73]

The way that the interpretation of fault developed in the administrative courts was very similar to civil law in that there was a steady move from a very protective approach for the medical practitioner to one enabling easier compensation for the victim. Over time the approach of the administrative courts in clinical negligence cases was consistently to facilitate the proof of a *faute lourde* in an effort to help the compensation of victims.[74] In 1959 the Conseil d'Etat thus stated that *faute lourde* would be applied only where an accident arose as a result of a medical (rather than a paramedical) act and that liability for damage resulting from the defective organisation or functioning of medical services would only be subject to the proof of a *faute simple*.[75] The courts commonly stated that faults occurring during medical acts were faults in the functioning of the medical service, in order to ensure that liability would be based on *faute simple*,[76] or alternatively took a generous view of what actually constituted a *faute lourde*.[77] The use of *faute lourde* was finally abandoned by the Conseil d'Etat in medical negligence cases in 1992.[78]

In addition, from the 1970s both the civil and administrative courts started using the technique of loss of chance with respect to the causal link between the medical act and the victim's injury in order to facilitate the awarding of compensation,[79] and this technique continues to be used, somewhat controversially, today. Hence, in some circumstances where

---

[71] Tribunal de Grande Instance Meaux, 13 Dec. 1961, Gaz. Pal. 1962.2.44; Paris, 4 May 1963, JCP 1963.II.13291.

[72] Cass. civ. (1), 1 April 1968, D. 1968, 653, note Savatier; Penneau, doctoral thesis, at 131.

[73] Paris, 4 July 1932, D. 1933.2.113; Paris, 25 April 1945, S 1946.2.29; Paris, 26 April 1948, D. 1948, 272: as long as this did not involve the judge in an evaluation of medical science.

[74] The tendency for the administrative courts to move away from liability for *faute lourde* in fact started in the area of medical liability, before extending to other areas of public service provision: Brisson and Rouyere, above n. 57.

[75] CE 26 June 1959, D. 1960, 112, note J. Robert.

[76] CE 4 Oct. 1968, Leb. 478. Y. Gaudemet, *Traité de droit administratif*, vol. 1 (Paris: LGDJ, 2001) at 812.

[77] CE 9 July 1969, Leb. 364; Y. Gaudemet, *ibid.* at 812.

[78] CE 10 April 1992, AJDA 1992, 355, concl. H. Légal.

[79] Cass. civ. (1), 18 March 1969, JCP 1970.II.16422 note A. Rabut; Cass. civ. (1), 27 Jan. 1970, D. 1970, somm.70; CE 19 May 1971, RDSS 1971, 525, note Moderne.

the claimant is unable to prove the causal link between the doctor's act and the damage, the courts base liability on the loss of a chance of recovery or survival (*perte d'une chance de guérison ou de survie*). In such cases, damages will be set at a percentage of the total loss, reflecting the court's assessment of the percentage chance that the patient had of avoiding the loss if it were not for the fault. This technique is used by the courts in a number of cases where there is a doubt as to the link between the doctor's act or omission and the loss.[80] The court must however be satisfied that there is a genuine chance of recovery or survival which has been lost because of the fault of the defendant.

4.4   Possible factors behind the development of liability rules

As Penneau observes,[81] the adaptation in certain cases of the fault principle in order to facilitate the compensation of victims can be seen as a reaction of the courts to the increase in medical risk which came with the rapid advances in medical science after the second world war. The evolution of medical liability rules therefore reflects the same movement which occurred at a much earlier date for industrial accidents, most notably with the introduction of statutory no fault compensation for employment related accidents in 1898,[82] and the well known development of strict liability in tort for damage caused by objects or things under article 1384–1 of the *Code civil*. At the time that Saleilles was pushing for a move away from fault based compensation for industrial accidents,[83] the position in relation to medical law did not raise the same concerns, the equivalent leap in technological and scientific techniques not having yet occurred in this area. The later development in the area of medical accidents can also perhaps be explained by the particular difficulty in establishing fault and a causal link in clinical liability cases, and the concern not to distract the doctor from his primary task of treating the patient by

---

[80] Where there has been a diagnostic error (CE 6 Feb. 1974, AJDA, 1974, 456: loss of chance for a patient of avoiding a serious operation or amputation), a delay in treatment (CE 10 Nov. 1976, n° 97760 and n° 97787: delay in treatment of a broken leg led to a loss of chance for the patient of avoiding the need for a replacement hip), or where the equipment or surveillance of the patient was inadequate (Cass. civ. (1), 13 Oct. 1992, Resp. civile et assur. 1992, n° 162: inadequate surveillance in a delivery room led to the loss of a chance of a newborn baby of avoiding brain damage).

[81] Penneau, doctoral thesis, at 116. Also see Penneau, above n. 4, at 1.

[82] Law of 9 April 1898.

[83] R. Saleilles, *Les accidents du travail et la responsabilité civile: essai d'une théorie objective de la responsabilité délictuelle* (Paris: Arthur Rousseau, 1897).

imposing excessive liability.[84] However, as Penneau remarks, the progress to strict liability in other areas of tort law at a much earlier date no doubt finished by exerting pressure on the rules relating to medical liability, and was therefore a factor in the evolution of the concept of fault in this area from the second half of the twentieth century.[85]

The first signs of changes in medical liability rules occurred at the same time as the second wave of doctrinal criticism of fault liability, this time in the area of professional services, which was led by Starck.[86] The evolution of the fault principle in medical law from the end of the 1940s corresponds to a period where there was rapid progress in medical techniques and a consequential increase in the number of accidents due, for example, to the use of more ambitious surgical procedures, and to the increased use of radiology.[87] This would appear to be reflected in the increase in the number of claims by patients. Statistics are sparse, but figures from the group insuring 90% of private practitioners show a steady rise in the number of claims from the 1940s to the end of the 1970s.[88] There would then appear to be a levelling out of claims from the beginning of the 1980s.

Other factors have also doubtlessly played an important role. Medical liability insurance became available from the start of the twentieth century and began to be more widely used from the 1930s following legislation which made it possible to insure for all degrees of fault, even *faute lourde*.[89] The availability of unlimited insurance cover was rare in the 1930s,[90] but had become common by the 1960s.[91] Viney, in her works on civil liability, has frequently emphasised the link between the increasing availability of liability insurance and the development of no fault

---

[84] Penneau, above n. 4, at 3.

[85] Penneau, doctoral thesis, at 124.

[86] B. Starck, *Essai d'une théorie générale de la responsabilité civile, considérée en sa double fonction de garantie et de peine privée* (Paris: doctoral thesis, 1947); Penneau, doctoral thesis, at 140–7.

[87] J. Penneau, doctoral thesis, at 121 and 142, citing J. Bernard, *Rapport au 2e congrès international de morale médicale*, vol. 1 (Paris: Ordre national des médecins, 1966) at 261.

[88] Statistics from GAMM (Le groupe des assurances mutuelles médicales). The number of claims to the insurance companies concerned rose from 35 in 1944, to 123 in 1954, 254 in 1964, 338 in 1973, 1,158 in 1980, to 2,000 in 1988. The statistics unfortunately only show the evolution in the number of practitioners insured with the group from 1980. Penneau infers however that the increase in the number of claims made was greatly in excess of the increase in the number of practitioners insured. From 1980 the proportion of insurance claims made in proportion to the number of insured has remained stable, at around 1.4%: Penneau, above n. 4, at 2.

[89] Law of 13 July 1930. G. Viney, *Traité de droit civil. Introduction à la responsabilité*, at 30.

[90] R. Savatier, 'Les assurances illimitées de responsabilité' [1934] *Assurances terrestres* 490.

[91] G. Viney, *Traité de droit civil. Introduction à la responsabilité*, at 30.

liability. She thus writes that 'one of the principal reasons for the case law development [of no-fault liability] has been to make liability coincide as far as possible with insurance cover'.[92]

The increase in cases before the courts and the evolution in the concept of fault must be seen against a background of important changes in the provision of health services which became progressively more widely available to the population from the end of the First World War. Legislation in 1928, and then in 1930 introduced for the first time a social insurance scheme which financed health care and pensions for workers.[93] This was extended to the wider population in 1946. In 1941 access to hospitals, rather than being restricted to local residents, became open to the whole population.[94]

The increasing number of claims should also be seen in a context of a rapid rise in investment in and capacity of medical services and in the consumption of medical care. The number of hospital beds increased by 20% in the public sector and doubled in the private sector from 1950 to 1970, and the total patient capacity of hospitals increased by 40% over the same period, and by a further 50% from 1970 to 1980.[95] The number of hospital patients increased by 50% from 1960 to 1970. The expansion in capacity was accompanied by a marked increase in investment in medical equipment especially from the 1970s. This is revealed in the changes to the structure of hospital budgets. In 1945 the cost of accommodation for patients represented 93% of the total budget, whereas in 1985 it had fallen to 65%. In 1985 the investment in technology took up 35% of the budget, compared to only 7% just after the Second World War. In 1990 there were 173,100 doctors in activity in France compared to 65,000 in 1970.[96] In terms of expenditure on care per head of population, this has tripled in real terms from 1970 to the present day.[97] From the beginning of the 1960s to the mid 1970s there was a considerable financial investment by the State in the hospital system, and permits for the construction and extension of hospitals increased twelve-fold during this period.[98]

In addition, the evolution in society's perception of the doctor/patient relationship and the decline of medical paternalism probably also played

[92] Ibid. at 41. See also G. Viney, *Le déclin de la responsabilité individuelle* (Paris: LGDJ, 1965) at paras. 246–55.
[93] Law of 5 April 1928 on social insurance; Law of 30 April 1930.
[94] Law of 21 Dec. 1941.
[95] N. Destais, *Le système de santé. Organisation et régulation* (Paris: LGDJ, 2003) at 34. The overall capacity was however reduced by 20% from 1980 to 1990.
[96] *Ibid*. at 42.   [97] *Ibid*. at 67.   [98] *Ibid*. at 33.

a role in changing the attitudes of both the courts, which became less deferential to the medical profession, and of the public, which increasingly saw the doctor as a mere provider of services.[99] This change in attitudes in fact seems to have started much earlier than the consumerist movement from the 1970s. Indeed, the change in the doctor/patient relationship was identified as a factor in the increase in claims as early as 1900.[100] This evolution can doubtlessly be explained in part by the changing level of education of the population, but also by developments in the way medicine was practised. Hence, in his *Traité du droit médical* published in 1956,[101] Savatier suggests that with the increase in complexity of medical techniques, the patient was more often treated by a medical team rather than by an individual doctor. This inevitably led to an erosion of the close relationship between the doctor and his patient. Medicine became more anonymous, and so the patient became more willing to sue.[102]

Personality rights and self-determination are not referred to in judgments on medical liability and do not form the formal basis of court decisions. Nor is the development of such rights referred to by doctrinal writers as being a factor in the development of liability rules. However, the right to bodily integrity is recognised as a fundamental human right and was expressly inserted in 1994 into the *Code civil*.[103] The Conseil constitutionnel has recognised that the right to compensation for physical injury is a constitutional right where the injury has been caused by fault.[104] Moreover, even if there is no specific reliance in the formulation of the case law rules on personality rights, we can speculate on the underlying connection between the developments in medical liability rules and the growth in the idea of patient rights and of patient consumerism.[105] It is perhaps no coincidence that the first signs of a move away from liability for fault occurred at the same time as the appearance of such ideas. On an international level, the Universal Declaration of Human Rights 1948 included the right to a sufficient standard of living to ensure health and adequate medical care.[106] The foundation of patient rights in France

---

[99] On this change in conception, see, for example, F. Ponchon, *Les droits des patients à l'hôpital* (Paris: PUF, 1999) at 107; Penneau, doctoral thesis, at 123; C. Evin, 'L'indemnisation des accidents médicaux' [2001] *Revue générale de droit médical* 72; Maurès at 3.

[100] See Maurès at 3.   [101] Above n. 42.   [102] *Ibid*. at 23.

[103] Loi bioéthique n° 94–653 of 29 July 1994.

[104] Conseil constitutionnel, 22 Oct. 1982, D. 1983, 189. Y. Lambert-Faivre, above n. 7, at 161.

[105] On the growth of patient consumerism, see F. Ponchon, *Les droits des patients à l'hôpital* (Paris: PUF, 1999).

[106] Art. 25.

can be found in the preamble to the 1946 constitution which stated that
the nation 'guarantees health protection to all.'[107] As was recognised at
the time, the text emphasised the rights of individuals rather than the
duty of the community.[108] This principle was put into effect by an important reform of the hospital system in 1958 which developed research and
training, and for the first time created full time posts for doctors in public hospitals. Further legislation in 1970[109] introduced the principle that
patients were free to choose their doctor and hospital, and rationalised
health care provision across the public and private sectors. A 1974 decree
established rules on the functioning of hospitals, particularly relating to
admissions, conditions of stay and discharge and this text introduced
the fundamentals of patient rights in hospitals.[110] This was followed by a
charter for patients drawn up in 1975.[111] The consumer/patient movement
became particularly pronounced from the 1990s. Legislation in 1996[112]
required the presence of two patient representatives on hospital governing boards. The same legislation required a conciliation commission to
be set up in every hospital.[113] Consumers' associations in hospitals also
started appearing from the early 1990s. These associations provide support to patients suffering from particular illnesses, together with help
with administration and even financial difficulties. They can also offer
assistance in possible legal action.

The development of patient rights is reflected in the Law of 4 March
2002. One of the principal aims of this legislation is to establish a system
of 'health care democracy' (démocratie sanitaire).[114] The Law confirms the
provisions with respect to patient representation and, in addition, allows
licensed associations to intervene as civil parties in actions in the criminal courts for infractions harming the collective interests of consumers.

It is difficult to assess whether increased specialisation amongst legal
practitioners has had any influence on the number of claims being made.
There is relatively little statistical data available on the degree of specialisation of French avocats. Legislation from 1971 lists fifteen areas

---

[107] 'garantit à tous … la protection de la santé'.
[108] J. Rivero and G. Vedel, 'Les problèmes économiques et sociaux de la Constitution du 27 octobre 1946', fascicule XXXI, Droit social 13.
[109] Loi n°70–1318 of 31 Dec. 1970, JO 3.1.1971.
[110] Décret n°74–27 of 14 Jan. 1974, JO 16.1.1974.
[111] An updated version was published in 1995.
[112] Ordonnance n°96–346 of 24 April 1996, JO 24.4.1996.
[113] Despite the name, the role of these commissions is not to provide a conciliation service but to provide orientation to patients on their options following a medical accident.
[114] Arts. R 1114–1 to R 1114–17 Code de la santé publique.

of specialisation which an *avocat* is permitted to feature on his letter head provided he has shown evidence of a genuine specialisation in this area. However, these specialisations are very general, and medical law and medical liability law are not contained in the list. The National Bar Council, in a rough survey of the register of Parisian lawyers in 2000,[115] found that there were sixty-eight practitioners claiming expertise in medical law according to the official register (16,000 *avocats* were registered at the Paris Bar in that year). There is nothing to stop law firms claiming specialisation in medical (liability) law in the telephone directory, or on internet sites. It is perhaps relevant that the number of *avocats* registered in France had increased five-fold from 1970 to 2000.[116]

4.5   Significant developments in liability rules in the 1990s

The later developments in patient consumerism which I have identified came at the same time as a particularly pronounced movement away from fault in the 1990s by the courts. This was clearly a reaction by the French courts to the increased awareness of medical risk and a desire to facilitate the compensation of victims. It was doubtless in part triggered by the strong public reaction to the blood transfusion and growth hormone scandals from the late 1980s. French courts were inevitably influenced by the increasing tendency towards strict liability which has been prevalent in the context of industrial accidents from the mid-nineteenth century in France and which presented a striking contrast with the principally fault based liability regime applying to medical negligence cases at the time. The evolution in liability rules away from the fault principle had the effect of pushing the legislature towards reform as a means of alleviating the actual or perceived financial burden on medical practitioners and their insurers. This may well indeed have been one of the motives behind the courts' decisions.[117]

There was a marked move by both the administrative and the civil courts in the 1990s to improve the claimant's position in defined circumstances.

---

[115] Conseil National des Barreaux, report of 8 July 2000 (www.cnb.avocat.fr).

[116] Conseil National des Barreaux, *Présentation des résultats des études de la profession*, Convention nationale de Nice, Oct. 2002 (www.cnb.avocat.fr).

[117] This of course is not specifically admitted by the French courts. However, Pierre Sargos, principal adviser to the Cour de cassation and very influential figure, saw the introduction of a statutory scheme of compensation as a solution to the increase in financial pressure on doctors and insurers. P. Sargos 'L'aléa thérapeutique devant le juge judiciaire' JCP 2000.I.189.

Where the patient contracted a bacterial infection during his stay in hospital or within thirty days of his leaving, the Conseil d'Etat introduced a presumption of liability on the part of the hospital. The defendant would only be able to avoid liability by establishing that the victim was infected by the germ on his arrival at the hospital.[118] In three judgments handed down in 1999, the Cour de cassation established the same principle for infections contracted in private hospitals, the establishment was strictly liable, and would only be able to avoid liability in the unlikely event that it was able to establish that the infection was contracted by the patient elsewhere.[119]

The Cour de cassation developed further exceptions to the principle of fault based liability. Thus, where the medical act involved the use of equipment, the court held that the contract between the practitioner/institution and the patient included an implied term that that equipment is free from defect. Where the patient was injured by defective equipment, the doctor/institution was strictly liable in contract.[120] The Cour de cassation also consistently held that simple errors of manipulation by a surgeon during an operation would automatically be considered as negligent. A term would be implied in the contract between the surgeon or clinic and the patient providing that the surgeon guarantees the accuracy of his gestures.[121]

In addition, both the administrative and civil courts placed on the doctor the burden of proving that he had informed the patient of the risks involved in treatment.[122] The courts thereby in certain circumstances allowed a claimant who was unable to establish the fault of the practitioner or service to obtain damages for the loss of the chance he would have had of avoiding the risk if he had been given the opportunity to refuse his consent to the treatment.[123]

Most notably, the administrative courts, since 1993, admitted claims for what are commonly referred to as *'aléas thérapeutiques'*. This

---

[118] CE 9 Dec. 1988, *Cohen*, Leb. 431; CE 1 March 1989, *Bailly*, Resp. civile et assur. 1989, no.199.

[119] Cass. civ. (1), 29 June 1999, JCP 1999.II.10138, rapport Sargos, Gaz. Pal. 29–30 Oct. 1999, 37, note J. Guigue.

[120] Cass. civ. (1), 9 Nov. 1999, *Resp. civile et assur.* 2000, no.61.

[121] Cass. civ. (1), 26 June 1972, JCP 1972.IV.60; Cass. civ. (1), 25 May 1983, JCP 1984.II.20281, note Dorsner-Dolivet.

[122] Cass. civ. 1re, 25 Feb. 1997, Gaz. Pal. 1997.1.274; CE 5 Jan. 2000, JCP 2000.II.10271, note Moreau.

[123] Damages will be calculated as a percentage of the actual loss suffered. Y. Lambert-Faivre, above n. 7, at 706, who criticises the use of the loss of chance principle in this context; J. Bell, S. Boyron and S. Whittaker *Principles of French Law* at 412–4, where the operation of the loss of chance principle is referred to in another context.

refers to accidents occurring as a result of a medical act rather than the patient's illness but which are not due to the fault of a medical practitioner or medical institution. Liability here was thus based on risk rather than fault.[124] The Conseil d'Etat imposed liability on public hospitals for such accidents provided certain criteria were fulfilled. Hence, in the 1993 case *Bianchi*[125] a patient who became paralysed after an operation under general anaesthetic sued the hospital. The Conseil d'Etat found the hospital liable since the injury occurred as a result of the medical act even though no negligence was established. The court however laid down a set of strict criteria to be fulfilled in such cases. The harm suffered had to be a known risk of the medical act and have no connection with the patient's pre-existing condition. The type of harm suffered had to occur rarely (so common side effects will not be compensated) and be of an extremely serious nature.

In contrast, the Cour de cassation was unwilling to impose liability on medical defendants for loss resulting from this form of accident.[126] The unfortunate result was that whether or not the claimant received compensation depended on whether he was treated in the public or the private sector.

The introduction of legislation on the compensation of victims of medical accidents reflected the widespread feeling that the current system was unsatisfactory.[127] In many situations, the victim still faced the difficult task of establishing the fault of the defendant, and the difference between

---

[124] On the notion of risk in French administrative law, see L. Brown and J. Bell, *French Administrative Law* (Oxford: Clarendon Press, 1998) at 184, 289.

[125] CE 9 April 1993, *Bianchi*, Leb. 127, concl. M. Daël; JCP 1993.II.22061, note J. Moreau; and also CE 3 Nov. 1997, JCP 1998.II.10016, note Moreau.

[126] Cass. civ. (1), 8 Nov. 2000, D. 2000.IR.292. See Y. Lambert-Faivre, 'La réparation de l'accident médical. Obligation de sécurité: oui; aléa thérapeutique: non' D. 2001 chr. 570. There are several reasons for this reluctance. The civil courts are bound to work within the provisions of the civil code. The articles of the code which could be used to found liability in these cases (arts. 1135 and 1147) would not allow the courts to limit liability to cases where the harm suffered by the patient is of a serious nature. The burden of liability placed on medical practitioners, and hence on their insurers, would also be very heavy. The civil courts perhaps also fear that it will be extremely difficult to define the notion of *aléa thérapeutique* to keep it within tight boundaries. There is perhaps a danger of the principle of liability for fault being eroded by an ever wider definition of *aléa*. P. Sargos (conseiller in the Cour de cassation) 'L'aléa thérapeutique devant le juge judiciaire' JCP 2000.I.202.

[127] See, for example, C. Larroumet, 'L'indemnisation de l'aléa thérapeutique', D. 1999 chr. 33; P. Sargos, above n. 126, C. Evin, 'L'indemnisation des accidents médicaux' [2001] *Revue générale de droit médical* 71; Y. Lambert-Faivre, 'L'indemnisation du préjudice des victimes d'accidents médicaux. N'est-ce pas temps d'adopter un système d'indemnisation

the rules in the administrative and civil courts added to the complexity of the system and led to injustice. There was also a fear that the approach of the courts in constantly extending the liability of the defendant would lead to the practice of defensive medicine, although no evidence of this was produced. The decision of the Cour de cassation in the *Perruche* case in 2001,[128] where damages were awarded in an action for wrongful life, and the line of cases that followed, were seen as the most extreme manifestation of a developing compensation culture. From the start of the 1990s insurers reacted to the increasing liability of practitioners by withdrawing their insurance offers or by renegotiating policies, and this tendency became particularly marked from 1998 in areas perceived as high risk, such as obstetrics and surgery.[129] In addition there was concern that France would follow the same route as the American system, condemned as the ultimate 'litigation culture'.[130] There was indeed in France a generally held perception of a litigation crisis with respect to medical accidents, with a considerable increase in the number of claims. Statistical evidence of such a crisis is however very limited, and any such increase would certainly not appear to be on the same scale as that experienced in the United Kingdom.[131]

---

cohérent et stable?' Gaz. Pal. 2001.1.13 ; G. Viney and P. Jourdain, 'L'indemnisation des accidents médicaux: que peut faire la Cour de Cassation?' JCP 1997.I.181.

[128] See below p. 104.

[129] S. Guiné-Gibert, 'L'assurance responsabilité médicale des acteurs de santé. Historique: comment en est-on arrivé à la situation actuelle' [2004] *Revue générale de droit médical* 157 at 158.

[130] See, for example, the introductory remarks to the report of the *Commission des affaires sociales du Sénat* of 19 April 2001, on a private member's bill presented by Mr Huriet, which notes the fear by health professionals of the arrival of an American style claims culture in France. The true risk of this happening in reality seems very small: see L. Engel, 'Vers une nouvelle approche de la responsabilité. Le droit français face à la dérive américaine' *Esprit*, June 1993, 29.

[131] Statistical data on the number of medical negligence actions in France is rather sparse. A study carried out in 1994 found just over 1,000 new cases brought in 1990 to 1991, and 1,500 in 1992. (Study for the *Agence nationale pour le development de l'évaluation médicale* by D. Thouvenin, cited in D. Thouvenin, *La responsabilité médicale* (Paris: Flammarion, 1995). There were 2,503 declarations made to medical insurers in 2002, down from 3,004 in 1994, source: GAMM, *annual reports*, cited in Y. Lambert-Faivre, above n. 7, at 840. These figures compare rather favourably with recent trends in the UK, where a modest 392 actions in 1996 to 1997 had exploded to 5,765 actions in 2002 to 2003: *Making Amends: a consultation paper setting out proposals for reforming the approach to clinical negligence in the NHS* (London: Department of Health, 2003) at 58.

4.6 *The new statutory compensation scheme*

The changes to the compensation system introduced by the Law of 4 March 2002 are the culmination of thirty years of proposals for reform.[132] However, despite a number of private members bills, the bill filed with Parliament on 5 September 2001 was the first time that the government had presented a proposal for legislation.

The reforms are introduced as Part IV of the Law *relative aux droits des maladies et à la qualité du système de santé* (Patients' Rights and Quality of the Health System Act), entitled *Réparation des conséquences des risques sanitaires* (Compensation for Loss Resulting from Medical Accidents).

The Law guarantees full compensation to victims of serious medical accidents and introduces new procedures aimed at avoiding litigation and at speeding up compensation payments. I will deal with both these elements in turn.

4.6.1 The guarantee of compensation for victims of serious medical accidents

The Law states the basic principle that health professionals[133] and organisations are only liable for damage caused by their acts of prevention, diagnosis and treatment where they are at fault. However, there are two exceptions to this where strict liability will apply. Hence, health organisations will be strictly liable for any loss caused to the patient by a bacterial infection contracted during a visit to their premises. The organisation will only be able to avoid liability in this latter case by showing that the infection was caused outside the medical establishment.[134] This exception therefore reflects the position taken by both the civil and administrative courts on infections. Secondly, liability for defective medical products[135]

---

[132] A no-fault compensation fund for medical accidents in France was first suggested by A. Tunc at the second international conference on medical ethics in 1966. This was followed by various reports commissioned by the government in the 1980s and 1990s and a number of private member bills. For a brief history of French proposals for reform, see C. Evin, 'L'indemnisation des accidents médicaux' [2001] *Revue générale de droit médical* 71.

[133] A health professional is defined broadly to include a wide range of professions. Hence, the list includes, amongst others, doctors, dentists, midwives, pharmacists, nurses, physiotherapists, radiologists, dieticians. Further see art. L 1142–1 of the *Code de la santé publique*, referring to the professions mentioned in Part 4 of the same code.

[134] Art. L 1142–1.

[135] A medical product (*produit de santé*) is defined in the fifth book of the *Code de la santé publique* as including medicines, cosmetics, poisonous substances and preparations, contraceptives, certain dietary products and various regulated medical devices and products.

will be governed by the 1985 Product Liability Directive and the 1998 French Product Liability Act.[136]

The provision relating to liability for bacterial infections, amongst others, led to uproar from medical insurers who claimed that medical insurance, which was made compulsory by the legislation, had been made technically impossible.[137] Large numbers of insurers withdrew from the market. The result was the Law of 30 December 2002[138] which made various amendments to the earlier legislation. Amongst these changes, it states that bacterial infections which cause permanent incapacity[139] of over 25% or death would be compensated by a State fund and would not therefore be a burden on insurers. Despite these changes, by 2004 there still remained an insufficiency in the number of insurance offers for clinics, and complaints by private practitioners as to the level of premiums.[140]

To qualify for compensation under the Law the harm suffered by the victim must be of a sufficiently serious nature. An accident will be considered as sufficiently serious where the victim experiences a predefined minimum level of injury as a result of the accident. This level of injury will be assessed with particular reference to the victim's level of permanent disability or the duration of any temporary inability to work. The degree of permanent disability is expressed in percentage terms[141] by reference to a chart of invalidity levels which takes into consideration the nature of the disability, the general condition of the victim, his age, his physical and mental faculties, his skills and professional qualifications. The minimum level of invalidity required to benefit from the scheme is set at 24%.[142] A medical accident will also fulfil the criteria of seriousness where the patient suffers a temporary inability to work for six months, or, exceptionally, where the victim is declared permanently inapt to exert his chosen profession, or where the accident causes him 'particularly serious problems', which can include financial problems. The requirements to qualify under the scheme inevitably exclude a large number of victims. A level of permanent disability of 25% would correspond to the loss of

---

[136] Loi no. 98–389, 19 May 1998, now arts. 1386–1 to 1386–18 *Code civil*.
[137] Y. Lambert-Faivre, 'La responsabilité médicale: la loi du 30 décembre modifiant la loi du 4 mars 2002' D. chr. 2003, 361.
[138] Loi n° 2002–1577 du 30 Dec. 2002, JO 31.12. 2002.
[139] For an explanation of this term see below p. 191 (art. L1142–1 *Code de la santé publique*).
[140] S. Guiné-Gibert, 'L'assurance responsabilité médicale des acteurs de santé. Historique: comment en est-on arrivé à la situation actuelle' [2004] *Revue générale de droit médical* 157 at 159.
[141] Art. L 434–2 *Code de la sécurité sociale*.
[142] Art. D.1142–1 *Code de la santé publique*.

an eye.[143] A level of permanent partial incapacity of 24% represents fewer than 4 per cent of medical accidents.[144]

Where the liability of a health care professional or organisation is established, the victim will be compensated for the full extent of his loss by the insurers of that medical practitioner or organisation. The Law states that civil liability insurance is compulsory for private medical practitioners and organisations, and producers of medical products.[145]

Where the liability of a health care practitioner or organisation is not established the patient will receive compensation representing the entirety of his loss from a State financed compensation fund. However, to qualify for compensation, the accident must be sufficiently serious and the injury must have been caused by a medical act as opposed to being the natural consequences of the patient's medical condition. The Law therefore adopts the criteria for compensation for *aléa thérapeutique* which had been established by the Conseil d'Etat.

Although the Law does not provide for compensation for victims of less serious accidents, the Law does provide that the Regional Commissions, in addition to their role of deciding on the compensation of serious accidents, offer a conciliation service which is available to all victims.[146] In this role, the Commissions can delegate functions to independent mediators.

4.6.2   Procedure for obtaining compensation

The Law provides that the organisation or health professional must inform the victim or the victim's dependants or legal representative of the cause of any damage within fourteen days of the discovery of the damage or of the victim's specific request for information.[147]

To obtain compensation, the victim must apply to one of the newly established Regional Conciliation and Compensation Commissions. These regional commissions are presided over by a judge, accompanied by a panel which is comprised of representatives of patients, health professionals and administrators, representatives of the new national compensation fund together with insurers.[148]

The Commission must first be satisfied that the loss suffered by the applicant is of a sufficiently serious nature. It will then consider the advice of expert witnesses[149] and will provide an opinion on the circumstances

---

[143] M. Lorrain, Senate debates, 6 February 2002.
[144] F. Jegu, 'La loi du 4 mars 2002 et l'aléa thérapeutique' [2004] *Revue générale de droit médical* 143.
[145] Art. L 1142–2.   [146] Art. L 1142–5.   [147] Art. L 1142–4.   [148] Art. L 1142–6.
[149] The Law establishes a new national list of medical experts. Any expert used must be drawn from this list. Arts. L 1142–11 to L 1142–12.

of the damage, its causes, its nature and extent and on the compensation system applicable.

Where the Commission decides that the damage was caused by the negligence of a health professional or health organisation, or by the producer of a medical product, that person's insurer must make an offer of compensation to the applicant within four months of the Commission's decision, and once this offer is accepted, payment must be made within one month of that acceptance.[150] Should the insurer refuse to make an offer, or the compensation payable exceeds the insurance cover provided, the victim will receive compensation from the State fund, which may then sue the insurers for the amount paid out. The applicant can always refuse the insurer's offer and take action through the courts. Should he do this and the court decides that the offer made by the insurer was 'manifestly insufficient', the court may order the insurer to make an additional payment to the fund of up to 15% of the compensation allocated to the victim.[151]

Where the accident was not caused by fault, the applicant will receive an offer of compensation from the State fund within four months of this finding, and payment will be made within one month of the acceptance of this offer by the victim. The victim can always choose to pursue an action against the fund through the courts should he consider that the amount of compensation proposed is inadequate.

The Law establishes a National Commission for Medical Accidents ('ONIAM').[152] This Commission has the task of ensuring the consistency of the decisions taken by the Regional Commissions, and decides on the admission of experts to the national list of medical experts.

Finally, the Act unifies the limitation periods for claims in the administrative and civil courts at ten years from the date that the injury suffered has finished evolving.[153] When the victim applies to the Regional Commission, this has the effect of suspending the running of the limitation period.[154]

4.6.3 How is the new scheme working?

In 2004 there were 3,553 applications for compensation under the scheme, compared to 1,907 in 2003.[155] The annual report on the working

---

[150] Art. L 1142–14.   [151] Art. L 1142–14.   [152] Art. L 1142–10.

[153] Art. L 1142–28. This new limitation period therefore replaces the limitation period for contract actions of thirty years from the knowledge of the damage (art. 2262 *Code civil*), and of four years for actions in the administrative courts.

[154] Art. L 1142–7.

[155] Only fourteen of the twenty regional commissions were functioning in 2003.

of the scheme for 2004[156] observes that there was a backlog of claims in certain regions, particularly in the Paris region. The average time for dealing with an application was steadily increasing, but for the year 2004 it still remained within the six-month limit set by the legislation.[157] Just under half the applications examined by the regional commissions were rejected due to the threshold of seriousness not being attained, or because the accident occurred before the legislation came into force. ONIAM paid out nearly €4 million in compensation in 2004, and incurred total expenditure of €9 million. The ONIAM report for 2004 predicts that expenditure on compensation in 2005 will reach €50 million, for a total expenditure of €61 million.[158] The conciliation service for minor injuries remained unpopular, and only 149 applications for conciliation were received in 2004.

4.6.4 The effect of the 2002 legislation on the compensation of victims

It is uncertain to what extent the new legislation will actually improve the position of the majority of victims of medical accidents. Hence, all but the most seriously injured are excluded from the compensation scheme in view of the high level of incapacity that is required.[159] Statistics for road accidents show that 97% of victims who suffer permanent injury would fall below a 25% threshold.[160] Apart from potentially excluding large numbers of victims, any exclusion based on a rate of permanent disability is also extremely arbitrary. It is clear that the assessment of the level of injury will be an extremely litigious point, and the difficulty of this assessment can only be increased by the fact that the Law rather strangely provides that experts are to advise the Commission only after, and not before, it is established that the accident is sufficiently serious.

---

[156] Office national d'indemnisation des accidents médicaux (ONIAM), *Rapport d'activité 2e semestre 2004* (Paris: La documentation française, 2005).

[157] In the first semester 2003 the average time to deal with an application was 76 days. This had risen to 211 days in the second semester 2004.

[158] ONIAM, *Rapport d'activité 2e semestre 2004,* at 8.

[159] The exclusion of the less seriously injured has been heavily criticised by academic commentators. See Y. Lambert-Faivre, 'La loi n° 2002–303 du 4 mars 2002 relative aux droits des malades et à la qualité du système de santé. L'indemnisation des accidents médicaux' D. 2002 chr. 1367 at 1370; C. Radé, 'La réforme de la responsabilité médicale après la loi du 4 mars 2002 relative aux droits des malades et à la qualité du système de santé' Resp. civile et assur. 2002, 4 at 5.

[160] Y. Lambert-Faivre, above n. 159, at 1371. Statistics taken from the *Fédération Française des Sociétés d'Assurances* (FFSA) 2000.

The new legislative regime is extremely complex. An application to the regional commissions and a court action for damages can be made either one after the other or in parallel. Added to this, different liability rules will apply to court actions based on damage caused by defective products, which will fall under the 1985 product liability directive and the transposing French legislation.[161] In addition, although in some ways the Law goes some way to unifying rules in civil and administrative law, no attempt has been made to remove the dual jurisdiction. The legislation has been criticised for transferring a decision on liability, a judicial role, to administrative bodies whose exact legal status is uncertain.[162] Indeed, the Commissions will be required to decide on potentially very complex issues of fault and causation. There is also an inevitable danger that the courts and commissions adopt different interpretations of key concepts, particularly that of fault, and also of 'particularly serious problems' (*troubles particulières de l'existence*) which is relevant, following the December 2002 amending legislation, to assessing the degree of seriousness of the injury.[163]

Despite the fact that the legislation seeks to remove claims for compensation for medical accidents from the court system, the court process will inevitably continue to play a very significant role. This is obviously the case for victims of less serious accidents, who have to date proved reluctant to use the new conciliation services set up by the Law. The Law also provides that the only way to contest a rejection of an application for compensation by the regional commissions will be through court action.[164] Insurers will also have recourse to court action where they wish to contest the liability of the insured[165] and the ONIAM has the possibility of taking action against health professionals or their insurers where they have had to pay compensation to the victim due to a refusal of the insurer to cooperate.

For many victims the new rules may actually result in a reduction rather than an increase in protection. Indeed, the perhaps surprising consequence of the introduction of a scheme for which one of the principal aims was to facilitate the compensation of victims is that it in fact reinforces the principle of liability for fault.

5   The role of fault liability following the legislative reforms

Fault continues to play a very significant role even within the new statutory scheme since the victim's loss will be compensated by the doctor's or

---

[161] Arts. 1386–1 to 1386–18 *Code civil.*
[162] G. Mémèteau, *Cours de droit médical* (Bordeaux: les Etudes hospitalières, 2003) at 442.
[163] Art. D 1142–1.   [164] Art. L 1142–8.   [165] Art. L 1142–15.

medical service's insurance where the fault of the medical practitioner or service is established.

For victims who do not qualify under the new scheme because their accident does not fulfil the requirement of seriousness, fault returns to being in principle the sole basis of liability. It must be supposed that the courts will be unable to continue to employ strict liability to assist victims of medical accidents as they had done before the new legislation.[166]

Hence, where bacterial infections are contracted outside a medical organisation, for example in a doctor's private surgery,[167] and so do not fall within the 2002 Law, then the claimant will now have to establish the fault of the defendant, instead of relying on the strict liability principles which the Cour de cassation had previously established.[168]

In addition, those victims of medical accidents in a public hospital which are not due to the fault of the establishment or staff will be unable to obtain compensation for *aléa thérapeutique* where the injury falls beneath the required threshold of seriousness required to fall within the Law, although given that the case law already required the victim to have suffered harm 'of a very serious nature', the effect here may not be significant.

However, even though it would appear that the 2002 legislation will have an effect on the rules developed by case law, the statutory rules do retain strict liability in certain limited cases. Hence, as we have seen, health clinics and hospitals will be strictly liable for less severe bacterial infections. Their only defence will be to show that the infection came from a source exterior to the hospital.[169] The *Code de la santé publique* also provides that any loss directly due to a compulsory vaccination will be compensated by the State. It also states that the State will be strictly liable for loss incurred by a blood donor during donation.[170]

The position of liability for defective products should also be considered as a separate case. The legislation provides that the fault principle does not apply to cases where the liability of doctors or health services is engaged due to a defective health product. In cases of product liability

---

[166] This appears to be confirmed by recent case law: Cass. civ. (1), 4 Feb. 2003, Juris-Data n° 2003–017447, Resp. civile et assur. 2003, comm. 143; Cass. civ. (1), 1 March 2005, Juris-Data n° 2005–027240, Resp. civile et assur. 2005, 158; Cass. civ. (1), 29 Nov. 2005, Juris-Data n° 2005–031018, Resp. civile et assur. 2006, comm. 59.

[167] Since the Act only makes a medical *organisation* strictly liable.

[168] This point is considered by P. Mistretta, 'La loi no. 2002–303 du 4 mars 2002 relative aux droits des maladies et à la qualité du système de santé. Réflexions critiques sur un droit en mutation' JCP 2002.I.1075 at 1081.

[169] Art. L 1142–1.   [170] Art. L 1222–9.

articles 1386–1 to 1386–18 of the *Code civil* will apply. These provisions impose liability on the producer for harm caused by a defective product which he has put into circulation.[171] Following decisions against France by the Court of Justice in 2002[172] and in 2006,[173] French law now complies with the directive by providing that the supplier will be able to avoid liability under the product liability rules by identifying his supplier or the producer of the product.[174]

It could also be argued that the statement in the 2002 legislation that the fault principle does not apply to liability of doctors relating to health products also includes situations where injury is caused to the patient by defective products/materials used (but not supplied) by the medical practitioner. In such cases, the Cour de cassation has consistently imposed liability on the practitioner on the basis of a contractual obligation to guarantee the safety of products and materials used.[175] The Conseil d'Etat has taken the same line in administrative law. Doctrinal writers are divided as to whether strict liability can continue to be applied in such cases.[176]

The new legislation would also not seem to have any effect on the presumptions of fault. One significant case in point here is the duty imposed on the doctor to warn the patient of the risks of treatment. The 2002 legislation states that the burden of proof is on the defendant to show that he has provided the required information on the risks.[177]

In addition, other situations where the courts have applied a presumption of fault would not appear to be affected by the new legislation. Hence, both the civil and administrative courts will often employ a presumption of fault where damage arises as a result of a simple standard act of medical care. Fault here will be presumed from the contrast between the simple, benign nature of the act and the serious consequences.[178] A presumption of fault will also be applied in cases of burns received from

---

[171] But enable him to avoid liability in certain circumstances, notably where he can show a 'development risk'.

[172] Case C-52/00, *Commission v. France*, 25 April 2002, [2002] ECR I-3827.

[173] Case C-177/04, *Commission v. France*, 14 March 2006.

[174] Loi n° 2006–406 of 5 April 2006, JO 6.04.2006, art. 1386–7 *Code civil*.

[175] Cass. civ. (1), 7 Nov. 2000, D. 2001 somm. 2236, obs. D. Mazeaud.

[176] For the continuing application of strict liability in such cases: G. Mémeteau, *Cours de droit médical* (Bordeaux: Les études hospitalières, 2003) at 402, also Y. Lambert-Faivre, above n. 7, at 812. Contra: J. Penneau, *La responsabilité du médecin*, above n. 4, at 27; P. Jourdain, 'La réforme de l'indemnisation des dommages médicaux et la place de la responsabilité médicale' in P. Jourdain *et al.*, *Le nouveau droit des malades* (Paris: Litec, 2002) at 92.

[177] Art. L 1111–2.   [178] CE 23 Feb. 1962, Leb. 122.

hospital equipment,[179] and in cases of errors in analysis by the hospital's laboratory.[180]

5.1 Specific examples of fault liability today: errors, technical faults and lack of consent

A fault will be considered as any defect in conduct that a normally diligent and competent doctor placed in the same circumstances as the person who made the error would have avoided. His behaviour will be assessed by reference to the level of knowledge that existed at the time of the act leading to the damage.[181] In administrative law, the liability of doctors is now based on the usual fault criteria assessed by whether the defendant meets the standard expected of the reasonable practitioner.[182]

5.1.1 Errors

A distinction is made between mere errors and fault. Errors in diagnosis will not constitute faults unless they demonstrate a lack of reasonable care. However, the approach to errors tends to vary depending on the circumstances of the case. Hence, in cases of accidents due to mistakes in the manipulation of instruments and equipment, for example during surgery, cases have confirmed the existence of a fault where the harm suffered by the patient was not a natural consequence of the medical act in question.[183] This therefore comes very close to the application of a principle of *res ipsa loquitur*.[184] The defendant will in such cases be able to avoid liability by showing that the part of the patient's body which was affected already had an anomaly which rendered the harm inevitable.

5.1.2 Negligent diagnosis and treatment

It is interesting to compare the approaches of the English and French courts in respect of what the French doctrinal writers refer to as '*fautes techniques*', that is negligence by the doctor in the course of diagnosis or treatment. Three points deserve to be emphasised here. First, in

---

[179] CE 1 March 1989, D. 1989 IR 106.
[180] CAA Paris, 24 March 1998, Juris-Data n° 050463.
[181] Cass. civ. (1), 6 June 2000, RDSS 2000, 750, obs. L Dubouis. G. Mémèteau, *Cours de droit medical,* at 379.
[182] CE 10 April 1992, JCP 1992.II.21881, note J. Moreau.
[183] Cass. civ. (1), 7 Jan. 1997, Bull. civ. 1, no. 6, p. 4; Cass. civ. (1), 23 May 2000, Bull. civ. 1, no. 153, p. 100.
[184] G. Mémèteau, *Cours de droit medical,* at 376.

such cases the action or decision of the doctor or medical practitioner is assessed in France by reference to the state of medical knowledge at the time of the act in question (*la règle de l'art*). The requirement is that the knowledge should be tried, tested and accepted by the scientific community.[185] One potential difference here between the English and French rules is in how knowledge accepted by the scientific community is defined. Hence, the French courts require that the knowledge be accepted by the largest part of that community (*la partie la plus considerable de la communauté scientifique*[186]), which provides a potential contrast with the English law as stated in *Bolam v. Friern Hospital* that it is sufficient if the practice is accepted by 'a body of medical opinion'.

Secondly, the French courts have shown themselves to be willing on occasions to call into question current medical practice and to find a fault even where the doctor has respected that practice.[187] Hence, the court can reject the validity of medical guidelines and usual practice if it considers that their infallibility has not been established. Thus, the French courts have applied the approach advocated by the House of Lords in *Bolitho v. City and Hackney Health Authority* of willingness to call into question the logic of medical practice. Inevitably this will only be done in rare cases.[188] Indeed it is recognised that the role of the judge is not to assess the scientific merits of the expert's opinion, and he must not substitute his unqualified opinion for those of the experts. Where he does disregard expert evidence, it will generally be where the expert has gone beyond the mission that was conferred on him or because, since the expert evidence has been produced, other factors have come into play which change the pertinence of that opinion.[189]

Finally, under French civil procedures, the expert is appointed by the court. Therefore, unlike in English law, where each party still generally appoints his own expert witness, the French judge will not systematically

---

[185] Cass. civ. (1), 12 Nov. 1935, Bull. civ. 1, no. 265; Paris, 23 March 2001, Juris-Data n° 141837.

[186] M. Harichaux, 'Responsabilité médicale', para. 26, in J.-J. Veron, (ed.), *Dictionnaire permanent bioéthique et biotechnologies* (Montrouge: Editions legislatives, 1994–); Cass. crim. 3 Nov. 1988, D. 1989, somm. 317, obs. J. Penneau.

[187] Cass. civ. (1), 6 June 2000 RDSS 2000, 750, obs. L. Dubouis; JCP 2000 10447, obs. Méméteau. Rapport Cour de cassation 2000, 380. This is not a recent phenomenon: Paris, 4 July 1932, D. 1933.2.113; Paris, 25 April 1945, S 1946.2.29; Paris, 26 April 1948, D. 1948, 272.

[188] Penneau, *Faute et erreur,* at 98.

[189] M. Harichaux, 'L'obligation du médecin de respecter les données de la science (à propos du cinquantenaire de l'arrêt Mercier)' JCP 1987.I.3306.

be called on to consider an expert opinion which defends an act or decision of the doctor.

5.1.3   Consent

The duty to obtain the consent of the patient to a medical act is imposed by article 16–3 of the *Code civil*, and confirmed by the 2002 Law. Failure to obtain this consent will constitute a fault, subject to exceptions based on the urgency of the act and the refusal of treatment by the patient.

To enable the patient to give consent, he must be adequately informed of the risks inherent in the medical act. French law is demanding in terms of the content of such information. Case law has established the principle that the medical practitioner must notify the patient of all serious risks, even if these are very rare. If he fails to do so, this will be considered as a fault. The legislation confirms this principle and provides that the doctor must warn the patient of any frequent or serious risk which is normally foreseeable (*risques fréquents ou graves normalement prévisibles*).[190] There is some ambiguity in the meaning of 'frequent or serious risks which are normally foreseeable' and whether it extends to rare risks.

Where the doctor fails to warn the patient of a risk involved in the medical treatment which then arises, the French courts often award damages to the patient on the basis that, as a result of the absence of warning, the patient has lost a chance of refusing the treatment. The patient will normally only be awarded compensation representing a fraction of his full loss to reflect the doubt as to whether he would in fact have refused the treatment if he had been presented with the relevant information concerning the risk.[191] Consequently, often only a very low level of damages is recovered by the claimant. Full damages will only be awarded where the patient is able to present evidence which establishes that he would certainly have refused the treatment. However, the Cour de cassation has on occasions denied the liability of the doctor on the basis that the treatment was unavoidable, and so the lack of information could not be considered as causing the loss, even if the lack of warning constitutes a fault.[192]

---

[190] Art. L 1111–2 *Code de la santé publique.*

[191] Cass. civ. (1), 29 May 1984, D. 1985, 281.

[192] Cass. civ. (1), 13 Nov. 2002, JCP 2003.IV.1008. However, even here he may be able to obtain some form of compensation. Hence, the patient may be able to recover damages for the psychological harm suffered due to inevitable consequences of the medical act which he was not able to prepare for; Penneau, *La responsabilité du médecin,* at 35. He will also be able to obtain damages for the economic loss suffered where, if he had been better informed, he would have been able to arrange to undergo the treatment at a time where he would have had less serious consequences.

The technique of awarding damages for loss of a chance is in fact often used as a way of bypassing difficulties in establishing the existence of a causal link between a technical fault or a fault in diagnosis and the physical harm to the claimant. Liability in such cases is founded on a failure to warn even though in reality it is a technical fault that is being sanctioned.[193]

Where the doctor negligently failed to warn the patient of the risks of the treatment but no physical harm actually resulted from the medical act, the question also arises whether the patient should be entitled to damages reflecting the violation to his personal autonomy in depriving him of the possibility of giving his informed consent. Whilst French doctrinal writers are critical of the artificial use of loss of chance which seeks to compensate for the physical harm suffered instead of the 'moral' harm of the infringement of the patient's autonomy,[194] cases where the doctor has been found liable for the interference with his individual autonomy are extremely rare,[195] and there would appear to be no cases where the patient has suffered absolutely no harm as a result of the act.[196] Certainly, the Cour de cassation and the Conseil d'Etat have to date refused to compensate specifically for this loss of autonomy.[197]

5.2   The particular case of wrongful life and wrongful birth

There have been important developments in recent times concerning the question of whether damages are recoverable for wrongful birth and wrongful life. The Law of 4 March 2002 attempts (not necessarily effectively) to overrule a controversial line of cases by the Cour de cassation which allowed claims for wrongful life. The case law developments will be examined before considering the effect of the 2002 Law.

Where a healthy child is born as a result of a negligently performed sterilisation or abortion, the courts consider that there is no recoverable loss.[198] Both the Cour de cassation and the Conseil d'Etat have been prepared to

---

[193] D. Thouvenin, 'Les masques de la faute' D. 1999 chr. 559 at 564.

[194] D. Thouvenin, 'Les masques de la faute' at 564.

[195] CAA Paris, 9 June 1998, *affaire Guilbot*, *Petites Affiches*, 23 April 1999, p. 23 ; Cass. Civ. (2), 19 march 1997, *Mutuelle du Mans Assurance*, Bull. civ. 2, no. 86.

[196] S. Porchy, 'Lien causal, préjudices réparables et non-respect de la volonté du patient' D. 1998 chr. 379 at 380.

[197] S. Boussard, 'Comment sanctionner la violation du droit à l'information de l'usager du système de santé?' *Revue du droit public* 2004, 168 at 196.

[198] Cass. civ. (1), 25 June 1991, JCP 1992.II.21784, note J.-F. Barbieri; CE Ass. 2 July 1982, Leb. 266.

award damages to the parents for the birth of a disabled child following a negligent diagnosis on the risk of disability (wrongful birth).[199] Damages have been awarded on this basis for the resulting additional financial cost to the parents, and for their upset/disappointment (*prejudice moral*).

Where the claim is by the child himself there has been a difference in approach between the Conseil d'Etat and the Cour de cassation. The Conseil d'Etat has consistently refused to award damages to the child, stating that there is no causal link between the fault of the doctor and the disability.[200] However, the Cour de cassation, in the well-known *Perruche* case[201] allowed a claim for damages for wrongful life. This decision was confirmed by five subsequent judgments of the highest civil court[202] and was seen as the most extreme example of the Cour de cassation's drive to facilitate the compensation of patients from the beginning of the 1990s. The *Perruche* decision incited a great deal of controversy. Doctrinal writers were split into two camps: those who opposed the decision on the basis that there was no causal link between the negligent advice of the doctor and the disability, or on the basis that the decision awarded damages for being born, and was the same as acknowledging that that particular life was not worth living. Other commentators approved the decision as giving the disabled person, through financial compensation, and in the absence of sufficient financial help from the State, a chance to lead a more dignified life.

The case also gave rise to considerable criticism from doctors who threatened to no longer perform certain pre-natal examinations and started industrial action, and also from associations of parents of disabled children. There was considerable press coverage of the case, most of it negative. The French Parliament quickly rushed through legislation to ban wrongful life actions in the form of the first article of the Law of 4 March 2002, which is stated to be 'dedicated to solidarity towards handicapped people', and stipulates that no one can use the fact of being born as the basis for a claim. However, the parents of a disabled child are permitted by the legislation to sue the doctor or medical service, but to do so

---

[199] Cass. civ. (1), 26 March 1996, D. 1997, 35, note Roche-Dahan ; CE 14 Feb. 1997, *Quarey*, JCP 1997.I.4025, note G. Viney.

[200] CE 14 Feb. 1997, *Centre régional hospitalier de Nice*, AJDA 1998, 480.

[201] Cass. Ass. Plén. 17 Nov. 2000, JCP 2000.II.10438, rapp. P. Sargos. In English, see A. Morris and S. Saintier, 'To be or not to be: is that the question? Wrongful life and misconceptions' (2003) 11 Med. LR 167.

[202] Three cases decided together 13 July 2001: Cass. Ass. Plén. 13 July 2001, D. 2001, 2325, note P. Jourdain; two cases decided together 28 Nov. 2001: D. 2001. IR. 3587–8.

they must establish the existence of a *faute caractérisée*. The exact meaning of this notion of *faute caractérisée* is rather unclear since it is a new concept in French civil law and is not further defined by the legislation. It may be considered to be close to that of *faute lourde*, but which again is a concept which is not precisely defined. The legislation limits the scope of the loss for which the parents can claim compensation. Hence it states that no compensation may be awarded for the extra expenses incurred by the parents during the child's life due to the disability. The parents' compensation will therefore be limited to their *prejudice moral* which will compensate the disappointment/upset of the parents in having a disabled child. The Law states that the extra expenses caused by the birth are to be borne by the State.

Strictly speaking it is arguable that the legislative provisions do not actually prevent wrongful life actions. The Law provides that no one can claim as a loss the mere fact of being born. However, it is arguable that the *Perruche* decision did not define the loss as the fact of being born, but on the basis of the disability which the child has suffered.[203] On this basis the Law would not prevent future claims. However, the intention of the legislature was sufficiently clear for any continuation of the *Perruche* line by the Cour de cassation to be unlikely.

6   Conclusion

Liability rules in the context of medical accidents have been constantly evolving since the mid-nineteenth century, and this movement accelerated from the mid-twentieth century, to reach a head from the 1990s. This progression has been from a concept of fault which was very restrictive and thus favourable to the medical professional, to firstly a broader interpretation of this principle, and then a tendency away from liability for fault towards strict liability in certain circumstances. This movement has been almost exclusively the work of the French courts. As we have seen, there are a number of possible factors which have led to these changes. Most notably, the parallel evolution in the availability of health care over the period, and more particularly developments in medical science and techniques, have had the effect of increasing the number of accidents, of making it more difficult to identify individual fault, and of increasing the

---

[203] C. Radé, 'La réforme de la responsabilité médicale après la loi du 4 mars 2002' Resp. civile et assur. 2002, 4 at 9; F.-J. Pansier and C. Charbonneau, 'Commentaire de la loi du 4 mars 2002 relative aux droits des malades (1ʳᵉ partie)' *Les Petites Affiches*, 13 March 2002, 5.

expectations of patients. The development of liability insurance, particularly from the 1930s, represents another major factor in the progressive adaptation of the fault principle.

In some respects the 2002 legislation makes a significant move away from fault, by enabling the compensation of victims of serious accidents even where no fault can be shown. It is also significant in removing certain categories of claim from the litigation process. However, by asserting the principle that liability can only be based on fault, in other ways it marks a re-emphasis on traditional fault principles.

5

The development of medical liability in Austria

BERNHARD A. KOCH

1 Introduction

Even though medical malpractice cases appear in publications throughout the entire period under survey, medical liability as such does not seem to have emerged as a hot topic on the agenda of legal scholars until the last two decades of the twentieth century. While examples using doctors as tortfeasors[1] were used of course occasionally in textbooks or commentaries before then, such cases were seemingly not considered to deserve extraordinary attention. This may have been due either to the fact that these issues were not considered to deviate from standard cases of delict, or (more likely) because of the low frequency of such cases. This latter explanation can only be a guess, though, since proper statistics are missing, as are comprehensive case reports of that time.

Academic discussion on medical liability in Austria received somewhat of a boost when German scholars started to spend more time and ink on the topic in the 1970s.[2] It therefore seems to be rather the immediate cross-border than any transatlantic influence that stirred the Austrian debate. Since the early 1980s, and even more so in the 1990s, the frequency of Austrian contributions specifically on this topic has increased considerably. This is evidenced not only by the start of a journal on medical law, but also by the number of court cases.[3]

[1] The text in the following will predominantly only speak of 'the doctor' as the liable person, in order to simplify the presentation. In cases involving treatment at a hospital, it will most likely be the institution which will be liable for what went wrong inside, including misbehaviour by its staff.

[2] Earlier discussions in the 1960s were of course equally noted in Austria, for example the discussions at the 'Karlsruher Forum 1959'.

[3] Statistics are missing entirely, however, at least in publicised form. Proper data to assess the actual development is apparently also missing in Germany, where (as in Austria) trends tend to be cited on the basis of hearsay rather than proven in numbers: H.-L. Schreiber, 'Führt die Arzthaftungsrechtsprechung zur Defensivmedizin?' at www.medizinrechts-beratungsnetz.de/RTF/MRT2003/Vortrag_ProfDrHans-LudwigSchreiber.rtf.

This development may have happened in line with a probable change in attitude towards medical services. It was argued convincingly that the relationship between patients and doctors changed substantially in the second half of the twentieth century.[4] The family doctor is gradually becoming a phase-out model of comprehensive health care. Not only is the relationship between the growing number of doctors in a community on the one hand and its members on the other getting more and more anonymous, but also the 'one-stop-shop' concept of treatment by a local general practitioner is no longer valid in light of the latter's increasing readiness to refer patients to specialists (who are more and more likely to practise in the vicinity of the patients' homes). These developments, as well as an increased trust in the progress of medicine as a whole, at least contribute to the patient's willingness to question the quality of the services rendered by an individual doctor which did not come up to the patient's expectations, however (un)realistic these may have been.

A highly persuasive statement by a doctor on the consequences of the advance of medical science should also be cited in this context: 95 fatalities among 100 cancer patients were considered an inevitable matter of fate in the old days when a doctor was praised for the five survivors. With today's knowledge and technology, 50% may be cured, while even merely five patients with constant or deteriorating condition are nowadays often presumed to be a clear-cut indication of the doctor's failure.[5]

2   Health care system[6]

While public hospitals had already been installed in larger cities by Emperor Joseph II at the end of the eighteenth century, following French examples, the number of hospitals increased significantly in the second half of the nineteenth century, with almost one per local district by the end of the first world war.

---

[4] On the following, see W. Freiherr Marschall von Bieberstein, 'Überlegungen zur Haftung bei Heilbehandlung' in F. Hauss and R. Schmidt (eds.), *Festschrift für Ernst Klingmüller* (Karlsruhe: Verlag Versicherungswirtschaft, 1974) 249 at 259ff.

[5] Roemer, *Die ärztliche Aufklärungspflicht vom Standpunkt und aus der Erfahrung des Arztes*, cited by W. Freiherr Marschall von Bieberstein, above, n. 4, 250.

[6] The following information is based upon a historic overview contained at www.aeiouiicm.tugraz.at/aeiou.encyclop.s/s676277.htm.

At the end of 2000, the number of health care institutions remained at around 310 and subsequently went down to about 280 due to a restructuring of the system.[7] Interestingly, not only did the number of hospital beds decrease continuously in the last decades (from more than 84,000 in 1980 to 72,000 in 2000), but also the cumulative number of days that patients stayed in hospital went down by one-fourth.[8] At the same time, health care staff employed by hospitals nearly doubled in number.[9]

The number of medical professionals has increased continuously. Between 1960 and 2000, the numbers of general practitioners per 100,000 inhabitants almost doubled from 74.1 to 134.8; the number of specialists more than tripled.[10] At present, around 38,000 doctors practise in Austria, of whom about 11,500 are general practitioners. Around 16,000 doctors are specialists, and almost 4,000 work as dentists.[11]

Following a law introduced in 1870, the *Reichssanitätsgesetz*, doctors were not admitted to practise unless they had passed five years of university education. Since 1891, all practitioners are required by law to join a recognised professional organisation incorporated under public law (*Ärztekammer*, medical chamber), which from the outset also performed disciplinary functions. At present, there are nine provincial medical chambers (one for each province) which jointly form the Austrian Medical Chamber.[12]

a Social security

The first statutory social security regime was introduced in 1889, providing mandatory cover for all commercial and industrial employees (though excluding agricultural labourers). By the end of the first world war there were several hundred social security insurers (including small health insurance schemes for specific employees). After a series of structural changes during the last century, there are still twenty-four institutions

---

[7] Statistik Austria, *Statistisches Jahrbuch 2005* (Vienna, 2005) 108.

[8] This is mostly due to the fact that the payment scheme for hospitals has been changed from one based on the number of days spent in-house to a regime focussing on the specific kinds of disease and treatment at the beginning of the 1990s.

[9] From 9,492 in 1980 to 17,445 in 2000; from 39,655 nursing staff in 1970 to 73,528 in 2000. Compared to 1970, these numbers have almost tripled.

[10] From 49.9 specialists per 100,000 inhabitants in 1960 to 181.4 in 2000. Data derived from Statistik Austria, *Jahrbuch der Gesundheitsstatistik* (Vienna, 2005) 374.

[11] Statistik Austria, *Statistisches Jahrbuch 2005* (Vienna, 2005) 109.

[12] See www.aerztekammer.at/InternatB/structureAustria.htm. These medical chambers are governed by §§ 65ff. and 117ff. *Ärztegesetz* (law on medical doctors, ÄrzteG).

left at present (of which twenty-one are health insurers), grouped into one umbrella organisation.

Currently 97.6% of all Austrians are covered by social security.[13] Amongst other things, social security pays for all the costs of medical treatment, irrespective of its cause, and therefore also in cases of bodily harm tortiously inflicted by a third person.[14] In such a case, the victim's tort law claims are assigned by law to the competent social security insurer.[15]

In a medical malpractice scenario, therefore, the injured patient will receive treatment as well as other benefits,[16] either in kind or as direct monetary payments from the social security insurer, who in most cases will already have covered the initial treatment where something went wrong.

b   (Private) insurance

According to Statistik Austria, about one-third of Austrians took out (supplementary) private health insurance in 2000, which does not necessarily mean better treatment, but the free choice of doctor (not only those in contract with their social security provider) and more pleasant conditions during a hospital stay.[17] According to § 67 subs. 1 of the Insurance Contract Act (*Versicherungsvertragsgesetz*, VersVG), any claim against a third party that has caused the victim's loss is subrogated by law to the insurer to the extent that the latter has paid out compensation. This means that the active party in medical malpractice cases is the insurer, not the direct victim.

At present, neither employed nor self-employed health care personnel are required to buy liability insurance. Hospital staff are typically (but not always) covered by the institution's insurance policy.[18] The Austrian

---

[13] Hauptverband der österreichischen Sozialversicherungsträger (ed.), *Die österreichische Sozialversicherung in Zahlen* (14th edn., Vienna, 2004) 13. On the Austrian social security system, see e.g. W. Holzer, 'The Interaction of Tort Law and Social Security under Austrian Law' in U. Magnus (ed.), *Tort Law and Social Law* (Vienna: Springer, 2003) 7.

[14] W. Holzer, above n. 13, nos 11, 20.

[15] W. Holzer, above n. 13, no. 13.

[16] These include hospital care, nursing, but also – if applicable – loss of income to a certain extent.

[17] Federal Ministry of Social Security, Generations and Consumer Protection (ed.), *Social Protection Systems in Austria* (2003) 95, available online at www.bmsg.gv.at/cms/site/attachments/6/5/0/CH0339/CMS1064306288445/ sozialschutzsystemengl.pdf.

[18] See A. Fenyves and Ch. Hirsch, 'Zur Deckung der Ansprüche aus "wrongful life" und "wrongful birth" in der Arzthaftpflichtversicherung' *Recht der Medizin* (RdM) 2000, 10 at 16 note 74).

Medical Chamber recommends that all doctors take out liability insurance covering a minimum risk of €1.5 million.[19] Most insurers offer policies with such coverage, with premiums calculated according to the area of expertise (with plastic surgeons, gynaecologists, radiologists, and anaesthetists in the most expensive group) and the professional status (trainee, general practitioner, specialist). Standard annual premiums for specialists range from €450 to €750.[20] Such low figures clearly evidence how low insurers rank the actual risk of paying out the insured amounts, particularly if one considers that comparable policies in other professions are much more expensive.

3   Preliminary questions

a   Public or private law?

Only 21% of all Austrian hospitals are privately operated, the rest being run by legal persons governed by public law.[21] Nevertheless, liability of all these entities vis-à-vis their patients is considered to be of a contractual nature.[22] This is also true for tripartite relationships where a patient receives health care services as benefits in kind from her social security insurer.[23]

Quite a significant portion of the earliest available Supreme Court cases within the period under survey concern the question of whether patients can sue doctors employed by a state-run hospital. At the time, an 1806

---

[19] Yet, only half of all practitioners follow that recommendation; the rest remain uninsured against risks of personal liability. (They might, however, be covered by a hospital's insurance contract.) The percentage is substantially higher with high risk specialists such as plastic surgeons, radiologists, gynaecologists, and anaesthetists. B. Wohlgenannt, *Die Arzthaftpflichtversicherung in Vorarlberg* (diploma thesis, University of Innsbruck, 1998) 155.

[20] This data is based on the study by B. Wohlgenannt cited above at n. 19, 127ff. In a quick survey for this report, at least one insurance broker offered coverage for the high-risk group with an annual premium of €491 (before applicable discounts!): www.sie-wir.com/ aerzte/haftpflicht3.htm.

[21] Statistik Austria, *Jahrbuch der Gesundheitsstatistik* (Vienna, 2005) 394. About one-third is operated by the provinces ('Länder'), 8% by local communities, 12% by social security organisations, and 15.4% by orders or churches.

[22] E.g. OGH 4.10.1951 *Entscheidungen des Obersten Gerichtshofes in Zivil- und Justizverwaltungssachen* (SZ) 24/262.

[23] W. Holzer, 'Die Haftung des Arztes im Zivilrecht' in W. Holzer, W. Posch and P. Schick, *Arzt- und Arzneimittelhaftung* (1992) 1 (18–19); D. Engljähringer, *Ärztliche Aufklärungspflicht vor medizinischen Eingriffen* (Vienna: Orac, 1996) 17 ff., both with further references.

decree[24] was still in force which excluded tort law actions against civil servants performing the duties of their office. The courts nevertheless admitted the claim by arguing that healing a patient was not one of the official duties covered by this decree: 'His office entitles and obliges the doctor to practise medicine in the hospital. When it comes to the treatment given to patients, however, he is not responsible to the authorities, but to the individual patient, as does any other expert according to the rules of private law.'[25]

b   Contract or tort law?

The Austrian General Civil Code (*Allgemeines Bürgerliches Gesetzbuch*, ABGB) contains a separate section on 'liability and compensation' (§§ 1293–341) which not only deals with tortious liability, but also with contractual liability.[26] Nevertheless, the two varieties show significant differences. In essence, it is easier for the claimant to succeed with a claim for contractual liability. Apart from the fact that contractual duties of care go much further, it is up to the defendant to prove that he was not at fault when violating his contractual obligations (§ 1298 ABGB). Furthermore, a contractual defendant is vicariously liable for all auxiliaries that he used in performing his obligation (§ 1313a ABGB), whereas in the law of delict proper, his auxiliaries must have fulfilled certain (narrow) qualifications. These advantages can also be decisive in a medical malpractice case, e.g. when a patient is treated by an employed doctor. The latter will only be liable in tort if he has not contracted with the patient directly, whereas the hospital (or any other employer) will be vicariously liable for violations of contractual duties of care which extend to the doctor if he performs such duties on behalf of his employer.[27]

---

[24] Hofdekret vom 14 März 1806, Justizgesetzsammlung 758, das Gesetz vom 12 Juli 1872, Reichsgesetzblatt Nr. 112, womit zur Durchführung des Artikels 9 Staatsgrundgesetzes vom 21 Dezember 1867, Reichsgesetzblatt Nr. 144, über die richterliche Gewalt das Klagerecht der Parteien wegen der von richterlichen Beamten in Ausübung ihrer amtlichen Wirksamkeit zugefügten Rechtsverletzungen geregelt wird.

[25] OGH 4.6.1914, J. A. Glaser and J. Unger *et al.* (eds.), *Sammlung von zivilrechtlichen Entscheidungen des k.k. Obersten Gerichtshofes, Neue Folge* (Vienna: Manz, 1900–1919) (hereafter 'GlUNF') no. 6,948: *Zentralblatt für die juristische Praxis* (ZBl) 1914, 851; 17.6.1914, GlUNF no. 6,969: ZBl 1914, 960; 22.12.1914, GlUNF no. 7,159: ZBl 1915, 362.

[26] *Cf.* H. Koziol, 'The Borderline Between Tort Liability and Contract' in H. Koziol (ed.), *Unification of Tort Law: Wrongfulness* (The Hague: Kluwer Law International, 1998) 25.

[27] See B. A. Koch and H. Koziol, 'Compensation in the Austrian Health Care Sector' in J. Dute, M. Faure and H. Koziol (eds.), *No-Fault Compensation in the Health Care Sector*

4   Discipline and patients' rights

a   Disciplinary boards

Apart from courts of law, Austrian doctors are also answerable to the disciplinary commission in their region, which operates under the supervision of the disciplinary council of the Austrian Medical Chamber (§§ 135 ff. ÄrzteG). A rather vague statutory provision defines disciplinary offences as any conduct which may adversely affect the reputation of Austrian doctors, or any violation of professional duties (§ 136 ÄrzteG). As express examples of such misbehaviour, the statute mentions disobedience with a professional ban as well as criminal conduct which has been sanctioned by any national or foreign court with a sentence of at least six months' imprisonment or a minimum fine of 360 daily rates (or €36,340). Apart from temporary injunctions, possible sanctions range from written reprimands to a permanent ban on practising medicine. If a doctor works for a legal entity of public law, only the disciplinary rules for civil servants apply (to the exclusion of the aforementioned provisions of the *Ärztegesetz*). Unfortunately (or fortunately for the doctors concerned), decisions of the disciplinary commissions are not publicised, so their impact on liability issues cannot be properly assessed.

b   Patients' rights movement

As early as 1920, the Hospitals Act (*Krankenanstaltengesetz*, KAG) already spelt out that treatment should conform to the state of medical science, and that patients must not be treated without their proper consent. In 1957, the follow-up act to this earlier statute brought further explicit references to patients' rights, though without calling them as such. The term 'patients' rights' was introduced into the Act in 1993 as a heading to § 5a, which lists inter alia the right to information before, during and after the treatment, the right to sufficient visiting hours and the like.[28] A more comprehensive listing, both in scope (beyond hospitals) and in substance (with further points), was envisaged with the so-called 'patients' rights charters' that were adopted in all provinces around the turn of the millennium.[29] These

---

(Vienna: Springer, 2004) 89 (no. 1ff.); B. A. Koch, 'Austrian Cases on Medical Malpractice' [2003] *European Journal of Health Law* 91.

[28] On the history, see e.g. E. Kalbhenn, *Patientenrechte und Patientenvertretung in Österreich*, at www.patientenanwalt-kaernten.at/downloads/patientenrechte_oesterreich.pdf.

[29] Formally, these charters were introduced by way of a treaty between the federal republic and the respective province. See, for example, www.patientenanwalt.com/

documents expressly underline such fundamental patients' rights as the right to treatment and nursing, the respect of dignity and integrity, the right to self-determination, information and documentation.

Apart from these developments on the substance of patients' rights, several institutions have been created on the level of the federal provinces to safeguard patients' rights during the last two decades of the period under survey.

c   Patients' ombudsman

All federal provinces have introduced a so-called *Patientenanwaltschaft* (a patients' ombudsman institution), which handles complaints by patients, assists them in obtaining compensation, and acts as a mediator in disputes between patients and health care institutions or doctors. The Viennese *Patientenanwaltschaft*, for example, handles about 1,300 to 1,600 files per year, 40% of which include claims for compensation. In about 40% of these latter cases, negotiations by the *Patientenanwaltschaft* lead to indemnification payments.[30]

d   Conciliation panels

Furthermore, all provincial *Ärztekammern* (medical chambers) have installed so-called *Schiedsstellen* (conciliation panels[31]) which serve as a forum for both patients and doctors to resolve disputes involving medical treatment.[32] The services offered by the panels are entirely voluntary for either side and do not preclude subsequent[33] proceedings before a court of law. Cases are brought to the attention of the panel by an informal request, either by the patient or by the doctor or his liability insurer. Decisions are

---

fileadmin/dokumente/09_english_documents_legal_information/PatientsCharter_ Guaranteeing_the_Rights_of_Patients.pdf.

[30] See the 2002–2003 report of the *Patientenanwaltschaft* of Vienna, at www. patientenanwalt_vbg.at. The percentages in other provinces seem to be quite comparable, see e.g. the 2003 report by the Patientenanwaltschaft of Lower Austria, at www. patientenanwalt.com.

[31] The literal translation would be 'arbitration panel'. Despite their name, however, they do not offer arbitration in the formal sense, since their decisions are not binding.

[32] On details, see M. Leitner, 'Schiedsstelle in Arzthaftpflichtfragen' RdM 1998/7; M. Roth and J. Sperl, 'Außergerichtliche Konfliktlösung in medizinischen Schadensfällen' [2000] *Anwaltsblatt* (AnwBl) 387.

[33] Upon filing, the parties must declare that they will not file a lawsuit before the panel has rendered its decision (and at the same time waive the defence of the statute of limitations).

rendered as mere (non-binding) recommendations, typically involving a lump-sum payment to the patient if the latter was successful. The number of claims filed is rising; statistics show that the majority of these claims are decided in the patient's favour.[34]

e   Compensation funds

A federal law introduced in 2001[35] initiated the creation of compensation funds (*Patientenentschädigungsfonds*) for hospitals.[36] As compensation funds fall within the jurisdiction of the provinces themselves, the federal legislator can only lay down the principles for its provincial counterparts, which led to some differences in the models ultimately adopted by the various provinces.[37] The fund is financed by contributions from the patients (i.e. the potential victims!) themselves, who must pay an extra €0.73 per day spent in hospital.[38] The fund is not meant to replace liability regimes; quite the contrary: it is designed specifically for cases of hardship, where liability cannot be clearly established, or if a rare, but severe complication has occurred, or in cases with extraordinarily severe complications (even if the patient had been warned of these before). Proof of causation is still required, whereas fault or other factors relevant for establishing liability need not be proven by the patient. It is up to the *Patientenanwalt* to assist patients in filing such claims, which is particularly odd in light of the fact that the *Patientenanwalt* is at the same time the head of the commission that makes decisions about payments out of the fund. As cases do not reach the commission before the *Patientenanwalt* has decided against the

---

[34] In Upper Austria, for example, patients were successful in 1,250 cases out of 2,200 filed in the thirteen years of the panel's existence (www.gesundesooe.at/patient/dhtml/service/bzwf/site_index.php).

[35] § 27a subs. 5 and 6 Public Hospital Act (*Bundesgesetz über Krankenanstalten und Kuranstalten*, KAKuG), in the version of Federal Law Gazette (*Bundesgesetzblatt*, BGBl) I 90/2002.

[36] To some extent, this was modelled after the Viennese fund created earlier; see V. Pickl, 'Verschuldensunabhängige Entschädigungsmodelle in Wien und Kärnten' in W. Radner (ed.), *Die ärztliche Aufklärungspflicht in Rechtssprechung und Praxis* (Linz: Trauner, 1999) 67 at 69–74. Practitioners outside hospitals are not covered by this fund.

[37] W. Kossak, 'Der Entschädigungsfonds gem. § 27a Abs 5 und Abs 6 Krankenanstaltengesetz' RdM 2002/25.

[38] The fund's means vary from province to province. In 2003, the funds in Vienna and Lower Austria stood at almost €1 million each (with payments totalling about €400,000 in the latter province during that year). In comparison, the monies collected in the same period in the Burgenland amounted to only one-tenth. See the report by the *Patientenanwalt* of Lower Austria at www.patientenanwalt.com.

merits of tort law liability, the success rate of these claims is rather high.[39] Payments out of the fund are capped, but these amounts vary from province to province.[40]

5   Key elements of liability

a   Wrongfulness[41] and informed consent

The fact that someone was injured by the behaviour of another indicates that the latter acted wrongfully, which is particularly true in cases of bodily harm. Nevertheless, wrongfulness under Austrian law does not follow from the negative outcome per se, but needs to be linked to some behaviour which the law disapproves of.[42]

As medical treatment, by its nature, aims at affecting the patient's bodily or mental integrity, such an outcome will therefore serve as a primary indication of wrongfulness unless the conduct of the doctor was justified, in particular by the patient's own consent,[43] which can only be given on the basis of proper information, or in cases of emergency. In order for

---

[39] Of the 49 cases brought before the commission in Lower Austria in 2003, 41 were decided in the applicant's favour.

[40] While the maximum in Vienna stands at €70,000, awards in Lower Austria must not exceed €21,000 (in cases of extraordinary hardship €36,000).

[41] On the concept of wrongfulness in Austria, see H. Koziol, 'Wrongfulness under Austrian Law' in H. Koziol (ed.), *Unification of Tort Law: Wrongfulness* (The Hague: Kluwer Law International, 1998) 11.

[42] This is the core of the so-called doctrine of 'Verhaltensunrecht', which prevails in Austria. See H. Koziol, above n. 41, nos. 4/2 ff.

[43] E.g. OGH 23.1.1986 SZ 59/18; 21.9.1989 SZ 62/154; 12.11.1992 JBl 1994, 336; 31.1.1995 JBl 1995, 453 (comment by J. Steiner); 30.1.1996 RdM 1996/24; 3.9.1996 SZ 69/199. See also W. Holzer, in P. Schick (ed.), *Die Haftung des Arztes in zivil- und strafrechtlicher Sicht unter Einschluß des Arzneimittelrechts* (Graz: Leykam, 1983) 63 (at 64–7); W. Holzer, above n. 23, 3 ff.; P. Barth 'Hat der Patient bei eigenmächtigen medizinischen Eingriffen Anspruch auf Ersatz seines Körper- und Gesundheitsschadens?' RdM 1999/110 at 111–12; D. Engljähringer, above n. 23, 110 ff. *Contra* F. Harrer, in Schwimann, *Praxiskommentar ABGB*, vol. VII (2nd edn., Wien: Orac, 1997) § 1300 no. 43, with further references, who opposes 'such depreciatory and disturbing equation of healing with infliction of bodily harm'. See also H. Honsell, 'Die Aufklärungspflicht des Arztes in Deutschland, Österreich und der Schweiz' (1995) 63 *Schweizerische Versicherungszeitschrift* 329; E. Pitzl and G. Huber, 'Ärztliche Heilbehandlung und Körperverletzungskonstruktion' RdM 2000/105. Such criticism is not convincing, however. A tailor commits the delict of damaging property if she processes cloth without the owner's prior consent. Nevertheless, no one would consider such judgment (which is in full accord with all defence of lawfully protected interests) as a criminalisation of craftsmanship. *Cf.* E. Karner, *Der Ersatz ideeller Schäden bei Körperverletzung* (Vienna: Springer, 1999) 119.

the consent[44] to be valid, a conversation[45] must have been held between the doctor and the patient at a point in time which enabled the latter to thoroughly consider the possible advantages and disadvantages of the treatment.[46]

If such grounds for justification are missing, the doctor has violated § 110 of the Austrian Criminal Code (*Strafgesetzbuch*, StGB), which penalises the treatment of another 'without that person's consent, even if carried out according to common standards of the science of medicine', unless permission could not be awaited due to imminent and 'serious' danger to her life or health.[47]

As the patient's consent is required to refute the indication of wrongfulness in the sphere of the doctor, it is up to the latter to prove that such consent was validly given on the basis of adequate knowledge of the risks involved.[48] While the doctor himself will typically be under a duty of

---

[44] On the nature of the patient's consent, see W. Holzer, above n. 23, 5 ff.; D. Engljähringer, above n. 23, 140 ff.; T. Juen, *Arzthaftungsrecht* (Wien: Manz, 1997) 52 ff.; S. Dullinger, JBl 1998, 11 ff.; OGH 19.12.1984, SZ 57/207.

[45] A mere standard form, letter or leaflet is not enough; the patient must have the option of asking questions. See e.g. OGH 31.1.1995, JBl 1995, 453 (comment by J. Steiner); 30.1.1996, RdM 1996/24. *Cf.* W. Holzer, 'Schadenersatzrechtliche Konsequenzen der ärztlichen Aufklärungspflicht aus österreichischer Sicht' in *Festschrift Gitter* (Wiesbaden: Chmielorz, 1995) 375 at 384–5; E. Pitzl and G. Huber, 'Behandlungsaufklärung – Risikoaufklärung – Aufklärungsbögen' RdM 1996/113; J. Schramm and M. Stempkowski, 'Die zahnärztliche Aufklärungspflicht' RdM 1997/136 at 138; T. Juen, above n. 44, 71 ff.; A. Heidinger, 'Die ärztliche Aufklärungspflicht in der Rechtsprechung des Obersten Gerichtshofes' in F. Harrer and A. Graf (eds.), *Ärztliche Verantwortung und Aufklärung* (Vienna: Orac, 1999) 17 at 39 ff.

[46] If there is no imminent danger, a rule of thumb might say that the higher the risks involved, the more time the patient will need. F. Harrer, above n. 43, § 1300 no. 40; D. Engljähringer, above n. 23, 166 ff.; W. Holzer, above n. 23, 32; W. Holzer, above n. 45, at 382; J. Schramm and M. Stempkowski, RdM 1997/138; A. Heidinger, above n. 45, 37–8. See also OGH 23.6.1994, RdM 1995/1 (comment by C. Kopetzki): information conveyed on the day before the operation is still regarded as timely. Similarly OGH 14.4.1998, RdM 1998/21.

[47] See R. Reischauer, *Der Entlastungsbeweis des Schuldners* (Berlin: Duncker & Humblot, 1975) § 1299 no. 23b. Established court practice, e.g. OGH 23.6.1982, SZ 55/114 (comment by W. Holzer); 23.1.1986, SZ 59/18; 7.2.1989, SZ 62/18; 21.9.1989, SZ 62/154; 12.9.1990, SZ 63/152; 25.1.1994, SZ 67/9. *Cf.* § 8 subs. 3 of the Austrian Hospitals Act (KAG), which provides that a patient who is admitted to a hospital must specifically agree to any action taken if there is enough time to ask for such consent without imminent danger to the patient's life or health. Further code provisions which require a medical practitioner to inform her patient are e.g. § 5 AIDS Act, § 8 Venereal Diseases Act, § 7 Reproductive Medicine Act, as well as § 8 Blood Safety Act. See R. Resch, 'Zur Rechtsgrundlage der ärztlichen Aufklärungspflicht', RdM 1996/170.

[48] By expressly overruling previous practice (though dating back as long as the mid-1950s: 29.2.1956, SZ 29/16), the Supreme Court confirmed this distribution of the burden of

his own to inform the patient (as in a contractual relationship[49]), he may exonerate himself in other cases by establishing that he had good reason to believe in the patient's valid consent having been expressed to someone else (e.g. a colleague at a hospital).

Adequate information about possible risks and complications needs to be given early enough in order to allow the patient sufficient time to make up her mind.[50] While such disclosure has to be documented in writing (if only for evidentiary reasons[51]), a mere standard form alone cannot satisfy the obligation to communicate the risks of the treatment. Letting the patient sign a written piece of information without discussing it in itself constitutes a breach of said duty.[52]

---

proof in 1992: OGH 12.11.1992, JBl 1994, 336; see also 11.1.1996, RdM 1996/11; 12.3.1996, RdM 1996/25; 20.3.1997, RdM 1997/29. See further G. Gaisbauer, 'Zur Beweislast für Einwilligung des Patienten und Erfüllung der ärztlichen Aufklärungspflicht' JBl 1994, 352; W. Holzer, above n. 45, 385; *contra* R. Reischauer, above n. 47, § 1299 no. 26 at 333–4; but see Reischauer, 'Die Arzthaftung in der Rechtsprechung' [1997] *Versicherungsrundschau* 146; A. Haslinger, 'Probleme der ärztlichen Aufklärung und Patienteneinwilligung' [1994] AnwBl 866 at 871; K. Hofmann, 'Die Aufklärungspflicht des Arztes im Lichte der Rechtsprechung des Obersten Gerichtshofes' [1998] *Österreichische Richterzeitung* (ÖRZ) 80; S. Dullinger, 'Zur Beweislast für Verletzung/Erfüllung der ärztlichen Aufklärungspflicht' JBl 1998, 2 at 9 ff., 16). Dullinger's arguments were expressly rejected by OGH 23.2.1999, JBl 1999, 531; 11.3.1999, RdM 2000/2; 30.3.1999, RdM 2000/4; 23.11.1999, JBl 2000, 657 (comment by P. Jabornegg). See further E. Karner, above n. 43, 114 ff.; A. Kletečka in his comments to OGH RdM 1999, 120 ff.; P. Jabornegg in his comments to OGH JBl 2000, 662 ff.

[49] *Contra* R. Resch, RdM 1996/173 ('duty to inform based on delictual protection of legal interests'); A. Heidinger, above n. 45, 26, § 49, para. 1 ÄrzteG does not oblige the hospital's staff practitioners personally by informing their employer's patients. *Contra* R. Reischauer, above n. 47, § 1299 no. 26. Paragraphs 2 and 3 of section 49 specifically consider (and do not rule out) the case that some or all of the doctor's duties are delegated. This is typically true for hospitals. Consequently, there are not only practical reasons against the strict duty of each and every doctor to inform every single patient without exception.

[50] F. Harrer, above n. 43, § 1300 no. 40; D. Engljähringer, above n. 23, 166 ff.; W. Holzer, above n. 23, 32; W. Holzer, above n. 45, 382; J. Schramm and M. Stempkowski, RdM 1997/138; A. Heidinger, above n. 45, 37–8. See also OGH 23.6.1994, RdM 1995/1 (comment by C. Kopetzki): information given on the eve of the operation is still timely. Similarly OGH 14.4.1998, RdM 1998/21.

[51] A. Heidinger, above n. 45, 9. Hospitals are further required by § 10 subs. 1 subpara. 2 letter a of the Hospitals Act (KAG) to record the fact that their patients have been informed. The doctors who are in charge of the treatment in general are also required to ensure that such documentation is made (subs. 3 of the same).

[52] See e.g. OGH 31.1.1995, JBl 1995, 453 (comment by J. Steiner); 30.1.1996, RdM 1996/24. *Cf.* W. Holzer, above n. 45, 384–5; E. Pitzl and G. Huber, 'Behandlungsaufklärung – Risikoaufklärung – Aufklärungsbögen' RdM 1996/113, J. Schramm and M. Stempkowski, 'Die zahnärztliche Aufklärungspflicht' RdM 1997/136 at 138; T. Juen, above n. 44, 71 ff.; A. Heidinger, above n. 45, 39 ff.

Even though there is no pre-determined checklist of items that need to be disclosed to the patient, the practice of the Austrian Supreme Court has brought about a set of guidelines on how to observe the patient's right of self-determination and at the same time the ultimate goal of her well-being. Upfront, one has to look at the circumstances of the case, which should guide a doctor to inform the patient "according to conscientious medical practice and experience ... in the light of the characteristics of the clinical picture".[53]

A 1982 decision is generally considered to be the leading case in this field, when the court tried to comprehensively summarise previous case law and to develop it further.[54] A rule of thumb upfront would read that the more urgent it is for the patient's health, the less extensively she needs to be informed, especially if she appears to be overly anxious and might back out of the treatment, which in turn would constitute a much higher risk to her health.[55] On the other hand, if the treatment is not impera-tive (such as purely diagnostic measures),[56] information must be given as extensively as possible.[57] Typical risks always have to be disclosed, even if the chances of such complications are remote.[58] Whether or not a risk is 'typical', therefore, is not determined by statistics, but rather by the fact 'that such risk is particularly connected with the operation at issue, that it cannot be avoided completely even if utmost care is employed, and that it would surprise an uninformed patient since she would not consider such risk otherwise'.[59] Even under this rule, it is not necessary that a patient knows of each and every complication that one could possibly mention. Under this test, typical risks only have to be mentioned if knowledge

---

[53] E.g. OGH 23.1.1986, SZ 59/18; 29.1.1997, RdM 1997/18.

[54] OGH 23.6.1982, SZ 55/114. *Cf.* the overview given by K. Hofmann, ÖRZ 1988, 80; see fur-ther A. Heidinger, above n. 45, 24 ff.; B. A. Koch and H. Koziol, above n. 27, 61–5.

[55] See e.g. already OGH 20.4.1904, GlUNF no. 2,672; W. Holzer, above n. 23, 26 ff.; D. Engljähringer, above n. 23, 215 ff. with further references.

[56] W. Holzer, above n. 45, 383–4; OGH in SZ 59/18; 8 Ob 620/91; 2 Ob 124/98v (the last two as yet unpublished); OGH, JBl 1999, 531; RdM, 1999/11 (comment by A. Kletečka).

[57] E.g. OGH in SZ 63/152; JBl 1991, 455; RdM 1994/1 (comment by C. Kopetzki); SZ 67/9; JBl 1995, 245; RdM 1994/25 (comment by C. Kopetzki); SZ 69/199; RdM 1997/4; RdM 1998/18; see further G. Gaisbauer, 'Ärztliche Aufklärungspflicht bei kosmetischen Eingriffen' [1993] ÖJZ, 25.

[58] E.g. OGH in SZ 62/154; JBl 1990, 459; RdM 1997/18; D. Engljähringer, above n. 23, 189 ff.

[59] Established practice, e.g. OGH 19.12.1984, SZ 57/207; JBl 1985, 548; EvBl 1985/85; RdW 1985, 272; 21.9.1989, SZ 62/154; JBl 1990, 459; VersR 1990, 879; 25.1.1994, SZ 67/9, RdM 1994/25 (comment by C. Kopetzki); JBl 1995, 245; 31.1.1995, JBl 1995, 453 (comment by J. Steiner), RdM 1995/15 (comment by C. Kopetzki); EvBl 1995/149; 11.1.1996, RdM 1996/11; 16.1.1996, RdM 1996/12; 30.1.1996, RdM 1996/24; 12.3.1996, RdM 1996/25; 3.9.1996, RdM 1997/4, SZ 69/199, EvBl 1997/86; 24.10.1996, RdM 1997/28.

thereof could influence the patient's decision.[60] Statistical probabilities are but one factor:[61] the paramount test is whether the patient might be specifically interested in the particular risk at issue,[62] and to what extent the knowledge thereof might influence her decision.[63] Even dangers which are completely insignificant therefore have to be communicated to the patient if it is apparent that she might be particularly interested in such consequences.[64] Only in 'borderline cases' is it possible to completely abstain from informing the patient, which is the case if the latter would be excessively alarmed and might overreact in a way completely disproportionate to a rational evaluation of the benefits and risks involved.[65] Information is further not required if the patient has validly waived such rights.[66]

Even if the patient was not adequately informed and could therefore not give any valid consent to her treatment, she will nevertheless have to bear her own loss if the defendant can prove that the patient would still have gone ahead with the treatment had she known all possible complications thereof.[67]

b   Fault

In contrast to most other European jurisdictions, Austria still (at least in theory) adheres to a subjective standard of fault.[68] In general, therefore, the abilities of the individual tortfeasor to avoid the damage are decisive. It is, however, presumed by § 1297 ABGB that everyone has average abilities unless a person is younger than fourteen years of age or mentally handicapped.

---

[60] OGH 24.10.1996, RdM 1997/28.

[61] This does not mean that rare risks never have to be disclosed: OGH, RdM, 1994/1 (comment by C. Kopetzki). Even if the risk of infection is close to one in a thousand, the patient still has to be informed if the doctor realises that the patient would otherwise believe that the treatment is without any danger at all. See also OGH, RdM 1998/19 (2%). But see F. Harrer (above note 43) § 1300 no. 36; D. Engljähringer, above n. 43, 201 ff.

[62] OGH 29.1.1997, RdM 1997/18.   [63] OGH 24.10.1997, RdM 1997/28.

[64] OGH 29.1.1997, RdM 1997/18.   [65] OGH 23.6.1982 (above note 47).

[66] On the requirements of such a waiver see D. Engljähringer, above n. 23, 218 ff.; OGH 23.6.1982, SZ 55/114; 19.12.1984, SZ 57/207.

[67] OGH 23.1.1986, SZ 59/18; 21.9.1989, SZ 62/154, JBl 1990, 459; 12.9.1990, SZ 63/152; 14.1.1992, JBl 1992, 391; 31.1.1995, JBl 1995, 453 (comment by J. Steiner). But see H. Koziol, above n. 41, no. 8/72, who does not grant the doctor such a possibility of justifying his acts if 'the practitioner has substantially violated his duties', for example if he 'completely failed to disclose risks'.

[68] W. Wilburg, *Die Elemente des Schadensrechts* (Marburg: Elwert, 1941) 17, 43 ff.; R. Reischauer, *Der Entlastungsbeweis des Schuldners* (Berlin: Duncker & Humblot, 1975) 201 ff.; H. Koziol, 'Liability Based on Fault: Subjective or Objective Yardstick?' [1998] *Maastricht Journal* 111 ff.; OGH 19.9.1984, JBl 1985, 625.

There is a very important exception to that general rule. According to § 1299 ABGB, 'experts'[69] have to abide by an objective standard of care.[70] Medical practitioners are required to attain the standard of a prudent and experienced specialist in their respective area of expertise,[71] which is determined according to the state of medical science at the time the harmful event occurred.[72] Therefore, someone who carries out an activity that requires the knowledge or abilities of an expert, which is particularly true for a surgeon or other medical practitioner,[73] has to bear responsibility for possessing such qualities even if he personally cannot come up to such a standard.[74]

Patients can expect the safest possible treatment, though it need not necessarily be the best from an objective point of view. Doctors cannot be held liable merely for choosing a method of treatment if there is an alternative approach taken by other colleagues, as long as the chosen method is acknowledged by a significant number of his peers. It is therefore deemed safe as long as it is recognised by at least one distinguished school of medical science, unless another school holds it to be unsafe and dangerous.[75]

While it is generally up to the claimant to prove fault together with any other requirement to establish the defendant's liability (§ 1296 ABGB),

---

[69] This is by law defined as someone who 'publicly professes a function, a skill, a business or craft; or who, voluntarily and without necessity, takes on a business which requires special knowledge or exceptional diligence and gives everyone to understand that he believes himself to be capable of the necessary diligence and required exceptional knowledge' (§ 1299 ABGB).

[70] On liability of experts in general, see H. Koziol, 'Fault under Austrian Law' in P. Widmer (ed.), *Unification of Tort Law: Fault* (The Hague: Kluwer Law International, 2005) no. 25 ff.; furthermore H. Koziol, *Österreichisches Haftpflichtrecht*, vol. II, (2nd edn., Wien: Manz, 1984) 182 ff.; H. Koziol, 'Characteristic Features of Austrian Tort Law' in H. Hausmaninger et al. (eds.), *Developments in Austrian and Israeli Private Law* (Vienna: Springer, 1999) 159 (173–4).

[71] OGH 4.1.1906, GlUNF no. 4,449; 9.2.1915, GlUNF no. 7,305; 7.9.1915, GlUNF no. 7,557; R. Reischauer, above n. 47, § 1299 no. 25; K. Hofmann, 'Qualitätsmängel bei der medizinischen Behandlung als Tatbestand in der Rechtsprechung' [1999] ÖRZ 82; T. Juen, above n. 44, 86 ff. *Cf.* § 49 subs. 1 *Ärztegesetz*: 'A physician is required to conscientiously and indiscriminately treat any person, healthy or ill, whom he admits to consult or to treat. He thereby has to ensure the well-being of the ill and the protection of the healthy according to the science of medicine and according to experience, as well as pursuant to any applicable rule.'

[72] *Cf.* OGH 29.6.1989, SZ 62/125.

[73] *Cf.* B. A. Koch and H. Koziol, above n. 27, 72–3.

[74] A medical malpractice example was already used by F. Zeiller, *Commentar über das allgemeine bürgerliche Gesetzbuch für die gesamten Deutschen Erbländer der Österreichischen Monarchie*, vol. III/2 (1812) 713.

[75] OGH 16.3.1989, SZ 62/53.

§ 1298 ABGB provides for a reversal of the burden of proving fault if the claim is based upon a breach of a contractual duty or of a statutory rule prescribing certain behaviour for the protection of the interest ultimately harmed. The latter has to be proven by the claimant. So the reversal only applies to the subjective aspect of fault, whereas the proof of an objective violation of a standard of care remains the task of the claimant.[76]

If a patient can therefore prove that she was injured because the practitioner did not abide by professional standards and thereby breached his contractual obligations, or that he has breached a specific statutory rule of conduct aimed at preventing harm, it is up to the defendant to prove that there was no fault attributable to his sphere of responsibility which led to such breach.[77] If the doctor cannot rebut this presumption of fault, he will have to compensate all harm suffered (including non-pecuniary loss[78]) according to standard rules of damages. While the prevailing theory holds that § 1298 ABGB applies to all degrees of fault, the Supreme Court insists that the claimant can only avail herself of this rule in cases of slight negligence, whereas it is up to her to prove the defendant's grave fault.[79]

c   Proof and causation

As a general rule, it is up to the claimant to prove the requirements to hold the defendant liable. A patient therefore also needs to convince the court that her (further) injuries or diseases were caused by the defendant hospital or doctor.[80]

In medical malpractice cases, such proof is hard to obtain, which is even more true if it is not active behaviour that the patient complains of, but if she claims that the defendant has failed to render some action which would have been due under the circumstances. In such cases of omission, a claimant need not prove causation with absolute certainty. It suffices to show a high probability that she would not have suffered the injuries at stake if the defendant(s) had acted as necessary under the

---

[76]   Contra H. Koziol, above n. 41, no. 16/28.

[77]   On the burden of proof, see e.g. OGH JBl 2000, 657 (critical comment by P. Jabornegg).

[78]   § 1325 ABGB deals with damages for personal injuries in general. See R. Reischauer, above n. 47, § 1325 nos. 10 ff.; F. Harrer, above n. 43, § 1325 no. 66; see also OGH 31.10.1974, SZ 47/117.

[79]   See OGH 28.4.1970, SZ 43/80.

[80]   B. A. Koch and H. Koziol, 'Austria' in M. Faure and H. Koziol (eds.), Cases on Medical Malpractice in a Comparative Perspective (Wien: Springer, 2001) 57 (at 73–4 with further references).

circumstances.[81] The latter could in turn rebut such proof by showing that another possible cause was more likely to have triggered the damage to the claimant.[82]

In some of the more recent medical malpractice cases, the standard of proof was lowered even further in the patient's favour in so far as the likelihood of medical malpractice merely needs to outweigh any other possible cause for the deterioration of the patient's condition,[83] whereas defendants in turn have to prove 'with utmost probability' that such other possible cause did indeed produce the harm.[84] This is supported by the argument that patients are typically not in a position to deliver any exact proof of causation.[85]

Lack of adequate documentation may also come to the patient's aid. Her contract with a doctor or a hospital undoubtedly obliges them to document at least key aspects of diagnosis and treatment.[86] Furthermore, § 51 ÄrzteG[87] inter alia requires doctors to record the 'type and degree of … diagnostic and therapeutic services' and to preserve such documentation for at least ten years. This provision was at least in part enacted in order to facilitate the patient's proof of causation in cases of damage.[88] Any breach of such a duty can reverse the burden of proof, since a person who acts in violation of the law shall not benefit from such conduct.[89] If there is

---

[81] OGH 18.10.1966, 8 Ob 213/66; 16.3.1989, SZ 62/53; 31.5.1990, SZ 63/90; 17.6.1992, JBl 1993, 316; 8.7.1993, JBl 1994, 540 (comment by R. Bollenberger); 25.1.1994, SZ 67/9; 31.1.1995, JBl 1995, 453 (comment by J. Steiner); 7.11.1995, SZ 68/207; 5.5.1998, JBl 1999, 246 (comment by C. Bumberger).

[82] Juen, above n. 44, 132.

[83] OGH 31.5.1990, SZ 63/90; 5.5.1998, JBl 1999, 246 (in both cases, the court was satisfied with the proof that the 'probability of the injuries occurring as a consequence of the doctor's malpractice was more than insignificantly higher'); 17.6.1992, JBl 1993, 316 (at 319). See Juen, above n. 44, 131 n. 604; F. Harrer, above n. 43, 1300 nos. 54–5.

[84] OGH 10.10.1991, JBl 1992, 522 (at 523); 31.5.1990, SZ 63/90; 5.5.1998, JBl 1999, 246.

[85] OGH 17. 6.1992, JBl 1993, 316: 'An omission therefore was the cause of the loss if lawful behaviour had made the occurrence of the loss less likely than the omission of such behaviour.'

[86] OGH 25.1.1994, SZ 67/9; T. Juen, above n. 44, 69ff., 125ff. with further references.

[87] This rule was already included in the predecessor statute of the present 1998 law (§ 22a ÄrzteG 1984).

[88] T. Juen, above n. 44, 125.

[89] H. Koziol, 'Der Beweis des natürlichen Kausalzusammenhanges' in A. Koller (ed.), Haftpflicht- und Versicherungstagung 1999 (St. Gallen: University of St. Gallen, 1999) 79 at 91. Cf. OGH 25.1.1994, SZ 67/9: 'If a doctor fails to fully comply with his duty to record the treatment and thereby makes it more difficult for the patient to prove any wrongdoing, such proof will be made easier to compensate for the difficulties caused by the lack of documentation in order to ensure a fair distribution of evidentiary positions in the relationship between doctor and patient.' See also OGH 7.11.1995, SZ 68/207; 1.12.1998, RdM 1999/12.

no documentation showing the steps taken, e.g. information given to the patient, it is therefore presumed that no steps were taken to inform her.[90]

Courts also tend to waive standard requirements of proving causation if it is evident that something was objectively wrong within the sphere of the defendant, though not equally clear from an evidentiary point of view that this led to the claimant's harm. In such cases, the burden of proving causation is reversed in that sense by assuming the latter in the case of the former.[91]

Some Austrian courts have rather recently started to adopt[92] a proposal by Franz Bydlinski[93] to split the loss in cases where the defendant may have caused the claimant's injuries, but where another possible cause lies in the latter's own sphere. Since it seems unfair either to let the defendant bear the full risk of liability by (further) lowering standards of proof or to leave the full loss with the claimant, Bydlinski proposed to spread the risk between the two parties according to the ratio of the respective probabilities,[94] but only if it is proven that the defendant violated a duty of care and behaved highly dangerously under the circumstances. Therefore, in the medical liability scenario, if a patient suffers injuries in the course of some treatment and it remains unclear whether this happened due to some precondition of the patient herself or whether the injuries were caused by the (undisputedly) negligent behaviour of the physician, both sides will have to share the uncertainty and therefore the loss.[95]

---

[90] E.g. OGH 16.8.2001, RdM 2002/27; 25.1.1994, SZ 67/9; 12.8.2004 RdM, 2004/124.

[91] E.g. OGH 18.3.1931, ZBl 1931/198; 11.6.1952, JBl 1953, 18; 16.1.1991, JBl 1991, 453; 10.10.1991, JBl 1992, 522; 25.1.1994, SZ 63/90.

[92] OGH 9.11.1989, JBl 1990, 524 (with critical comment by W. Holzer); *cf.* also OGH 7.5.1985, JBl 1986, 576 (comment by E. Deutsch); 7.11.1995, SZ 68/207 (only distribution of the damage ensures 'a solution to the problem which is in accordance with principles of justice'). Others have expressly rejected his theory in earlier cases and continued to stick to their all-or-nothing approach: OGH, 10.10.1991, JBl 1992, 522; 8.7.1993, JBl 1994, 540 (comment by R. Bollenberger).

[93] *Probleme der Schadensverursachung nach deutschem und österreichischem Recht* (Stuttgart: Enke, 1964) 86 ff.; 'Aktuelle Streitfragen um die alternative Kausalität' in *Festschrift Beitzke* (Berlin: de Gruyter, 1979) 3 (at 30ff.); 'Haftungsgrund und Zufall als alternativ mögliche Schadensursachen' in *Festschrift Frotz* (Vienna: Manz, 1993) 3. See also H. Koziol, 'Problems of Alternative Causation in Tort Law' in H. Hausmaninger *et al.* (eds.), *Developments in Austrian and Israeli Private Law* (Vienna: Springer, 1999) 177 at 180 ff.

[94] R. Bollenberger in his comment on OGH 8.7.1993, JBl 1994, 540 (at 545); H. Koziol, above n. 89, 79 at 97, 99 ff.; B. A. Koch and H. Koziol, above n. 27 78–80, with further references. *Cf.* F. Bydlinski, JBl 1992, 349. But see W. Holzer, above n. 23, 15 ff.

[95] F. Bydlinski, *Probleme der Schadensverursachung* (Stuttgart: Enke, 1964) 89.

While the question of intervening causation in general is still debated in Austria,[96] at least one issue thereof seems to have been settled. In cases of an established predisposition of the patient coinciding with proven tortious acts of the practitioner, liability is generally split between the parties.[97] If one could predict that a hypothetical course of events would have led to similar harm, even without the defendant's acts, the latter is only held responsible for the fact that such damages have occurred earlier than anticipated. If, for example, a wrongful and faulty treatment brings about the same symptoms that would have arisen anyway due to the patient's predisposition, liability only covers the losses incurred in the time period starting from their actual occurrence until the predicted moment when their cause would have manifested itself anyway (so-called *Verfrühungsschaden* or – if the tortious act has aggravated a precondition – *Verschlimmerungsschaden*).[98] All this has to be proven by the defendants, who have to meet high standards of proof as imposed by the Austrian courts for such defence.[99]

6   Who is held liable?

It is obvious that the doctor or any other health care professional is liable for any fault on his side which led to the patient's (further) harm. Such direct responsibility may be founded in contract or in tort, as indicated earlier.[100] Hospitals or hospital managers may also have to account for their own fault, e.g. for lack of proper organisation within the hospital or the like.

Much more debated – and rather recently disputed in practice – however, is the question of the extent to which someone should be vicariously liable for the behaviour of someone else. The answer differs significantly between a contract relationship and a matter exclusive to the law of delict.

---

[96] See generally H. Koziol, *Österreichisches Haftpflichtrecht*, vol. I (3rd edn., Vienna: Manz, 1997) nos. 3/58 ff.; R. Reischauer in P. Rummel (ed.), *Kommentar zum Allgemeinen Bürgerlichen Gesetzbuch*, vol. II (2nd edn., Vienna: Manz, 1992) § 1302 nos. 14–15; F. Harrer, above n. 43, § 1302 no. 32 ff. (all with further references).

[97] H. Koziol, above n. 96, no. 3/78.

[98] OGH 3.9.1996, SZ 69/199; 5.5.1998, JBl 1999, 246 (comment by C. Bumberger). *Cf.* Juen, above n. 44, 35 ff.; Reischauer, above n. 47, § 1299 no. 23b at 328; R. Reischauer, 'Ärztehaftung in der Rechtsprechung' [1997] VR 141 at 144.

[99] It is therefore not sufficient if the parties to the patient's contract can only prove a 'preponderant probability' of the intervening predisposition as to the injuries at issue. Instead, such probability must almost amount to certainty (in as much as possible): OGH 5.5.1998, JBl 1999, 246 at 248 (comment by C. Bumberger); 3.9.1996, SZ 69/199.

[100] See supra p. 113.

In the latter case, a principal is only liable for the behaviour of those auxiliaries who are unfit or dangerous, and even then only if they acted within the scope of their duties (§ 1315 ABGB). In a contract case, on the other hand, § 1313a ABGB extends vicarious liability to all helpers as long as these acted in fulfilment of the principal's contractual duties vis-à-vis the injured person (which may be a third party protected under the contract, such as the unborn child in the mother's womb).

§ 1313a ABGB was introduced into the ABGB in 1916 in the course of amendments which aimed at incorporating certain ideas of the (then new) German Civil Code into Austrian law. Before, the employer was only liable for *culpa in eligendo* beyond the cases covered by §§ 1314[101] and 1315 ABGB.

Discussion became heated in this field after two decisions rendered in 1999 on borderline issues between personal and vicarious liability. Both cases involved specialists who had agreed to perform surgery on their respective patients by using the facilities of a hospital. Even though they operated there regularly, they were not employed by the hospital. They were so-called 'Belegärzte'. They only rented the space and equipment of the operating theatre and contracted for the temporary assistance of the hospital's personnel. In one case, a staff member of the hospital who assisted with the surgery negligently caused injuries to the defendant's patient.[102] The other case involved the negligence of a fellow specialist for anaesthesia (who was not employed by the hospital, but hired directly by the defendant).[103] In both cases the surgeon was held liable, since the actual wrongdoers were acting under his (at least general) direction and control (even though they were not his employees).[104]

Some commentators fight this conclusion by pointing to the fact that surgeons are not even allowed to give drugs to their patients.[105] The latter argument is irrelevant, however. Vicarious liability does not require that the principal could himself have performed the tasks that he delegated

---

[101] This provision is almost obsolete. It holds the employer liable for housing employees without a testimonial.

[102] OGH 27.10.1999, SZ 72/164.   [103] OGH 23.11.1999, JBl 2001, 5.

[104] This was particularly disputed as regards the anaesthetist, who was acting within her area of expertise on the same professional level as the defendant. See the comment by C. Kopetzki, above n. 61, and the critical remarks by H. Bruck and H. Pfersmann, 'Wie weit reicht die Haftung des operierenden Chirurgen?' JBl 2001, 64. On the general notion of who should count as an assistant in the meaning of § 1313a ABGB: R. Reischauer, (above n. 96), § 1313a no. 9; H. Koziol, *Österreiches Haftpflicht*, 340–2.

[105] C. Kopetzki in his comment to this case in RdM 2000/8.

to another, which would exclude vicarious liability in most aspects of modern-day life where division of labour is essential. The focus should rather be on the expectations of the parties to the contract in question, and thereby in particular on the perception of the patient who typically contracts with a surgeon for an operation and thereby entrusts the latter with the entire organisation thereof, including the appointment of other necessary personnel. Seen from that perspective, there is hardly any difference from building contracts, where parts of the work (in particular specialist work) are subcontracted, and in those scenarios it is undisputed that the general contractor will be liable for the behaviour of the subcontractors, even if the former could not himself perform the kind of work delegated to the latter.[106]

Even though § 49 para. 2 ÄrzteG allows doctors to include auxiliaries acting under their supervision and control (for whom they are vicariously liable according to § 1313a ABGB), a practitioner must not delegate his contractual duties to someone else, not even to another doctor of the same expertise, without the patient's consent. If he nevertheless does,[107] he will have to account for all negative consequences which would not have occurred, had he performed his obligations himself. If the patient agrees to substitution or if it becomes unavoidable, the doctor will only have to account for fault in selecting the substitute (*culpa in eligendo*),[108] not for the latter's fault in executing the substituted task.[109]

7   Damages

Under Austrian law – unlike most other legal systems – the extent of compensation generally depends upon the degree of fault (§ 1324 ABGB).[110] There is, however, a special rule for cases of bodily injury, which is of particular interest in cases of medical malpractice. According to § 1325 ABGB, all tortfeasors, irrespective of the degree of their fault, have to indemnify the injured person for costs of medical care and loss of

---

[106] *Cf.* OGH 10.2.2004, JBl 2004, 648 (comment by M. Lukas).

[107] § 49 para. 3 ÄrzteG to a limited degree allows such delegation, but at the same time explicitly states that he will remain fully responsible for such delegation.

[108] *Cf.* OGH 4.2.1959, JBl 1960, 188 (gynaecologist liable for asking another doctor – but not a specialist in the same field – to take over).

[109] R. Reischauer, above n. 47, § 1299 no. 30; W. Holzer, above n. 13, 54–5.

[110] If the injurer therefore acted with slight negligence, he has to pay only the 'actual loss', but neither lost profits nor non-pecuniary harm. Moreover, in the case of property damage, the loss has to be assessed in an objective way according to the market value (§ 1332 ABGB).

earnings;[111] in addition, they must compensate non-pecuniary loss 'as is adequate under the circumstances'.

8   Exemption clauses

While liability for slight negligence can be excluded by advance agreement, exemption clauses are invalid altogether with respect to intentional behaviour, whereas they remain effective with respect to gross negligence unless agreed upon individually between the parties.[112]

9   Conclusions

The number of medical malpractice issues before the courts has increased substantially in the last quarter of the period under survey, and academia has reacted thereto correspondingly. Nevertheless, the way courts handle such issues has apparently not changed dramatically in the course of time. Early cases of, say, the first years of the twentieth century read quite like modern-day reasoning when it comes to comparing the arguments used.

However, certain moves towards a more patient-friendly decision-making process cannot be denied, even though they remain – at least on the face of it – within the limits designated by earlier practice (they simply move closer to such limits). Changes in the way courts handle causation issues, for example,[113] seem to be in line with the increase in public awareness of such problems.

The most significant changes from the perspective of patients did not happen in tort law proper, but were at least 'inspired' by its development. The introduction of independent ombudsmen and conciliation panels can certainly be considered a success, despite certain teething troubles. These institutions to some extent cushion the readiness of modern patients to seek consequences for what they deem unfair, even against the so-called 'gods in white', who are no longer unconditionally adored.

---

[111] Compensation for loss of earnings in principle has to be awarded as a rent payment; a lump sum is only awarded under special circumstances. See H. Koziol, 'Damages under Austrian Law' in U. Magnus (ed.), *Unification of Tort Law: Damages* (The Hague: Kluwer Law International, 2000) 7 at 19.

[112] For more details see H. Koziol, above n. 96, no. 18/1 ff. and OGH ZVR 1999/37. Even wrongdoing with slight negligence cannot be excluded between an entrepreneur and a consumer.

[113] See above at pp. 123–6.

Unfortunately, I could not find any explicit evidence in the literature which traces back the changes to certain specific developments in society or in law. In addition to my introductory remarks, I will nevertheless try to summarise some factors which I personally believe did have at least some influence on the advances and expansion of medical malpractice law, at least during the last three decades. The following list is certainly not complete, however, and it would be particularly helpful to launch a sociological study investigating the changes in public attitude towards the medical profession and its occasional failures. To my knowledge, there is no such survey in Austria as of yet.

Decreasing admiration of members of the medical profession, coupled with *increased expectations* of medical services: due to changes in society (including, in particular, advances in public education and access to medical school and professions), the status of doctors has turned from highly esteemed members of the community to 'mere' professionals whom nobody hesitates to bring before a court any longer. As mentioned earlier, their services are no longer considered to be acts of grace in an effort to aid the patient, but patients increasingly take it for granted that they contract for a complete recovery by hiring a doctor, even though the scientific probabilities of healing may not even be close to such often exaggerated laymen expectations.

More and faster information available, both on the progress of medical science as well as on the downsides and failures thereof: news about a heart transplantation some 6,000 miles away would not have reached Austria and spread there as quickly some decades before 1967. A broader range of media (following greater demand from the general public) has taken on (at least allegedly) sensational topics in quite a different way from the way the few newspapers did at the beginning of the twentieth century. I personally still remember certain tabloid reports of the late 1970s and early 1980s touching upon sensitive issues of health care (though not necessarily on specific cases of malpractice), which at the time was deemed to be outrageous and sensational. Investigative journalism and undercover reporting from hospitals, for example, was probably not the way the general public learned about the medical profession before the second world war (and certainly not before the first world war). Rankings of doctors did not appear until maybe some ten years or so ago, but now they are a standard series in one of Austria's most popular magazines.

Academic treatment of medical malpractice issues in Austria received a boost in the 1970s and certainly in the 1980s, as already mentioned. This was, to a considerable degree, inspired by German publications in this field shortly before this time. As these topics became more and more discussed by doctrine, such information was almost simultaneously passed on to students, who left law school at least equipped with arguments they could use in such cases. Whether or not this really had a measurable impact on the trial practice can only be a matter of pure speculation, however. At least in the most recent past, specialisation in medical law has turned into a distinct trend at law schools, which have started to offer specific course packages in this field.[114] At the same time, demand in the job market for such specialisations has grown markedly (though not excessively).

A very important development which has certainly pushed the number of malpractice cases much higher was the *introduction of patient ombudsmen and conciliation panels*, which themselves were but a response to a previous increase in patient complaints. With the new and easier administration of such claims, however, more and more patients dared to come forward with their cases (whether or not these were actually founded from a legal perspective). If these complaints are included in the counting, the number of malpractice cases (irrespective of their success[115]) has certainly been pushed way up high by the introduction of such institutions, even though doctors have surely not become more careless over time. Current statistics show that the caseload these institutions have to handle is still on the rise, which may be further supported by increased newspaper reporting on their work, but also by active information campaigns not only by these institutions themselves, but also by their targets. Any average hospital homepage, for example, includes a prominent link to patients' rights issues and at least links from there to the administration of claims.

---

[114] The University of Vienna introduced a special group of electives in 1999, which is one of the most popular so-called 'baskets' chosen by students. The Vienna law faculty established a special chair in medical law in 2002.

[115] As statistics show, more than 70% of all complaints filed with the ombudsmen are unsuccessful. See the references above at n. 30 and 32.

6

The development of medical liability in the Netherlands

EWOUD HONDIUS

1 Introduction: interest of Dutch law

Why could the development of medical liability in the Netherlands be of interest for European legal development? Apart from the fact that, of course, the Netherlands are one of the twenty-seven member states of the European Union, three arguments may be presented.[1] First, from a purely legal point of view, it may be of interest to study how a legal system which once was firmly entrenched in the French legal family, has gradually reached out for the German legal family, culminating in the adoption of the new 1992 Civil Code, which in many aspects has been influenced by German law.[2] Rather than qualify Dutch law as belonging to the German

---

[1] Moreover, being one of the six founding members of the European Union and one of the three members of Benelux, the Netherlands have probably had more influence than some other nations. Being the European Union's fifth trading power – after Germany, the United Kingdom, France and Italy – the Netherlands are also of some importance from an economic point of view, although this is perhaps less important in the realm of medical negligence.

[2] See E. O. H. P. Florijn, *Ontstaan en ontwikkeling van het nieuwe Burgerlijk Wetboek* (PhD thesis, University of Maastricht, 1994), 571–4: back in the nineteenth century, the old Code faced stiff opposition right from the beginning. Originally the criticism focused on the language and the structure of the Code. Later, the fact that the legislature did not keep up with developments in society was considered more important. Politicians were not interested in revision of the Code in the first decades after its adoption, except for a small number of cases in which a pressing social need had to be countered. This situation was caused by the fact that parliamentary procedures were time-consuming and because of frequent changes of government, which resulted in the fact that only bills that could be passed within one parliamentary year stood a chance to be taken into consideration. Only in the rare case that a minister was determined to try his utmost, a revision of the Civil Code could be brought about.

In the first decade of the twentieth century, the interest of government and Parliament in legislating in the field of private law was at its lowest. The disintegration of the idea of codification led to a shift of attention to judicial law-making, as had happened in France. In

legal family, however, it seems appropriate to suggest that the 1992 Code has a cosmopolitan nature, reflecting also the influence of other legal systems, such as the common law.[3] In its turn, the Dutch Code has influenced the new civil codes in Eastern Europe and the successors to the former Soviet Union (although this influence is sometimes overstated).[4]

Second, the Dutch patients' rights movement has resulted in a legal regulation in the Civil Code of the medical services contract, which may be of interest to other jurisdictions.

Finally, the Dutch judiciary has handed down some interesting judgments, such as the one in the *Kelly* case on 'wrongful life', which will be discussed at some length later.[5]

2 Public or private law

The Dutch health system has recently been privatised. As of 1 January 2006, the automatic public health insurance for the lesser incomes has been replaced by a system of compulsory private insurance. The liberalisation of insurance has been successful at least to the extent that hundreds of thousands of policyholders have made use of their new freedom by changing from one insurance company to another. Less reassuring is the fact that some 240,000 Dutch citizens are at present without insurance. When doctors and hospitals are going to refuse these patients treatment,

---

1913, a beginning was made with the systematic publication and annotation of case law. In 1919, the Dutch Hoge Raad handed down its landmark opinion in the case *Lindenbaum v. Cohen* (below n. 17), which recognised judge-made law as a source of law on the same level as statutory rules. These developments diminished the urgency of recodification, but they did not make it unnecessary.

One of the first, and by far the foremost, of those who still pressed for recodification, was Eduard Meijers, Professor of Private Law in Leyden. In 1947, it was decided that Meijers would be entrusted with drafting a new Civil Code. The decision is probably due to the influence of the Minister of Justice, Van Maarseveen, who personally took an interest in the project. Meijers immediately set to work and by the time of his death, in 1954, the whole project was nearly complete.

After the death of Meijers, first a triumvirate was appointed to finish the job, but later a large number of law professors were enlisted, which according to Florijn created large and often unsurmountable coordination problems.

[3] V. J. A. Sütö, *Nieuw Vermogensrecht en rechtsvergelijking – reconstructie van een wetgevingsproces (1947–1961)* (PhD thesis Leiden, The Hague: Boom, 2004).

[4] See my paper 'Export van Westers recht naar Oost-Europa: het voorbeeld van Litouwen', in *Import en export van burgerlijk recht/BW-krant jaarboek* 13 (Deventer: Kluwer 1997), 113–26.

[5] Below p. 147.

this will present a problem. In the Netherlands, there is a discussion as to whether or not human rights should 'invade' private law.[6]

3   Contract or tort

In this section some more general observations will be made about the development of Dutch civil law. Modern Dutch private law starts with the 1838 Civil Code. The 2004 bicentenary of the Code Napoléon has rekindled interest in the coming about of the separate Dutch Code, which on the one hand was heavily influenced by the French Code and on the other hand did show some characteristics of its own and over time also developed in a different way.[7] On the one hand the Dutch provisions on tort liability, articles 1401 ff. *Burgerlijk Wetboek,* read like a translation of articles 1382 ff. *Code civil.* On the other hand, the main provision, article 1401, instead of focusing on *faute,* did distinguish between *onrechtmatige daad* (illegal act) and *schuld* (fault). Moreover, the identical provisions, article 1384 *Code civil* and article 1403 *Burgerlijk Wetboek*, have been interpreted in widely divergent ways by the courts. Whereas in France the first section of this article has been used as the basis for introducing a strict liability for a wide variety of activities, the very same text in the Dutch Code was considered only a preface of the remainder of the article without an independent meaning by Dutch courts.

During the nineteenth century, Dutch law was at first heavily influenced by French law, especially academic writing. The other way round, French academics never showed the least interest in what happened in the Netherlands.[8] Towards the end of the nineteenth century, the new German *Bürgerliches Gesetzbuch* attracted considerable interest in Dutch legal circles and the interest remained ever after. With changing linguistic abilities – English replacing French as the first foreign language – the

---

[6] O. Cherednychenko, *Fundamental Rights, Contract Law and the Protection of the Weaker Party/A Comparative Analysis of the Constitutionalisation of Contract Law, with Emphasis on Risky Financial Transactions* (PhD thesis Utrecht, Munich: Sellier, 2007); C. Mak, *Fundamental Rights in European Contract Law/A Comparison of the Impact of Fundamental Rights on Contractual Relationships in Germany, the Netherlands, Italy and England* (PhD thesis Amsterdam, Alphen aan den Rijn: Kluwer Law International, 2007); J. M. Smits, *Constitutionalisering van het vermogensrecht*, paper for the Nederlandse Vereniging voor Rechtsvergelijking (Deventer: Kluwer, 2003), 1–163.

[7] J. Lokin, 'Die Rezeption der Code Civil in den nördlichen Niederlanden', *Zeitschrift für Europäisches Privatrecht* 2004, 932–46.

[8] See my paper 'Le Code civil et les Néerlandais', in *Le Code civil 1804–2004/Livre du bicentenaire* (Paris: Dalloz/Litec, 2004), 613–22.

interest has turned cosmopolitan, with influences coming also from common law sources.

On 10 January 2010, it will be eighteen years after the Dutch 1992 Civil Code entered into force. More precisely, books 3 (patrimonial law in general), 5 (on property rights) and 6 (general part of the law of obligations) as well as some titles of book 7 (specific contracts) – entered into force. Before, books 1, 2 and 8 had already come into force.[9] Has the new Code lived up to its promises? How have lawyers and non-lawyers coped with the introduction of new law? What has been the consequence for the always delicate balance between the law-making powers of the courts and the legislature? And what about the position of legal writing? Has the introduction of the Code deteriorated the position of the Netherlands in Europe, as was prophesied?

For years on end, the introduction of the new Code was dreaded by many Dutch lawyers, who disliked having to start their law studies all over again. Judges considered early retirement. Cram courses proved a remarkable commercial success. A new law review came into being.[10] But the introduction of the new Code did not prove to be the apocalypse, which some well-known antagonists had predicted.[11] To the contrary, it appears as if the Dutch were hardly impressed.[12] It would not be true to say that there have been no problems. But on the whole, the childbirth has been rather painless. This may be attributed to the fact that at the time of introduction, 1992, there already existed a good infrastructure.[13] Apart

[9] See A. S. Hartkamp, 'The Development of Dutch Private Law in a European Perspective', in E. Hondius, *Modern Trends in Tort Law, Dutch and Japanese Laws Compared* (Deventer: Kluwer 1999), 7, and B. Wessels, 'Civil Code Revision in the Netherlands: System, Contents and Future' (1994) 41 *Netherlands International Law Review* 163.

[10] *Kwartaalbericht Nieuw BW*, presently called *Nederlands Tijdschrift voor Burgerlijk Recht*

[11] J. M. van Dunné, E. A. A. Luijten, P. A. Stein, *Kosten en tekortkomingen van het Nieuw Burgerlijk Wetboek (boeken 3, 5 en 6)* (Rapport uitgebracht aan de vaste Commissie voor Justitie van de Tweede Kamer, Arnhem, 1990) 9, estimated the costs of the introduction at Hfl. 7,000 million (€3,200,000,000) for the first five years and Hfl. 15,000 million (€6,800,000,000) for the first twenty years.

[12] H. C. F. Schoordijk, 'Antwoord aan Barendnecht', *RM Themis* 1995, at p. 148: 'The New Civil Code has left me untouched, I hardly experience its introduction.'

[13] The parliamentary history of the new Code was easily accessible. In order to be able to handle a Code, it is necessary that the materials pertaining to its interpretation are readily available. When a codification period stretches over nearly fifty years, it can be imagined that the parliamentary proceedings are not easy to consult. A solution to this problem is to bring together all such materials. This is what was done in the case of the Civil Code: *Parlementaire Geschiedenis van het Nieuwe Burgerlijk Wetboek*, edited by C. J. van Zeben, J. W. du Pon, M. M. Olthof and later W. H. M. Reehuis and E. E. Slob.

from the question which value should be attached to the parliamentary proceedings when interpreting the law,[14] it is of interest that this history can be found, when one wants to find out its historical origin, what examples the legislature had in mind, which foreign legislation served as an example, etc. It should be added that the really novel and sometimes revolutionary provisions of the Code have as yet hardly been used. Also, the judicial tools have remained largely unaffected.

The introduction of provisions on the contract for medical services in the new Code will be dealt with below in Section 6.

4   Codes of conduct, disciplinary boards

The conduct of medical doctors is governed not only by liability rules, but also by codes of conduct, codes of ethics, etc., where the maintenance of the rules is left to disciplinary boards. In the Netherlands, the courts often rely on this form of self-regulation as establishing the standard of care.[15] This is particularly true in medical matters. It should be observed that the acceptance is greater if the self-regulation is bilateral, that is in agreement with in this case patients' organisations. In the Netherlands, such agreements are not uncommon.[16]

5   A history of liability in private law

In the Netherlands, medical liability is a rather new phenomenon. Although perhaps not unknown in the nineteenth century, it was then rarely brought into operation. In other liberal professions one finds similar developments. When did medical liability really begin to develop? There is no evidence that this was prompted by the American example. Rather, it is suggested, the rise of medical liability – including hospital

---

[14] *Cf.* W. H. M. Reehuis, 'De wil van de wetgever: over het gezag van wettekst en parlementaire geschiedenis', in *Rechtsvinding onder het NBW, Een Groningse kijk op het nieuwe vermogensrecht* (Deventer: Kluwer, 1992), 57–72, and for an English point of view my paper 'Looking at Hansards: Should Courts be Allowed to Switch on the Light? Some Observations on Constructing Statutes in the Light of their Parliamentary History', in A. Brzozowski, W. Kocot, K. Michalowska (eds.), *W kierunku europeizacji prawa prywatnego/Ksiega pamiatkowa dedykowana profesorowi Jerzemu Rajskiemu – Towards Europeanization of Private Law/Essays in Honour of Professor Jerzy Rajski* (Warsaw: Beck, 2007), 111–18.

[15] I. Giesen, *Alternatieve regelgeving en privaatrecht* (Deventer: Kluwer, 2007).

[16] See my paper 'Self-regulation in Consumer Matters on a European Level', in F. Cafaggi (ed.), *Reframing Self-Regulation in European Private Law* (Alphen aan den Rijn: Kluwer, 2006), 239–47.

liability – has developed first together with tort law in general and second on the crest of the patients' rights movement. The latter will be dealt with below in Section 6. Tort liability has developed rapidly in the Netherlands. The main thrust came from a case handed down on 31 January 1919, *Lindenbaum v. Cohen,*[17] the nearest Dutch equivalent to *Donoghue v. Stevenson.*[18]

6   The patients' rights movement

The Dutch regulation of the relation between patient and doctor or hospital all began with the patients' rights movement, which was started by two academics, Jaap Rang and Henk Leenen. The aims of the patients' rights movement were first set out in 1973 by Professor Jaap Rang in his inaugural lecture at Leyden University, entitled 'Patients' rights'. In his many publications, the late Henk Leenen has also actively sought codification of patients' rights. This led the government to ponder the question how to implement such rights. One possibility, to leave it to the medical profession itself, was rejected. Legislation seemed more appropriate. But what kind of legislation: should it be of an administrative nature, by requiring a licence allowing hospitals to practise only under certain conditions? Should it be criminal law, based on the idea that any medical treatment not consented to amounts to battery? Or should civil law prevail?

The Dutch legislature has opted for the private law solution and within this for contract and not tort as a basis. This approach has the advantage that it stresses the equality of health care provider and patient. Its drawbacks are that such equality often is non-existent, as in the case of children, the mentally ill, unconscious patients, etc. Also, the contract is a very one-sided affair with many patients' rights and only two rights for health care providers: those for payment and for the possibility to end the relation when a patient does not cooperate. Yet the contract option has the major advantage that a contract is based on party autonomy. This is a natural habitat for such patients' rights as the right to information, to consent and to access to medical records. The disadvantages set out above have partly been met by the Act. Psychiatric patients and minors who cannot formulate their will properly are to be represented under article 7:465. Article 7:464 declares the Medical Services Act of equal applicability for those situations in which the patient is examined by a medical examiner.

---

[17] Hoge Raad 31 January 1919, *Nederlandse Jurisprudentie* 1919, 161.
[18] [1932] AC 562.

The Act not only applies to the activities of physicians in relation to their patients, but applies to all contracts whereby a health care provider undertakes to provide medical treatment. The health care provider can be either a natural or a legal person, e.g. a hospital. This implies that the patient sometimes has two contracts; one with the hospital for nursing and care and one with the physician for examination and treatment. This is different if the physician is employed by the hospital. The fact that the hospital is seen as a health care provider, however, does not mean that it can interfere with the fiduciary relationship between doctor and patient. Medical treatment includes the treatment of dentists, midwives and so-called related nursing. Activities of pharmacists are excluded.

The formation of a medical services contract does not in itself raise any specific issues. Once a relationship has been entered into, a physician no longer has the right to terminate this relationship. Only if he has 'important reasons' is he entitled to do so, according to article 7:460. Having an affair with the patient and poaching a patient are two such circumstances which are mentioned in the explanatory report.

Quite a different question is whether or not a patient is entitled to specific costly treatment such as surgery. This is a budgetary question, which, as in other countries, has led to much political controversy. Unlike the situation elsewhere, Dutch courts occasionally have ordered hospitals to give a plaintiff a specific treatment,[19] although usually this will be denied.[20]

Under Dutch law, physicians are now obliged to inform the patient clearly and, if requested, in writing, about the proposed examination and treatment and about the developments concerning the examination, the treatment and the condition of the patient's health. Dutch law in this regard is now moving in the direction of German law, which has developed the right of informed consent earlier.[21] English law, on the other hand, has been reluctant to accept this American doctrine.[22] The right to be informed is not unlimited. Paragraph 3 of article 7:448 provides for a

---

[19] Court of Appeal, 's-Hertogenbosch 2 July 1990, *Nederlandse Jurisprudentie* 1990, 809.
[20] For instance Court of Appeal, The Hague 7 March 1991, *Tijdschrift voor Gezondheidsrecht* 1991, 394.
[21] C.C.M. Nadorp-van der Borg, 'Het recht van de patiënt op informatie in het Duitse civiele recht. Een voorbeeld?', *Tijdschrift voor Gezondheidsrecht* 1995, 1.
[22] *Hills v. Potter* [1984] 1 WLR 641. See also *Sidaway v. Board of Governors of Bethlem Royal Hospital and the Maudsley Hospital* [1985] AC 87. S.A.M. McLean, 'Litigating Disputes in Consent to Medical Treatment: The United Kingdom Position', in S.A.M. McLean (ed.), *Compensation for Damage/An International Perspective* (Aldershot: Ashgate, 1993), 35 at 42 saw some openings in this case for a development towards informed consent.

therapeutical exception. The patient not only has a right to be informed, but, under article 7:449, has a right not to be informed as well. If the dangers of not being informed, for the patient himself or for others, outweigh the benefits, information shall, however, be provided. The Act does not provide for a right to be informed for the patient's proxies.

Under article 7:450 physicians need prior consent for any act emanating from a medical services contract. For patients who are not competent, the Act assigns this authority to others. Minors who are not competent are represented by their parents. Though several authors have expressed their aversion against family members acting as proxies for a patient,[23] article 7:465 paragraph 3 appoints the spouse or the partner as proxy for the incompetent adult. In the absence of such persons, other family members will be appointed. This is only different if the patient has made a living will or appointed a proxy himself. The proxy will take all decisions concerning the health care of the patient. According to article 7:465 paragraph 4, the health care provider does not have to comply with the proxy's decisions in so far as they are incompatible with the level of care which a conscientious care provider has to provide.

Under the Medical Services Act, a living will containing a refusal is recognised. According to article 7:450 paragraph 3 the refusal has to be made in writing while the person still is competent. Furthermore the living will has to contain the clear wishes of the patient. The health care provider is allowed to deviate from the living will if he has legitimate reasons. Unlike in the United Kingdom, a patient can legally ask for euthanasia in his living will. The physician, however, won't be allowed to practise euthanasia if the legal requirements are not met.[24] He is never obliged to answer the request. The patient also has the possibility to appoint a proxy who will take all decisions concerning the health care of the incompetent patient. According to article 7:465 paragraph 3 this appointment has to be made in writing while the person is still competent. The health care provider does not have to comply with the proxy's decisions in so far as they are incompatible with the level of care a conscientious care provider has to

---

[23] See H. J. J. Leenen, *Handboek Gezondheidsrecht, Rechten van mensen in de gezond-heidszorg* (Alphen aan den Rijn: Kluwer, 1988), 178–81. J. K. M. Gevers, 'De onbekwame meerderjarige patiënt', *Nederlands Tijdschrift voor Geneeskunde* 1987, 2094 (*contra*) and E.-B. van Veen, 'Plaats voor een onbenoemde wettelijk vertegenwoordiger van onbekwame patinten?', *Tijdschrift voor Familie en Jeugdrecht* 1993, 6–10 (*pro*). See for the United Kingdom: P. D. G. Skegg, *Law, Ethics and Medicine, Studies in Medical Law* (Oxford: Oxford University Press, 1984), 72, 73.

[24] E.Ph.R. Sutorius, D. J. Jansen, 'De juridische status van het levenstestament', *Ars Aequi* 1991, 994.

provide. It is generally accepted that the proxy cannot ask for euthanasia unless there is a clear request (for example expressed in writing) from the patient himself.[25]

The Medical Services Act lays down several patients' rights relating to his privacy. These rights apply to both physical privacy as well as to confidentiality concerning data. Before setting out these rights, it should be observed that under article 7:454 a physician is allowed and even required to set up a medical record, which he shall preserve for at least ten years. Under article 7:455 the physician shall have to destroy the record at the patient's request, unless keeping the record is in the interest of another patient or required by statute. Unlike English law, the Medical Services Act's article 7:456 allows patients an unlimited access to all medical records, unless another person's right to privacy might thereby be infringed. For providing copies, the doctor may claim reasonable costs.

The right for physical privacy implies that the physician carries out his activities outside the perception of others, although other persons whose professional assistance is required are allowed to be present. Confidentiality concerning data implies that the physician will not supply data to others than the patient without his consent. Other professionals directly concerned with the treatment of the patient may receive necessary data as well. The supply of data, however, may take place without the patient's consent if these data are required by law, e.g. in case of certain contagious diseases. Provision without consent may also take place for statistic or scientific research. Article 7:458 paragraph 1 then, however, requires that it is impossible to ask the patient for his consent. The health care provider has to make sure that the data will not be convertible to the patient.

In case the patient is not content with the services supplied under the contract, several remedies are available. None of these remedies have been laid down in the Medical Services Act itself. First of all the patient can file his complaint with a grievance committee, e.g. of patients' organisations, organisations of the profession concerned or of the hospital itself. Furthermore the patient can always file a complaint with the disciplinary council. In case of severe mishaps the Public Prosecutor may decide to start a penal procedure. However, if the patient wants compensation, he will have to start a civil procedure on the ground that a breach of contract

---

[25] H. J. J. Leenen, 'Incompetente meerderjarigen, vertegenwoordiging van de patiënt', *Tijdschrift voor Gezondheidsrecht* 1988, 229; J. K. M. Gevers, 'De onbekwame meerderjarige patiënt', *Nederlands Tijdschrift voor Geneeskunde* 1987, 2095. For England, see now the Mental Capacity Act 2005.

has taken place. In case the health care provider is employed by a hospital or medical legal person, the employer will be summoned.

The question whether or not arbitration in medical matters should be introduced has arisen in the Netherlands.[26] Whereas in countries such as England the discussion seems to have been prompted by the high cost of ordinary litigation, in the Netherlands on the other hand, the absence of patient redress has been at the basis of the movement. This 'access to justice' argument has led the Dutch government to actively sponsor and subsidise a scheme of consumer arbitration tribunals, of which there are now twenty, most of them operating under the umbrella of a bipartisan consumer-industry organisation. The idea has been developed to integrate an arbitration tribunal for medical complaints in the existing consumer complaints board scheme. By the end of 1996, with the cooperation of the *Koninklijke Nederlandse Maatschappij voor de Geneeskunst*, an experimental patients' claims tribunal was set up. The experiment was successful and since 2001 the complaints tribunal operates permanently under the auspices of the general organisation of complaints tribunals. In 2008, the tribunal received fifty-four complaints and handed down thirty-four awards.[27]

7   Standard of care

In the 1970s, Dutch authors were at odds with one another as to the standard of care to be applied by physicians. Should they exercise the customary care or good care? The distinction may not at once be clear, but this will become so when one realises that in some regions or hospitals the customary care may be inferior to the care which is considered good care by the profession at large. Under article 7:453 of the Medical Services Act, the physician shall apply the care of a conscientious physician and he shall act in accordance with the responsibility emanating from the professional standard. Before this test was enacted, it had already been accepted by the Dutch supreme court, the *Hoge Raad*, in *Speeckaert v. Gradener*.[28] Article 7:453 does not seem to give physicians and courts much guidance as to what is a conscientious physician. One of the more specific provisions lays down that in principle the physician whom the patient has contracted with shall also perform the treatment. Here the

[26] W. R. Kastelein, *Van klagen naar klachtrecht/Het klachtrecht van de patiënt in de gezondheidszorg* (PhD thesis, Amsterdam/Gouda, 1992).

[27] Jaarverslag de Geschillencommissie (2009), 22.

[28] Hoge Raad 9 November 1990, *Nederlandse Jurisprudentie* 1991, 26.

model contract, which in advance of legislation has been drafted by the *Koninklijke Nederlandse Maatschappij voor Geneeskunst* (comparable to the British Medical Association) in cooperation with the *Landelijke Patiënten/Consumenten Platform*, a large patients organisation, may provide some useful additions.[29] Thus under article 11, the physician shall use fit materials and means; according to article 12, one physician shall be appointed as the contact person in case more of them are concerned with the treatment. Under article 32 the physician shall appoint a capable and competent locum. Article 36 entitles the patient to a second opinion and, on a different level, article 38 provides that the physician shall specify his bill.

Various questions may be raised concerning the standard of care. Let us take the following hypothetical case. A 45-year-old woman is taken to the hospital for treatment of a tumour in her breast. It is unclear whether this is a malignant growth or not. Under anaesthesia, the growth is taken away and the tissue is examined by a pathologist. The pathologist examines the tissue under low temperature (–20°C) and concludes that the tissue is malignant. Thereupon, the surgeon removes most of the breast. Afterwards, upon closer examination of the tissue, by using a parafine test, it becomes clear that the tissue was not malignant and that the breast had been removed needlessly. The woman sues the surgeon for damages. She claims: (i) that the pathologist has made a mistake in the diagnosis, for which the surgeon is responsible; (ii) that since the parafine test gives a clearer picture, this test should have been used instead of the freeze test; (iii) that the surgeon should have pointed out the risks involved in the freeze test. The surgeon invokes the following defence: as of the time of the surgery, there were available two methods to test a tissue. One method, chosen in this case, consisted of testing the tissue while the patient was under anaesthesia; in case the pathologist concluded the tissue to be malignant, the breast could be removed instantly under the same anaesthesia. The other method, generally not opted for by Dutch physicians, consisted of removing a tissue, then ending the operation, using the parafine test, and then, when the test was negative (as it was in the large majority of cases), operating on the patient again, this time to remove the breast. From American statistics it appears that the freeze test only gives an incorrect diagnosis in 1% of all cases. Although outside the Netherlands,

---

[29] As to the legal nature of the model contract see C. J. J. M. Stolker, 'De nieuwe Wet geneeskundige behandelingsovereenkomst en het juridisch belang van de Modelregeling arts-patiënt', *Nederlands Tijdschrift voor Burgerlijk Recht* 1994, 115–19.

it was generally advised to use the parafine test, the Dutch Association of Surgeons has advised its members to use the freeze test.

Of the various issues raised by this case, the one which is dealt with here involves the defence that it is the professional organisation of surgeons which has set the rules. Although in general, this should be a valid defence, this is not always the case. When professional organisations in other countries have set higher standards, a professional exercising the care of a conscientious physician should follow the foreign example according to article 7:453. Under English law, the application of the *Bolam* test would lead to a different result: 'in 1986 there was a respectable and responsible body of professional opinion who would not have warned in the circumstances with which this case is concerned'.[30]

Should doctors inform their patients as to the risks of the treatment they propose? This is the case in the Netherlands. According to article 7:453 of the Dutch Civil Code, a health care provider shall exercise the level of care expected from a conscientious health care provider. At first sight, this test is virtually identical with the English *Bolam* and the Scottish *Hunter* tests.[31] In fact, it is not. The 'standards of reasonably competent medical men at the time' are quite different from 'conscientious health care providers', because in the latter case it is the court which decides, not the medical colleagues as in the first case. The impact of informed consent is but one of the examples to show the difference. At this point I wish to enter a first personal reflection. The impact of the law on informed consent has in my personal observation been tremendous. Fifty years ago, patients may often have been informed adequately about their diseases and the treatment, as well as hospital discharge, but many were not informed at all. Whether this is only because of the introduction of an obligation in the Civil Code, or also because of changed ideas in the medical profession itself, is difficult to say, but there is no doubt that practices have changed fundamentally. Nowadays, information is the standard and failure to inform will generally be blamed.

Informing the patient is not the only point on which jurisdictions may differ where the standard of care is concerned. Diagnosis, advice and treatment are the three traditional medical functions. Here we find that Europe's small jurisdictions are sometimes running behind. The reason

---

[30] *Heath v. West Berkshire Health Authority* [1992] 3 Med LR 57, 59. This case law has been criticised by John Eekelaar, 'Consent to Treatment: Legal and Empirical Questions', in R. Dingwall (ed.), *Socio-legal Aspects of Medical Practice* (London: Butterworths, 1989), 21, 24. The same would apply to Scotland under the *Hunter v. Hanley* doctrine.

[31] See above pp. 42–6 and 60–2.

for this may be precisely the fact that they are small: as two authors have observed, 'where a legal system by its size tends to engender less litigation there are fewer occasions on which courts are presented with facts suitable to test or to clarify the application of existing legal rules'.[32] However, when precedents from the ordinary courts are lacking, there are other means of finding the law. One common solution in such case is to take into consideration the awards of disciplinary bodies. One must of course always bear in mind that disciplinary bodies and liability law serve different functions. But often, situations are very similar and practitioners may therefore profit from the body of disciplinary awards. It is therefore of interest that such awards are reported.

Another way of filling the gap is that of taking recourse to comparative law. French and German case law especially are so all-embracing, that it will not be difficult to find precedents which may be useful in other jurisdictions. Once again, these decisions have no decisive authority, but their arguments may have persuasive powers. In fact, small jurisdictions such as this author's home country often find inspiration from legislation, case law and doctrinal works from other countries. Small jurisdictions seem to have an advantage on this point which emanates from the very fact that they are small. In the larger jurisdictions, courts are less inclined to look abroad for guidance or inspiration. One of the hindrances is that of language. Not all French judges read German and the reverse is probably also true. It is therefore of some importance that case law is made available not only in the country's own language, but in other languages as well.[33]

In discussing the standard of care, I have so far only referred to the care of individual providers of health care. We should also take into account the standard of care of institutions, such as hospitals and – social and private – insurance companies. When looking at the statistics of complaints filed in various hospitals, one is sometimes appalled at the fact that in some hospitals much more, up to tenfold, complaints are lodged than in others. This may of course be a matter of complaint consciousness: urban patients may find it easier to complain than those in rural areas. But a better explanation is that the organisation of certain hospitals lags behind. No protocol has for instance been made for taking over of patients by the

---

[32] R. Zimmermann and S. Whittaker (eds.), *Good Faith in European Contract Law* (Cambridge: Cambridge University Press, 2000), 655.

[33] This is one of the major functions of the wave of European private law reviews such as *Europa e Diritto Privato*, the *European Review of Private Law (Europäische Zeitschrift für Privatrecht)*, the *Zeitschrift für Europäisches Privatrecht* and the *Zeitschrift für Gesamteuropäisches Privatrecht*.

day shift. It is therefore interesting that in new regulations of tort liability, such as the Swiss draft legislation (which seems to have no chance of adoption in the short term), liability for faults in the organisation are especially dealt with.

8   Proof and causation

The Medical Services Act does not lay down any rules as to the burden of proof. In tort law, the *Hoge Raad* has accepted a reversal of the burden of proof in a limited number of cases where safety norms have been infringed. Ever since 1953, a great number of cases have accepted this reversal, but only in traffic accidents and workmen's compensation. Medical liability cases have not been subjected to the reversal rule.[34] The *Hoge Raad* has, however, developed a line which comes close to a reversal of the burden of proof: the health care provider shall give the patient the documents which will enable him to prove the care provider's fault.[35] This rule is even applied where the patient complains that the physician has not given him sufficient information.[36]

Perhaps the reader will allow me a second personal reflection. At the time after these discovery cases had been handed down I had to teach a number of continuing legal education classes to nurses. To say that as the messenger of the bad news I was nearly molested is perhaps overstating the issue, but I certainly did not feel comfortable with their criticism. The cases just mentioned together with some other decisions were perceived as a legal plot against the medical profession. The shock effect they caused clearly helped to change the practices amongst members of the medical profession.

9   Who is held liable?

During surgery, a needle is left in a patient's stomach. The surgery is performed by the famous Professor Nuboer and his team, including nurses who are employed by the hospital. The patient cannot prove who acted negligently and therefore loses the case.[37] With Dutch physicians

---

[34] M. J. J. de Ridder, *Tijdschrift voor Gezondheidsrecht* 2006, 216–28.

[35] *Timmer v. Deutman*, Hoge Raad 20 November 1987, *Nederlandse Jurisprudentie* 1988, 500.

[36] *Schepers v. De Bruijn*, Hoge Raad 18 February 1994, *Nederlandse Jurisprudentie* 1994, 368.

[37] *Aarts v. Nuboer*, Hoge Raad 31 May 1968, *Nederlandse Jurisprudentie* 1968, 323.

exercising their profession either as independent professionals or as hospital employees, it has always been a major difficulty for patients to find out with whom they have contracted. The difficulty especially becomes apparent when a nurse has acted negligently. Who is the nurse's employer? Article 7:462 now solves this problem by making the hospital jointly liable in the event of any deficiency for any treatment carried out in the hospital. Under the present Civil Code, the hospital would therefore be liable in the *Nuboer* case. In the context of the ELD project, it is relevant to observe that even a case with a negative outcome for the development of medical liability may serve to promote law reform. The *Nuboer* case has always been considered a shame and has served as an incentive for the enactment of article 7:462 mentioned above.

10   The measure of damages

The law relating to damages is in itself highly developed and with reference to medical liability, many issues could be discussed at length. Instead, two specific issues related to medical cases will be discussed in some more depth. They involve what sometimes is called wrongful birth and wrongful life, and exemption clauses – the latter will be dealt with in the following section. 'Wrongful birth' typically is about a case where a health care provider has allegedly either committed an error causing a sterilisation not to have the desired effect or failure to provide information as to the remaining pregnancy risks. It is now well established case law in the Netherlands that this may consitute a breach of contract which will entitle the parents to compensation for damages. The leading Dutch case involving wrongful birth[38] is discussed in the General Introduction above (Chapter 1). What is perhaps less known is that the first cases were by no means uncontested. If the reader allows me a third personal reflection, I vividly remember one of the earliest, if not the first, cases. In the Radboud Hospital of the Catholic University of Nijmegen – as it was then called – a woman upon her request was sterilised by way of fallopian rings in 1979. Four years later the woman unexpectedly became pregnant and in 1984, at the age of 43, gave birth to a healthy child. The insurers of the hospital were prepared to compensate some baby clothes and other necessities, but not to pay for the child's upbringing, estimated at Hfl. 31,000 (some €14,500). The parents' claim for the child's upbringing was honoured by the District

---

[38] Hoge Raad 21 February 1997, *Nederlandse Jurisprudentie* 1999, 145 (note by C. J. H. Brunner).

Court of Arnhem.[39] Where do the personal reflections come in? I was at the time a member of the mixed legal-medical board which advised the insurer of the hospital in liability cases. During the entire existence of the board, the insurance company, although not formally bound, always followed our advisory opinions. The director never tried to influence our opinions. In this particular case, the director of the insurance company did not do so either, but he did address us to air his grave concern over the future of medical liability after the decision of the District Court. In retrospect this was a case where liability really changed.

Why did it change? Dutch cases usually don't give a clue – the exception being the *Hoge Raad*, where at least the conclusions of the Advocate General often give an insight into the reasons for a decision. In the case of the Arnhem District Court I am convinced that it was a mistake of the hospital's attorney which may have contributed to the court's decision. The mistake was to argue that the plaintiff could have had an abortion, thereby ending the pregnancy and her damages. This was a mistake not only because the attorney obviously acted against the views of the *Catholic* hospital which he represented. It also apparently irritated the court. There is no doubt that had the Arnhem District Court not compensated the plaintiff, some other case would have done so later. But if one wants a clear answer to the question, when the law on wrongful birth did change in the Netherlands, 14 December 1989 is as close as one can get.

Now turning to 'wrongful life', the leading case in the Netherlands is the *Kelly* case, *Leids Universitair Medisch Centrum v. Kelly Molenaar*.[40] The case involved a child born with a severe disability. The disability could be attributed to a genetic chromosomal defect of a hereditary nature in the father's family. During her pregnancy, Kelly's mother had brought the possibility of such genetic defect to the attention of her obstetrician. The obstetrician decided not to take any action. Had the mother been informed of the danger for her child, she would, she alleged, have opted for abortion. The obstetrician clearly had not lived up to professional standards. He and his employer, an academic hospital, admitted liability. That the mother herself was entitled to compensation, was no longer an issue in the procedure before the *Hoge Raad*. Rather, the award of compensation to the child has been hotly debated.

---

[39] *Flierman v. Stichting Katholieke Universiteit*, Rb. Arnhem 14 December 1989, n° 1988/3291.

[40] Hoge Raad 18 March 2005, *Nederlandse Jurisprudentie* 2006, 606 (note by J. M. B. Vranken).

Like the French *Perruche* case, the *Kelly* case led to a debate in Dutch law reviews – but unlike *Perruche* it has not resulted in a proposal for law reform and such proposal is now out of the question.[41]

The *Kelly* case is the first one in which the *Hoge Raad* pronounced itself on liability for a failed diagnosis with regard to an unborn child. It is not the first on questions relating to what is sometimes – wrongfully, according to most Dutch authors (who after dismissing this terminology still make use of it) – called 'wrongful birth' and 'wrongful life'. The first such case, which has achieved notoriety, is the case which in the *Ius commune* casebook on tort law is called the 'Missing IUD'.[42] In that case, liability was assumed for the costs of upbringing of a healthy baby, born after a contraceptive device installed by a doctor had failed to be successful.[43] The importance of this case is illustrated by the fact that it is one of the few Dutch cases taken up in the tort casebook, which aims at establishing a thesaurus of important cases for further use in Europe (Van Gerven).[44]

More in general, the *Kelly* case is in line with a long range of cases, in which the *Hoge Raad* has interpreted the Civil Code with some liberty. One other example is the *DES* case. From 1953–67 a drug called 'diethylstilbestrol', better known as 'DES', was prescribed as a sedative in the Netherlands, as it was in other countries. DES was supposed to prevent miscarriages, but instead happened to cause grave side effects. Daughters of the women who used the drug developed a special form of cancer in the uro-genital system. Not only did the victims suffer a medical plight, their legal plight also came to the fore. Could the manufacturers of the drug be

---

[41] This information was given to the author by circles close to the two Christian parties which together with the Labour Party form the present Dutch government.

[42] Hoge Raad 21 February 1997, *Nederlandse Jurisprudentie* 1999, 145.

[43] The key part of the *dictum* in the 'Missing IUD' case is the following:

> At issue is the medical fault of a physician who failed to fulfil his contractual obligation to treat the plaintiff woman. As a result of a combined reading of Arts. 6:74, 6:94 and 6:98 Civil Code the physician is therefore liable for all material damage which may be seen to be related to the fault, to the extent that it should be imputed to him in accordance with Art. 6:98. (…) The damage for which compensation is asked here consists of expenses which, by their very amount, must in principle be deemed to influence the financial situation of the family until the child comes of age. Such expenses are indisputably material damage. (…) Contrary to what the Court of Appeal considered, that is not inconsistent with the legal duty of parents to take care of and educate the child; rather it follows from it that the expenses incurred necessarily have to be made, and therefore constitute a financial burden and material damage.

[44] W. van Gerven, J. Laver, P. Larouche (eds.), *Tort Law* (The Common Law of Europe Casebooks series, Oxford: Hart, 2000), 133–6.

held liable? This question raises a number of issues: did the manufacturers commit a tort? Are the victims time-barred from instituting proceedings? How to sue a manufacturer when one cannot prove who brought the drug into circulation? It is especially the latter issue which has come to be associated with DES cases. DES being a generic drug, it was marketed by a large number of manufacturers. Twenty-five years later it is all but impossible to prove which manufacturer produced the particular drug which was used by the mother of any victim. Does this mean that victims cannot be compensated? Not necessarily.

In order to find an equitable solution, American courts have introduced the notion of market share liability. In the landmark case *Sindell v. Abbott Laboratories*,[45] the California Supreme Court, followed thereafter by a number of courts in other states, held that in case the manufacturer cannot be traced, all manufacturers are liable for their share in the market. This 'market share liability' has attracted much attention in Europe, but has not been applied by European courts. Would it be adopted by the Dutch courts which were called upon to decide the *DES* case? On 28 April 1986, six DES daughters sued ten pharmaceutical companies before the Amsterdam (District) Court. The case was dismissed, as it was in appeal, basically on the ground that none of the victims could prove which of the defendant manufacturers had brought the particular drug into circulation. In cassation, Advocate-General Hartkamp asked the *Hoge Raad* to annul the decision on the ground that it did not follow the market share liability theory. The court went one step further. The court first dismissed the Appellate Court's rejection of article 6:99 of the Civil Code[46] as an obstacle to the daughters' case. 'When constructing this article', said the court, 'the text, the purpose and the parliamentary history of the law should be taken into consideration'. According to the *Hoge Raad*:

> the situation occurring in the present case is covered by this text: it must be assumed by way of supposition that the companies which marketed Des in the relevant period are each liable therefore on account of fault on their part, that the entire damage of each injured party may have resulted from each of these 'events' – the marketing – and that at any rate the damage was the result of one of these 'events'. If the Court of Appeal (…) imposed the

---

[45] 607 Pacific Reporter 2d 924.

[46] The text of article 6:99 reads: 'Where the damage may have resulted from two or more events for each of which a different person is liable, and where it has been determined that the damage has arisen from at least one of these events, the obligation to repair the damage rests upon each of these persons, unless he proves that the damage is not the result of the event for which he himself is liable' (translation Haanappel, Deventer, 1990).

requirement that the alleged facts must include a 'specific act', it made a
requirement which does not find support in the text of article 6:99.

As to the purpose, the Court continued:

> The application of the article in a situation like the one involved in the
> present case is also in keeping with its purpose. The article aims at remov-
> ing the unreasonableness that the injured party would have to bear the
> damage himself because he is unable to prove whose act was the cause of
> his damage. This is the difficulty of providing evidence with which the
> injured parties are confronted in the present case.

Then comes the most difficult element: how to explain away the absence
of any reference to this kind of case in the parliamentary proceedings. It
should be mentioned that unlike the United Kingdom, where only since
the end of 1992 consultation of Hansard's, when constructing legislation,
has been allowed,[47] on the Continent this construction method has a long-
standing tradition. This is how the *Hoge Raad* countered this argument:

> It is true that in the 'Toelichting Meijers' and in the parliamentary docu-
> ments there is no mention of a situation like the one occurring in the pre-
> sent case in connection with the Des product, but it is likely that at the
> time this type lay beyond the range of conceivable situations. Therefore it
> may not be concluded from the fact that this situation was not discussed,
> that the article does not apply in such situation.

Another important point, argued the *Hoge Raad*:

> is that the system accepted by the Court of Appeal leads to an unaccept-
> able result. Even though in the present case it must be assumed by way of
> supposition that each of the Pharmaceutical Companies was at fault by
> marketing Des and that the Des-Daughters sustained serious injuries as a
> result of the use of Des by their mothers, in this system the Des-daughters
> will nevertheless be denied any claim for damages merely because they
> are unable to state from which producer the Des tablets taken by their
> mothers originated.[48]

---

[47] *Pepper v. Hart* [1993] 1 All ER 42.
[48] Why did the *Hoge Raad* not accept the American market share liability, as advocated by
its Advocate-General? This is the *Hoge Raad's* answer:

> (…) it is unsatisfactory that this system lays the risk of insolvency of one of the
> producers and also the risk that a producer has ceased to exist or can no longer
> be traced, with the victims and not with the producers. It is also burdensome
> that the victims will have to bring claims against as many producers as possible
> and that the market share of each of the producers will have to be established
> in the litigation between the victims and the producers. From the standpoint
> of victim protection, moreover, there is no need for market share liability in a

The Appellate Court had not applied article 6:99, because the DES daughters had not stated who belonged to the circle of persons who had marketed DES. The Appellate Court had not required that all such persons be summoned in the procedure, correctly so, according to the *Hoge Raad*, since it sufficed for an injured party to summon one of the persons liable. The Court continued:

> Likewise, it is not a requirement that the injured party alleges – and prove – which persons belong to the circle of persons liable. Even in the traditional situation falling within the scope of article 6:99, where several persons fire a rifle or throw stones in the same direction, such a requirement would already lead to an unreasonable result: if it is impossible to identify all riflemen or stone throwers, the injured party would have to bear his damage himself. In a situation like the one under review a requirement like the one just referred to would all the more lead to an unreasonable result: the injured party would have to bear her own damage if she is unable to identify all the producers which marketed Des in the relevant period, even though in fact such identification of producers will be virtually impossible.[49]

What about the defence that DES was also marketed by producers who are not liable? This is what the Court had to say on this point:

> it is conceivable that it will be established that in the relevant period Des was also marketed by one or more producers who are not liable

situation like the one occurring in the present case, since each of the producers is in principle liable for the entire damage, as has been ruled above.

[49] As to the burden of proof, the Court has stated the following:

> Each of the Des-daughters will have alleged sufficient facts by alleging with respect to each of the Pharmaceutical Companies, as in fact each of them did in the present proceedings:
>
> (i) that the Pharmaceutical Company in question marketed Des in the relevant period and is liable therefor on account of a fault committed by such company;
>
> (ii) that there are also one or more other producers – whether or not joined as defendants – who also marketed Des in the relevant period and who is/are also liable for it because of fault; and
>
> (iii) that she has suffered damage and that the damage is the result of the use of Des, but that it is no longer possible to establish from which producer the Des that was taken originated.
>
> In principle the burden of proof of the above rests with the Des-daughter in question.
>
> The concluding words of article 6:99 entail that as a rebuttal of his liability each of the Pharmaceutical Companies may allege and if necessary prove towards each of the Des-daughters that the damage of the Des-daughter in question is not the result of the use of any Des marketed by him.

therefore because there is no question of fault and that the damage of the Des-daughter in question may also have been caused by such producer.[50] This will not release the other producers from their liability for the entire damage unless in the given circumstances which include the degree of risk that the damage of the Des-daughter in question was caused by Des originating from a producer who is not liable, such liability would be unacceptable according to criteria of reasonableness and equity.[51]

The *DES* decision has met with a positive reception in the Netherlands. A majority of writers is happy with the result,[52] but the decision has also met with criticism.[53] Indeed, few Dutch lawyers would have predicted the outcome of this procedure, their type of argument still being based on Civil Code-related arguments. Since the present Civil Code at the time was of such recent origin (it entered into force on 1 January 1992), it was generally presumed that the Court would stick to these arguments. Instead, the *Hoge Raad* uses policy arguments, just as an American court would. Since such arguments always must play some role, it is better to bring them out into the open, in order that a decision can be judged on its real arguments. This is the major gain which *DES* has brought the Dutch.

I have given the *DES* case quite a lengthy treatment, because it serves as an example for a number of Supreme Court decisions in which the (new) Civil Code was constructed in a sometimes astounding liberal way. Other

---

[50] This case was not decided on the basis of the EC Directive on Product Liability and its implementation in the Dutch Civil Code. As the *Hoge Raad* stated, this is 'already for the mere reason that this is a case about liability for products which were marketed before 1985 while article 17 in conjunction with article 19 shows that the directive does not apply to these in any case'.

[51] As for recourse between the various manufacturers, the Court is curt. It says 'that the producers, who are jointly and severally liable to the injured parties for the entire damage, have mutual recourse, so that in principle they will not have to bear more damages, eventually, than their share in the total damage. Anyway, since recourse is not a point of discussion in the present proceedings, it need not be decided here in which proportion each of the producers will have to contribute to the damages.' And a little further: 'It need not be decided here whether the market share of each of the producers may be a relevant factor in the determination of the proportional contribution to be made by each of the producers.'

[52] J. Hijma, *Ars Aequi* 1993, 123; P. Ingelse, *Nederlands Juristenblad* 1992, 1403; J. Knottenbelt, *Nemesis* 1993/5, 23; G. J. Rijken and J. G. J. Rinkes, *Tijdschrift voor Consumentenrecht* 1992, 325; A. J. O. van Wassenaer van Catwijck, *Verkeersrecht* 1993, n° 19 and myself, *Tijdschrift voor Gezondheidsrecht* 1993, 382.

[53] By A. J. Akkermans, *Proportionele aansprakelijkheid bij onzeker causaal verband* (PhD thesis, Tilburg, 1997); L. Dommering-van Rongen, *Weekblad voor Privaatrecht en Notariaat* 6089; A. S. Hartkamp, in *Kabaal in Holland/Asscher-bundel*, (Arnhem, 1993), 76–8 and J. Spier, *Nederlands Tijdschrift voor Burgerlijk Recht* 1992, 193.

such cases have been handed down with regard to environmental liability, immaterial damages in case of death of a child,[54] reversal of the burden of proof, traffic liability, etc.

In the *Kelly* case, the following facts were considered relevant by the *Hoge Raad*.[55] Kelly's mother was born in 1966. In 1986 she had a miscarriage and in 1987 a curette. In 1988 she gave birth to a healthy daughter. In 1993, the mother became pregnant again. In 1994, she gave birth to a malformed child with a chromosomal defect, resulting in a physical and psychical disability. The pregnancy was under supervision of an obstetrician, whom the mother – in their first encounter – informed about a relative of her husband who had the same disability as Kelly would later appear to have. The mother asked whether she was eligible for a test. The obstetrician decided that this was not the case. Another relative of the husband also had the chromosomal defect; his wife was pregnant at the same time as Kelly's mother and her pregnancy was tested.

When Kelly's disability became apparent, her parents sued both the hospital and the obstetrician for damages: damages for the mother, the father and the daughter. The *Hoge Raad* decided that they all qualified for an award of damages. That the mother was entitled to damages was in itself, in the light of previous case law, not a very revolutionary view. That the father was likewise entitled to compensation was perhaps more

---

[54] Hoge Raad 22 February 2002, *Nederlandse Jurisprudentie* 2002, 240 (note J. B. M. Vranken).

[55] *Select bibliography*: W. H. van Boom, 'Compensatie voor geboorteschade – van aansprakelijkheid naar "*no-fault*"?', *Aansprakelijkheid, verzekering & schadevergoeding* 2006, 8; M. A. J. M. Buijsen, 'Over de toewijzing van de wrongful-life vordering in de zaak Kelly', *Nederlands Juristenblad* 2005, 830–4; T. Hartlief, 'Hollandse toestanden: de Hoge Raad over "wrongful life"', *Nederlands Tijdschrift voor Burgerlijk Recht* 2005, 232–48; W. R. Kastelein, 'Wrongful life claim', *Ars Aequi Katern* 2005, 5249–50; S. C. J. J. Kortmann and B. C. J. Hamel (eds.), *Wrongful birth en wrongful life* (Deventer: Kluwer, 2004); R. J. P. Kottenhagen, 'De wrongful life-vordering door de Hoge Raad erkend', *Tijdschrift voor Vergoeding Personenschade* 2005, 33–9; L. Ridderbroek, 'Wrongful life/Een wonderlijke vordering zonder ongewenste gevolgen', *Advocatenblad* 2005, 354–8; H. C. F. Schoordijk, 'Wrongful life mede vanuit rechtsvergelijkend perspectief', *Nederlands Tijdschrift voor Burgerlijk Recht* 2001, 212–18; C. H. Sieburgh, 'Schadevergoeding èn leven/Who is afraid of red, yellow and blue?', *Tijdschrift voor Privaatrecht* 2004, 1571–84; C. J. J. M. Stolker and M. P. Sombroek-van Doorm, 'De wrongful life-vordering: schadevergoeding of euthanasie?', *Nederlands Tijdschrift voor Burgerlijk Recht* 2003, 496–506; A. J. Verheij, 'Wrongful life: een goede uitspraak', *Gezondheidszorg Jurisprudentie plus* 2005, 73–9; B. van der Wiel and W. Wisman, 'Schadevergoeding bij "wrongful life"', *Bedrijfsjuridische berichten* 2005, 93–7; M. H. Wissink, 'Baby Kelly: één stap te ver?', *Gezondheidszorg Jurisprudentie plus* 2005, 61–8.

daring. But by far the most controversial decision was the Court's vision that Kelly was entitled to obtain damages.[56]

A major issue in this type of case is that of causation. In *McKay*, Lord Ackner held: 'The disabilities were caused by the rubella and not by the doctor (...). What then are her injuries which the doctor's negligence has caused? The answer must be that there are none in the accepted sense'.[57] In *Perruche*, the full French *Cour de cassation* in its Assemblée plénière came to a different conclusion: 'the negligence of the doctor and the laboratory in the performance of their contracts with Mme prevented her exercising her freedom to proceed to a termination of the pregnancy in order to avoid the birth of a handicapped child, the harm resulting to the child from such handicap was caused by that negligence and he can claim compensation for it'. Likewise, in *Kelly*, the *Hoge Raad* did not explicitly deal with the defence that there was no causal link between the fault of the doctor and harm resulting to the child.

Wissink finds the argument sympathetic but not convincing. Just suppose that Kelly's parents would not have alleged to have opted for abortion if given the choice, should Kelly's claim then have been denied and if so, is this an equitable result? The most convincing argument is to be found in the writings of Sieburgh.[58]

The Convention, if applicable at all, does not seem to prevent a court from accepting liability. The word 'resulting' does not preclude the acceptance of a causal link. Two further arguments which have been brought forward against allowing compensation are those of the human dignity and of the slippery slope.

The first-mentioned argument is that the award of expenses can only be based on the conception that the child itself must be regarded as damage or a damage element, and that such an award is contrary to the human dignity of the child, since its right to exist is thereby negated. This argument could be based on article 1 of the Oviedo Convention, which 'shall protect the dignity (...) of all human beings' ('*protègent l'être humain dans sa dignité*').[59] This line of reasoning must be welcomed. It is also applied

---

[56] An analysis of the award by the Court of Appeal may be found in T. Sheldon, 'Court Awards Damages to Disabled Child for Having been Born' (2002) 326 BMJ 784 and H. F. L. Nys and J. C. J. Dute, 'A Wrongful Existence in the Netherlands' (2004) 30 *Journal of Medical Ethics* 393.

[57] [1982] QB 1166, 1189.   [58] C. H. Sieburgh, above n. 55.

[59] The argument has basically already been dealt with in the 'Missing IUD' case, Hoge Raad 21 February 1997, *Nederlandse Jurisprudentie* 1999, 145:

in the *Kelly* case and even extended in that the *Hoge Raad* argues that to the contrary allowing compensation will enable Kelly to live as much as possible in human dignity.

Another possible argument against liability is that the next step along the slippery slope would then be that Kelly would sue her parents.[60] This argument is rejected by the *Hoge Raad*: 'Kelly is not entitled to a right not to be and has no right to interruption of the pregnancy of her mother. She is only entitled to compensation by the hospital and the obstetrician.' This means that the Convention's human dignity provision, which is applicable either directly or indirectly, does not stand in the way of allowing compensation, but to the contrary is used as an argument in favour of compensation.

Another argument of the hospital before the *Hoge Raad* was in order for a claim for damages to be eligible for allowance, there should be a situation to be compared to Kelly's disability. Well, such situation does not exist, is the argument, because non-existence for reason of abortion cannot be put forward in money. The *Hoge Raad* rejects the argument, arguing that the Dutch Civil Code's article 6:97 obliges the court to assess damages in a way which fits the character of the situation.

Can the Supreme Court's *Kelly* decision be reconciled with article 24 of the Convention on Human Rights and Biomedicine? The answer, it seems to me, to the extent that the Convention is applicable at all, is in the affirmative. A first hurdle to overcome is whether an omission to act may be equivalent to an act. It would appear that wherever a legislator speaks of 'acts', 'omissions' are included, unless the contrary is apparent. In Dutch law, for instance, article 6:169 BW specifically excludes mere

> As a further objection against the award of compensation of expenses for the care and education of the child, it has been alleged that such an award may result in the child being confronted later in life with the impression that it was not wanted by its parents, which may result in psychological damage to the child. The Hoge Raad does not regard this argument as convincing (...). In the first place, the argument interferes with the relationship between parents and child on a point which must, in principles, be left to be decided by the parents themselves. In the second place, to prevent an enlargement of the family is a wholly different matter than the issue of the acceptance of a child once it becomes an individual. The claim for compensation relates exclusively to the first, and not to the second point. In the third place, it may be assumed that parents are in general able to make it clear to the child that such an impression of rejection is incorrect, even apart from the fact that they themselves may contradict such an impression by raising the child with loving care.

[60] C. J. J. M. Stolker and M. P. Sombroek-van Doorm, 'De wrongful life-vordering: schadevergoeding of euthanasie?', *Nederlands Tijdschrift voor Burgerlijk Recht* 2003, 496, 503.

omissions.[61] Likewise, it seems evident that Kelly, the person involved, has suffered 'undue damage' as required by the Convention. Some doubt may concern the word 'resulting'. As we have seen above, the causal link between the obstetrician's failure to diagnose and the damage has been contested.

If we conclude that Kelly may fall under article 24, the question then is what value the arguments taken from the Oviedo Convention may be accorded. Two examples are the human dignity and the *tertium compatationis*. In my view these arguments should play a role,[62] but not in the sense that they would thwart liability.

The one remaining question is whether or not the Oviedo Convention is applicable at all. On the one hand, it does not purport to deal with all medical questions, but rather with the application of biology and medicine (*'protègent l'être humain dans sa dignité'*), as is stated in article 1 and repeated in article 27. Article 24 is to be found in Chapter VIII which is entitled 'Infringements of the provisions of the Convention' (*'Atteinte aux dispositions de la Convention'*). On the other hand, the Convention's provision on informed consent in article 5 does not specify a remedy. It might therefore be argued that article 24 does provide that remedy. But even if this argument is not accepted, I would still conclude that in the debate on arguments taken from international instruments the Convention could and should play a major role.

Once it is decided that the Convention either directly or indirectly plays a role, it is in particular the human dignity provision which may be used in favour of allowing compensation.

11   Exemption clauses

In health care, exemption clauses are not widespread. Unlike attorneys, medical doctors usually do not use stationery with a printed exemption clause at the bottom. Were they to employ such a clause, it is doubtful whether it would be valid. Under the Dutch Civil Code, the exemption clause

---

[61] 'A person who exercises parental authority or guardianship over a child of under fourteen years of age is liable for damage done to another by such conduct of that child *which must be considered as an act*, where this act, but for the child's age, could be imputed to him as an unlawful act' (*my italics*). See also article 6:165 BW for the liability of persons under fourteen themselves.

[62] Hartlief, above n. 55, at 247, argues that ethical arguments are usually not considered decisive by Dutch courts. An exception of course is the case of the Missing IUD, discussed above.

is plainly invalid: as the reason for introduction of the Medical Services Act is to protect the patient, abrogation of the patient's rights to his detriment is not allowed under article 7:478. Where jurisdictions have no such rule, the unfair contract terms legislation will usually take care of this.

Personally, I do not fully agree with the invalidity of all exemption clauses. If we take the example of a professional football player, who presents himself to a hospital for a knee operation, without disclosing the fact that an incorrect surgery could result in an income loss of €100 million, the hospital, for lack of causation, would not necessarily be liable to the full extent.[63] But if this is the case, why not codify this into the contract. Perhaps this is a clause dealing with liability, but it is not derogating from the law as I see it and therefore would not be subject to unfair contract terms legislation. This may be compared to §311(3) of the German Civil Code. Another point which is much debated at present is the question to what extent the loss of a chance should be compensated.[64]

12 The Nordic Patient Insurance Scheme

In the Netherlands, as elsewhere, in Europe and in Japan,[65] the Nordic Patient Insurance Scheme has attracted widespread attention.[66] In academic literature, proposals have been made to introduce the system in the Netherlands. The political parties, however, have never expressed any interest. In discussions, the cost element is usually brought forward as a deterrent. An attempt by the insurance company Centraal Beheer to even study the possibility of its implementation in the Netherlands met with such hostile reaction from part of the hospitals that it had to be called off. At present, there is no likelihood that a no-fault accident scheme will be introduced.

[63] C. J. J. M. Stolker, *Aansprakelijkheid van de arts/in het bijzonder voor mislukte sterilisaties* (PhD thesis Leyden, Deventer: Kluwer, 1988), 165–6; B. Sluyters, 'De WGBO, onderdeel van het burgerlijk recht', *Tijdschrift voor Gezondheidsrecht* 1996, 1, 7.

[64] T. Vansweevelt, *De civielrechtelijke aansprakelijkheid van de geneesheer en het ziekenhuis* (Antwerpen: Maklu, 1992).

[65] Y. Tejima, 'The Collaboration of Doctors and Lawyers/A Memorandum to Construct a Medical Accidents Deterring System', *Journal of Health Care, Medicine & Community* November 1995, with references to the Canadian Prichard report: 'Liability and Compensation in Health Care: A Report to the Conference of Deputy Ministers of Health of the Federal/Provincial/Territorial Review on Liability and Compensation Issues in Health Care'.

[66] B. A. J. M. de Mol, *Medisch letsel in het ziekenhuis no-faultverzekering/Een verkennende studie* (Doctoral thesis, Rotterdam, 1988).

13   Harmonisation at a European level

Medical liability is at present mainly a national affair. But there is also an embryonic body of European law. Here, a distinction should be made between the Council of Europe and its Convention on Human Rights, and the European Union and its regulations and directives. As for the Council of Europe, this in 1997 adopted the Convention on Human Rights and Biomedicine.

As for the European Union, the European Commission presented to the European Council a Draft directive on the liability for services in 1991. In the face of heavy criticism, the proposal had to be withdrawn. But at present, there is a renewed interest in this matter, and it is not inconceivable that the European Commission will once again propose harmonisation of liability, this time not of services in general, but of services in specific domains such as health care.

14   Conclusions

Having analysed a number of issues of Dutch medical liability, we may arrive at the conclusion that on these issues Dutch law is sometimes in the vanguard. This is the case with regard to wrongful birth and wrongful life, both of which may give rise to an action to recover the costs of upbringing of the child. The standard of care is on a high level. In other matters, such as liability for failure to inform and loss of a chance, German *viz.* French law are more advanced. There has been some discussion of introducing the Nordic Patient Insurance Scheme, but a serious proposal has never been brought forward.

How does medical liability develop? In the Netherlands, this has chiefly been the work of the legislature which has opted for the solution of laying down patients' rights in the Civil Code.[67] This development is different from that in most other countries, where the courts have had to do the work. The Dutch situation so far is rather unique among the jurisdictions in Western Europe; only Finland and France have had a slightly comparable legislation. The Dutch legislative action has been prepared by legal writing, which in medical matters is quite prolific and of high quality. The standards of health law are maintained by a law review (the

---

[67] E.H. Hondius and A. Hooft, 'The New Dutch Law on Medical Services' (1996) 43 *Netherlands International Law Review* 1; L.F. Markenstein, 'The Codification in the Netherlands of the Principal Rights of Patients: A Critical Review' (1995) 2 *European Journal of Health Law* 33.

Tijdschrift voor Gezondheidsrecht), a health law society (the *Vereniging voor Gezondheidsrecht*), an association of personal injury attorneys (the *Vereniging van Letselschade Advocaten LSA*), and a number of chairs in medical law at the universities.[68] Case law has also had a major impact, especially in the areas of the standard of care, proof and wrongful life.

---

[68] In Amsterdam, Groningen, Leyden, Maastricht, Nijmegen, Rotterdam, Utrecht and the Vrije Universiteit Amsterdam.

7

The development of medical liability in Spain

MARÍA PAZ GARCÍA RUBIO AND
BELÉN TRIGO GARCÍA*

1 Introduction

This report concerns the origin, the evolution, and the state of the situation regarding claims for damages in cases of medical malpractice in Spain. The birth and development of this issue shows a notable delay in relation to other European countries. In the first phase of evolution that ended in the 1970s, the judgments of Spanish courts regarding medical malpractice were scarce and sporadic. The literature from that period is also limited in quantity and writers had to support their work with texts and pertinent judicial sentences of other countries. It was not until the last third of the twentieth century that this trend began to change. In the 1980s there was an explosion of problems relating to medical malpractice, establishing, from that time onward, a series of questions that are, to a certain degree, similar to other legal systems.

Nevertheless, there are issues that are particular to the Spanish system such as the conflict associated with the determination of the correct jurisdiction (civil or administrative), in order to decide which of the two is competent for cases in which the physician or the hospital operate in the public domain. This issue was resolved with a law in 1992 that established that the competent jurisdiction in such cases is the administrative court.

* The authors wish to express their indebtedness to the Spanish Ministry of Education and Science for the award of the SEJ2004–02358 grant for the Project: 'Los daños morales en la UE: armonización sustantiva, ley aplicable y competencia judicial internacional' and to the Galician Government (*Dirección Xeral de Investigación, Desenvolvemento e Innovación*) for the award of the PGIDIT05CSO20201PR grant for the Projects: 'Dereito sanitario. Responsabilidade médico-sanitaria no marco da UE: aspectos civiles' and 'A autonomia da vontade no ámbito medico-sanitario: perspectiva legal e relación médico-doente' (PGIDIT 06CS20204PR). This paper has been drafted within the framework of these Projects. The authors thank Dr Lorel Scott for her assistance with the English translation of this report.

At the present time, there is a great quantity of Spanish judicial and literary activity relating to the issue of medical malpractice. The problems are similar to those that exist in the rest of Europe. It is noteworthy that the courts and the legal authors now consider concepts such as the standard of care, informed consent and the obligation of the physician to provide information, that are now legally recognised. Problems exist in some cases of medical practice regarding specific criteria used to identify the extent of damage or the causal link between the actions of the physician and the damage.

All of the topics mentioned and some others are included in this report which follows the design provided by the editor of this volume, Professor Hondius.

2   History

A   Court decisions

Medical liability jurisprudence began later in Spain than in other European countries. In the late nineteenth century, some criminal judgments were issued that related to medical errors, but no one ever sued for compensation because everyone thought at that time that doctors were not legally responsible. The first judgment of the Supreme Court of Spain (*Tribunal Supremo*, hereinafter STS) that some authors refer to as 'medical malpractice' is a case from 14 December 1917,[1] in which the plaintiff was a doctor who claimed compensation for non-pecuniary losses. Another similar case was from 3 June 1919.[2] It is important to note that these were not cases of medical malpractice claims of patients against physicians, but legal claims by physicians against patients in order to resolve financial payment issues.

The first case of medical malpractice that we have found in the Spanish Supreme Court (Civil Division) is a judgment of 3 December 1923.[3] It is a tort claim against a doctor (ophthalmologist) who had treated a patient. As a result of the treatment, the patient was left blind in both eyes. The facts of the case make it clear that the doctor erred in the diagnosis of the visual problem and prescribed an incorrect treatment that culminated in the complete blindness of the patient. There was also clear negligence in the medical attention provided. To be specific, the physician left town

---

[1] *Colección Legislativa. Jurisprudencia Civil* 1917, pp. 947 ff.
[2] *Colección Legislativa. Jurisprudencia Civil* 1919, pp. 442 ff.
[3] *Colección Legislativa. Jurisprudencia Civil* 1923, pp. 680 ff.

for several days during the treatment period. The judgment of the court of first instance decided that the doctor had acted with fault and was obligated to compensate the patient for damage. Nevertheless, both the appeals court and the Supreme Court denied liability on the part of the doctor. The Supreme Court considered that the decision of whether or not the doctor was at fault was a matter of the free interpretation of the court. Moreover, the judgment of the court could not be appealed. Today this decision would be unacceptable.

The 'leading case' is probably the judgment of the Civil Division of the Supreme Court of 21 March 1950.[4] The plaintiff was a woman who danced in the Tea-Dancing Club of Barcelona. She knew Dr Montaner, a physician with whom she spoke about the possibility of reducing the size of her breasts and improving their appearance. After a medical examination of the patient, Dr Montaner told her about Dr Mas Oliver, a plastic surgeon, who later performed the operation on 28 September 1940. The patient was in the clinic for several days and, upon release from the clinic, had to remain under the treatment of Dr Montaner until 15 January 1941. After the surgery and the treatment, the result of the plastic surgery was not as expected. In fact, the surgery and treatment left the patient with breasts of very unequal size, one breast was left without a nipple, and both breasts were full of scars. The patient requested the payment of compensation for material damage derived from the expenses of the clinic and medicines during her convalescence and other future damages arising from future operations to repair the physical damage that she had suffered at the hands of Drs Montaner and Mas Oliver. The Supreme Court ruled that the defendants were not liable to pay the damages because the surgery was correctly performed and the unfortunate result was produced by an infection that could not be attributed to the fault of the defendants.

The interesting aspect of this case is the reasoning of the attorney of the plaintiff that, although presented in 1950, is very similar to the arguments that can be found in the literature about medical malpractice and judgments of Spanish courts some fifty years later. The victim grounded her claim on a breach of contract by the two doctors. This breach of contract caused damage to her, and the doctors had to compensate this damage according to articles 1101 to 1108 of the Spanish Civil Code. The plaintiff understood that the contract with the physician and the surgeon obliged them to obtain a result – in this case, the reduction and beautification of her breasts. Furthermore, the plaintiff considered that the risk of failure

---

[4] *Colección Legislativa. Jurisprudencia Civil* 1950, pp. 401 ff.

was foreseeable and that the physicians did not warn the patient of the risks of the surgery. From that perspective, they committed a fault.

The first judgments that held the physicians liable for medical malpractice were of a criminal nature. They applied the principle that everyone who is criminally liable is also civilly liable. For example, the Supreme Court (Criminal Division, 15 March 1955) issued a judgment concerning a claim in which a doctor performed an illegal abortion that resulted in the death of the patient. The doctor, judged to be liable, was condemned to prison and prohibited from practising in any hospital. Moreover, he was sentenced to compensate the heirs of the patient for both pecuniary and non-pecuniary losses in spite of the fact that the patient herself had solicited the abortion. Another relevant judgment of the Criminal Division of the Supreme Court[5] dealt with a case in which a patient with an abdominal hernia was operated on by a physician who was later sued for damages associated with the operation. During the course of the operation, and without having previously obtained the informed consent of the patient, nor of his family, the doctor removed the patient's penis. Later, he explained that he had removed the penis because, during the operation, he had observed the existence of a tumour in the penis that required the removal of the organ. The surgeon was criminally condemned for flagrant imprudence and he was obliged to compensate the plaintiff with a significant amount of money.

The judgment of the Criminal Division of the Supreme Court issued on 17 January 1961 is also important. It concerned a case in which a motorcyclist moved forward incorrectly at a junction and hit another motorcycle which was carrying three persons. One of these three persons died a few days later from an illness which was the result of a tetanus injection that was administered by the physician who treated the patient for injuries from the traffic accident. The curious feature of the case was that the driver of the first motorcycle was found to be criminally guilty for a crime of imprudence which resulted in a death. He was also held responsible for the compensation of damages to the spouse and child of the victim, in spite of the fact that the direct cause of death was the treatment administered by the doctor (the tetanus injection) and not the accident.

One of the first judgments of the Civil Division of the Supreme Court that obliged a physician to compensate for damages is from 7 February 1973.[6] The case concerned a patient who underwent surgery, during

---

[5] STS 10 March 1959, *Colección Legislativa. Jurisprudencia Criminal* 1959, pp. 701 ff.
[6] *Colección Legislativa. Jurisprudencia Civil* 1973, pp. 431 ff.

the course of which a nerve was severed and, as a result, suffered grave pulmonary damage which made it impossible for him to ever return to work. This judgment is important because it dealt with various controversial issues in Spanish law. The judgment considered that the defendant responsible for patient compensation was not the surgeon, but the Public Administration (*Diputación*), the legal owner of the hospital where the surgery was performed. The court established the fault of the surgeon who worked for the hospital as the causal link between the action and the damage. The legal ground for the judgment was article 1903 of the Civil Code which establishes civil liability for the fault of others, even though the hospital is a public hospital. The first judgment pertained to civil jurisdiction. The Public Administration, as the defendant, argued that civil jurisdiction was not the competent arena but that the public nature of the hospital required a public procedure (administrative). This argument would be fully consistent with the laws in place today, but at that time the Supreme Court did not consider it to be so.

The judgment of the Civil Division of the Supreme Court from 12 December 1979[7] condemned the plaintiffs (physicians) to compensate a patient with tuberculosis to whom they had administered medicine that caused almost complete blindness. The court determined that the doctors had acted with grave negligence because they had not practised minimum precaution in order to avoid the serious consequences that arose. In spite of the fact that the doctors worked for a public hospital where the patient had been treated, the judgment was issued in the civil jurisdiction. In this case, only the doctors were held liable for the negligence, and not the hospital, because no one claimed against the hospital.

In the 1980s, the number of judgments that held physicians and hospitals liable for medical malpractice increased, although the first year in which we find an important number of judgments is 1988. The problem of conflict of jurisdiction was frequent during this period of time. In various cases in which the activity of the physician occurred in public medicine contexts, the issue of whether the proper jurisdiction was civil, labour, or administrative was debated. For example, some judgments held that the civil court was the competent jurisdiction.[8] On the other hand, some judgments held that the competent jurisdiction was the administrative

---

[7] *Colección Legislativa. Jurisprudencia Civil* 1979, pp. 585 ff.
[8] STS 20 February 1981, *Aranzadi Westlaw, RJ* 1981/564; STS 5 May 1988, *Aranzadi Westlaw, RJ* 1988/4016; STS 22 June 1988, *Aranzadi Westlaw, RJ* 1988/5124; STS 21 September 1988, *Aranzadi Westlaw, RJ* 1988/6847.

court.[9] The issue of competent jurisdiction was very important in this period because of the different consequences derived from the argument of cases in one or the other jurisdiction. The civil judgments relating to medical malpractice applied the civil code and insisted upon the requirement of fault of the physician in order to consider the physician liable. On the other hand, the judgments issued by the administrative courts applied the norms of Public Law that established the strict liability of the Administration. The problem should have ended in 1992 when Statute 30/1992 established that the competent jurisdiction in all cases in which the Public Administration is the defendant is the administrative court, but it did not.

B   Legal literature

The first Spanish book about medical liability was printed in 1944 and was entitled *The Professional Liability of a Physician* (*La responsabilidad profesional de médico*). It was introduced by a preface written by a very important Spanish doctor and well-known writer, Gregorio Marañón. He made the very strong argument that when a doctor acts in good faith, it is very difficult, if not impossible, to demand liability for damage. From his perspective, a patient must accept a margin of inconvenience and danger; a patient cannot demand responsibility for harm caused by a doctor. The author of the book was Eduardo Benzo Cano, a jurist, and he wrote from a legal perspective. From his point of view, there are three possibilities to consider. First, there is absolutely no medical liability. Second, the only situation in which medical liability could be considered is in the case of intent to harm. Third, any action performed with negligence, error, or malpractice is a possible case of medical liability. At that time there were no judgments of the Spanish Supreme Court about medical malpractice and, for that reason, the majority of judicial decisions cited by the author in this book were French. In some cases he also cited Italian and North-American cases.

In 1949 another book, written by M. Quintana Ferguson, entitled *The Civil Liability of a Physician* (*La responsabilidad civil del médico*) was printed in Madrid. The author presented a critique of Marañón's Preface (1944) and said that the law does not ask that the doctor is always correct, but the law does require that a doctor, like any other professional, should employ all

---

[9]   STS 4 July 1979, *Aranzadi Westlaw, RJ* 1979/3047; STS 29 July 1986, *Aranzadi Westlaw, RJ* 1986/6908.

of the means available in order not to cause damage or harm to the patient.[10] The doctor should act with diligence in order not to be held liable for negligence. If damage is caused, it does not necessarily imply criminality, but Quintana Ferguson does suggest that the doctor should compensate the patient for damages. This is the first Spanish text that treated the concept that preceded what we now call 'informed consent'. Quintana Ferguson stated that the doctor is obliged to obtain the patient's consent before initiating any treatment or intervention; no one should perform any activity that puts a human life at risk without the previous consent of the patient. For this consent to be valid, the doctor must provide necessary clear information so that the patient may have a reasonable idea about the nature of the illness, the typical types of treatment, the risks of surgery, the normal chances of success, and the difficulty of the operation. Quintana Ferguson proposed more than one idea that was ahead of its time. For example, he claimed that, in the case of a child, if the minor is fully conscious of the risks involved and refuses to be operated upon, it would be absurd to seek parental authorisation. If a doctor intervened and caused harm to the minor patient who did not consent, but whose parents did consent, the physician would nevertheless be liable.[11] He also stated that a physician must follow and keep pace with the developments in medicine if he or she does not want to be held liable. At that time, very few Spanish authors had addressed issues of medical liability in texts and there were no Spanish judgments concerning medical liability. As a consequence, all of the cases cited by the author were French.

In 1955, a Professor at Murcia University, J. Roca Juan, added some notes in the Spanish translation of the Italian book by A. Montel, *Problems of Liability and Damage* (*Problemas de la responsabilidad y del daño*). In his comments concerning Chapter XVII, which deals with the liability of the hospital and the surgeon, Roca Juan underlined the fact that, contrary to other European countries, there were no judgments in Spain and there was very little Spanish legal literature regarding this subject. He offered his opinion that the origin of medical liability lies in the omission of required professional diligence. The doctor's obligation is not to cure but to try to cure, applying his or her knowledge to that end. Roca Juan is the first Spanish author to mention a Spanish judgment about a medical case, the sentence of the Supreme Court of 1950, mentioned earlier.

---

[10] M. Quintana Ferguson, *La responsabilidad civil del medico* (Madrid: Trivium, 1949), p. 47.
[11] Ibid. at p. 92.

It was not until the 1980s that literature about medical malpractice began to appear in Spanish texts. The following books were published in that decade: *Responsabilidad civil médico-sanitaria*, by José Manuel Fernández Hierro (1984); *Los médicos y la responsabilidad civil*, by Joaquín Ataz López (1985); *Responsabilidad civil médica y hospitalaria*, by Javier Fernández Costales (1987); *La responsabilidad civil del médico. Aspectos tradicionales y modernos*, by Eugenio Llamas Pombo (1988); *La responsabilidad civil del profesional liberal*, by Mariano Izquierdo Tolsada (1989) and *La responsabilidad civil del médico*, by Luis González Morán (1990). Because neither a body of doctrine nor a body of court decisions regarding medical malpractice had yet been established in Spain, authors of leading Spanish texts in the field continued to cite French and Italian cases and literature. However, the founding Spanish judgments were cited.

Here we present a brief overview of some of the texts listed above in chronological order of publication. Fernández Hierro, in *Civil Medical Health Liability* (1984), wrote about the increment of claims of medical liability in Europe. He suggested that the same trend would probably appear in Spain within a few years. It is useful to note that the author provided an Appendix which includes the first criminal and civil medical malpractice cases decided by the Spanish Supreme Court and the courts of appeal. Ataz López, in *Physicians and Civil Liability* (1985), explained that, in the first phase of legal claims for medical malpractice in Spain, the complaints were typically presented in criminal courts. He asked whether all medical negligence, of whatever kind, deserved criminal punishment. His answer was a clear 'no', as he was of the opinion that not all medical malpractice cases required criminal procedures. He thought that many malpractice cases were not criminal but civil cases.

It is striking that in the Preface of Llamas Pombo's book, *Civil Liability of Physicians: traditional and modern aspects* (1988), Mariano Alonso Pérez stated in the first judgment that 'to speak about civil medical liability is to refer to a modern phenomenon, almost one of our own days'.[12] Llamas Pombo considered that 'informed consent' is nothing more than an element of the contract between the doctor and the patient and that the lack of informed consent is a supposed case of *culpa in contrahendo*. This idea was not followed, nor supported, in the subsequent literature.

---

[12] M. Alonso Pérez, 'Prólogo' in E. Llamas Pombo, *La responsabilidad civil del médico. Aspectos tradicionales y modernos* (Madrid: Trivium, 1988), p. xi.

The last book that we will discuss in this section was written by L. González Morán – *Civil Liability of Physicians* (1990). The author presented an analysis of Spanish judgments concerning medical malpractice. He mentioned that, until the 1970s, the few judicial decisions concerning doctors related to physicians who had claimed payment for their services. The first judgments relating to claims for compensation of patients against physicians were rejected by the Supreme Court (3 December 1923; 21 March 1950; 25 January 1965). From the 1970s on, the claims were situated in the field of Tort Law (7 February 1973; 28 December 1979). 1988 was the first year in which the Supreme Court pronounced an important number of judgments regarding medical malpractice. González Morán collected abundant judgments relating to non-pecuniary loss and specifically concerning death as a non-pecuniary loss for family members. The author clearly showed the conflict among the different jurisdictions (civil, criminal, labour and administrative) in medical malpractice suits when the defendant was a doctor employed by the Public Administration. González Morán maintained that the competent court for medical malpractice claims against the Public Health System is the civil court. We must note here that, in 1992, the Legislature passed a statute that made it clear that the competent court is not the civil court but the administrative court.

3   Statistics

According to statistics from 31 December 2008 provided by the Spanish Health Ministry, there were a total of 804 hospitals in Spain. Of these, 313 were public, belonging to different Public Administrations (state, autonomous communities, provinces, towns, etc.) and 491 were private hospitals. This means that 38.93% were public and 61.07% were private.[13] Regardless of the fact that there are fewer public hospitals than private ones, the public hospitals are the largest hospitals and have the best technological resources because, in Spain, most health care assistance is provided by public institutions.

Statistics provided by the National Institute of Statistics show that, in 2007, there were 208,098 doctors in Spain, of whom 117,360 were male

---

[13]   Read www.msc.es under 'Estadisticas Sanitarias'.

and 90,738 were female.[14] Many doctors work simultaneously in both systems, public and private.

According to the annual report of the Association for the Defence of the Patient (ADEPA)[15] from 2008, the Association recorded 12,276 cases of medical malpractice. Of that number, 508 patients died due to presumed medical negligence. According to the Association's report of 2007, a total of 12,662 cases of medical malpractice were documented. This represents a decrease of 346 cases in 2007. The number of deaths was 517, which means that 9 fewer patients died than in 2007. The most common complaints received concerned delay in the delivery of medical and hospital services, insufficient information given regarding these services, the lack of attention given in the emergency rooms of hospitals and serious cases of presumed medical negligence or errors. There are more claims in private health systems than in public health systems. The services most frequently denounced were accident and emergency and gynaecology.[16]

4   Public or private law: procedural norms

The division between public and private health care is very important in the Spanish regulations regarding health care liability. Today, when the doctor, the hospital, or the medical service sued are in the public health system, the liability lies in Administrative Law (articles 139–146, *Ley* 30/1992, from 26 November, *de Régimen Jurídico de las Administraciones Públicas y del Procedimiento Administrativo Común* (LRJAP),[17] modified by *Ley* 4/1999,[18] and its *Reglamento* (RD 429/1993)[19]). These rules provide for a vicarious liability system in which liability is channelled through the public body that operates the health care service. This

---

[14] See www.ine.esunder 'Profesionales Sanitarias Colegiados'.

[15] This is a private association that has no connection with the Public Administration that only receives funds from its members. The data that they collect may be viewed at www.negligenciasmedicas.com/index.html.

[16] In the legal literature it is argued that the acceptance of the actions relating to wrongful birth and wrongful life will possibly have negative repercussions for the medical professionals (gynaecologists in particular). These professionals, fearing the potential to be seen as liable for the birth of a disabled child, would practise defensive medicine.

[17] *Boletín Oficial del Estado* (hereinafter BOE) 27 November 1992, p. 40300.

[18] BOE 14 January 1999, p. 1739.   [19] BOE 4 May 1993, p. 13250.

prevents the victim from bringing claims against the civil servant or health care professional who directly caused the damage.[20] In this case, jurisdiction over litigation concerning liability lies in the administrative courts (*tribunales contencioso-administrativos*).[21] The conflict concerning competent jurisdiction can now be considered to be definitively resolved.[22]

On the other hand, when the doctor or the hospital are in the private health system, the Civil Code (CC) (articles 1101–8 concerning liability for breach of contract and articles 1902–3 concerning non-contractual liability) and also, theoretically, in both cases, articles 25–8 of the General Consumers Protection Act (*Ley general para la defensa de consumidores y usuarios*)[23] (especially article 28), can also be applied, regardless of the existence of a contract or not. The first two sets of rules refer to a fault liability system, while the second rule places upon the health care provider a strict liability regime. In these cases any litigation concerning the liability is tried by civil courts (*tribunales del orden civil*).

In both cases, when the doctor's actions are previewed in the Criminal Code, a criminal procedure should be initiated against the physician. The criminal procedure would suspend administrative or civil procedures. Nevertheless, a patient who suffers damage due to a criminal action on the part of the doctor has the legal option of demanding compensation in the criminal court. In these cases, the tort liability rules included in the Penal Code apply. Although this is not the usual course of action for health care claims in Spanish practice, some authors have observed that the legal reforms conducted in 1998 and 1999 have prompted an increase in penal lawsuits, which allow the victim to obtain a quick and free preliminary investigation into the case, a swift ruling on tort liability within the criminal proceeding itself, and moreover, an escape from the jurisdiction of the administrative court.[24]

---

[20] See in more detail below p. 000.

[21] Also *Ley* 29/1998, of 13 July, *reguladora de la Jurisdicción Contencioso-Administrativa* (BOE 14 July 1998, p. 23516).

[22] STS (Administrative Division) 20 December 2004, *Aranzadi Westlaw RJ* 2005/1597.

[23] BOE 24 July 1984, p. 21686. See now arts. 147 and 148 of the *Real Decreto Legislativo* 1/2007 of 16 November 2007, por el que se aprueba el texto refundido de la Ley general para la defensa de los consumidores y usarios (BOE 30 November 2007, p. 49181).

[24] M. Martín Casals, J. Solé Feliu and J. C. Seuba Torreblanca, 'Compensation in the Spanish Health Care Sector', in J. Dute, M. Faure and H. Koziol (eds.), *No-Fault Compensation in the Health Care Sector* (Vienna: Springer, 2004), p. 335.

5   The regulation of the professions

The Codes of Medical Ethics are norms of conduct that control medical activity. They are elaborated by the Colleges of Physicians that are professional associations of doctors. Each College of Physicians has its own code of conduct, although they are all very similar. The General Council of these Colleges of Physicians also have a Code of Ethics from 1999.[25]

The principal significance of the norms contained in these Codes is of a disciplinary nature. The non-performance of these rules and regulations by a physician may result in a charge of a disciplinary misdemeanour which may carry with it sanctions, including suspension or prohibition from continuing to exercise the profession.

These Codes of Conduct do not have a direct impact in the field of delict, although they are indirectly important for two fundamental reasons.[26] First, some of the norms which originally appeared only in these Codes have become actual legal norms integrated into statutes and directly applied by the courts. This has occurred, for example, with the issue of informed consent. It is now obligatory to inform the patient in an understandable manner about his or her illness. The obligation to obtain the consent of the patient for any medical activity appeared in these Codes much before it was incorporated into the 1986 General Law of Health (*General de Sanidad*).[27] The same has occurred in relation to the obligation to record and conserve the medical history of the patient, as well as in relation to the obligation to respect medical confidentiality. The most recent Codes of Conduct contain ethical norms concerning assisted human reproduction, the performance of useless practices, organ transplants, and/or medical experimentation with the patient.

The second reason why these Codes of Conduct are indirectly important to delict is that some of these ethical norms, even before being included in laws, had been used by the courts to determine if the activities of the physician had been performed in accordance with the *lex artis ad hoc*, that is to say, in order to establish if the physician had acted with due diligence.

---

[25] See www.wma.net/e/ethicsunit/organizations.htm.

[26] According to *Ley* 44, of 21 November 2003, relating to the Regulation of Health Professionals (*Ordenación de las profesiones sanitarias*), health professionals are obliged to practise the profession with loyalty and efficiency, and in observance of the technical, scientific, professional and ethical principles that are applicable.

[27] *Ley* 14 of 25 April 1986 (BOE 29 April 1986, p. 15207).

6   Personal rights and rights to self-determination

Following the Convention of the Council of Europe, the so-called 'Convention of Oviedo',[28] the legislators in Spain[29] have incorporated the notion of informed consent as a guarantee of respect for the right of self-determination. The legal regulation regards this issue as medical protocol. The informed consent should be written in certain cases (*cf.* articles 4, 8 and 9 of *Ley* 41/2002).[30] The legal regulation does not establish, however, the specific consequences of not performing these duties. There is only a reference to the general rules of liability. It may even be held that this protocol preferentially focuses on the exoneration of medical personnel.[31]

---

[28] Convention for the Protection of Human Rights and Dignity of the Human Being with regard to the Application of Biology and Medicine: Convention on Human Rights and Biomedicine (Oviedo, 4, IV, 1997); (BOE 20 October 1999, p. 36825); in effect in Spain since 1 January 2000.

[29] In the context of the State, *Ley* 41, 2002, of 14 November, *básica reguladora de la autonomía del paciente y de derechos y obligaciones en materia de información y documentación clínica* (BOE 15 November 2002, p. 40126). Almost all autonomous communities have already passed statutes on informed consent. Thus, Castilla la Mancha, *Ley* 8, 2000, of 30 November, *de ordenación sanitaria* (BOE 27 February 2001, p. 7296 amended by *Ley* 16/2001 of 20 December 2001, BOE 8 February 2002, p. 5241); Catalonia, *Ley* 21, 2000, of 29 December, *sobre los derechos de información concernientes a la salud y a la autonomía del paciente y a la documentación clínica* (BOE 2 February 2001, p. 4121), Galicia, *Ley* 3, 2001, of 28 May, *reguladora del consentimiento informado* (BOE 3 July 2001, p. 23537) (modified by *Ley* 3, 2005, of 7 March; BOE 19 April 2005, p. 13364 and *Ley* 8/2008 of 10 July 2008, (BOE 21 August 2008, p. 35080)), Aragón, *Ley* 6, 2002, of 15 April, *de salud* (BOE 21 May 2002, p. 18061); La Rioja, *Ley* 2, 2002, of 17 April, *de salud* (BOE 3 May 2002, p. 16210) amended, inter alia, by *Ley* 1/2006 of 28 February 2006 (BOE 23 March 2006, p. 11298; Navarra, *Ley* 11, 2002, of 6 May, *sobre los derechos del paciente a las voluntades anticipadas, a la información y a la documentación clínica* (BOE 30 May 2002, p. 19249) (modified by *Ley Foral* 29, 2003, of 4 April; BOE 20 May 2003, p. 19106); Cantabria, *Ley* 7, 2002, of 10 December, *de ordenación sanitaria de Cantabria* (BOE 7 January 2003, p. 551) amended subsequently, most recently by *Ley* 9/2008 of 26 December 2008 (BOE 24 January 2009, p. 8338); Valencia, *Ley* 1, 2003, of 28 January, *de derechos e información al paciente de la Comunidad valenciana* (BOE 25 February 2003, p. 7587); Castilla y León, *Ley* 8, 2003, of 8 April, *de derechos y deberes de las personas en relación con su salud* (BOE 30 April 2003, p. 16650); Baleares, *Ley* 5, 2003, of 4 April, *de salud de las Islas Baleares* (BOE 8 May 2003, p. 17438) amended subsequently, most recently by *Ley* 9/2008 of 19 December 2008 (BOE 27 January 2009, p. 9247); Extremadura, *Ley* 3, 2005, of 8 July, *de información sanitaria y autonomía del paciente* (BOE 5 August 2005, p. 27513); Murcia, *Ley* 3/2009 of 11 May 2009 (Boletin Oficial de la Región de Murcia, 20 May 2009, p. 22639).

[30] In other cases verbal information is sufficient, although the doctor must demonstrate that he or she provided the patient with information concerning all of the circumstances associated with the intervention. (*Cf.*, inter alia, STS (Civil Division) 29 September 2005, *Aranzadi Westlaw* 2005, 8891 and STS (Civil Division) 17 November 2005, *Aranzadi Westlaw* 2005, 7636.

[31] *Cf.* art. 10. 2° *Ley* 41, 2002: 'The responsible physician must keep in mind, in every case, that the more dubious the result that may occur as a result of an intervention, the more necessary is the previous written consent of the patient.'

Spanish courts had applied the notion of informed consent in order to increase medical liability relating to the general duty of information,[32] even before the approbation of the specific legal regulation.[33] In any case, the judicial construction of informed consent is still not clear regarding its foundation, its structure, or its consequences.[34] Some judgments from the beginning of the twenty-first century defined informed consent as a fundamental personal right.[35] However, the court did not ground these judgments in the perspective that informed consent is a fundamental right, but rather in the fault of the practitioners. The doctrine of informed consent is situated within the context of a new conception of medicine in which the autonomy of the patient is of principal importance. Spanish legal literature considers that patient autonomy relates to some fundamental rights, but does not view it as a new fundamental right.

The same Act regulates both the right of privacy of the patient as well as informed consent. Any and all persons with access to clinical information and documentation have the duty to respect confidentiality. At the same time, it is the right of the patient to demand that the medical personnel respect the confidentiality of the medical information (articles 2.7 and 7.1, *Ley* 41/2002).

Legal regulations concerning medical histories establish the manner in which the medical histories must be elaborated (articles 14, 15 and 16, *Ley* 41/2002). Minimally, the medical history must contain the informed consent document. The right of access to these medical histories, the duty to conserve them, as well as the usage of this information, including in court proceedings, must respect the right of privacy of the patient.

7   Contract or tort

In the public system of medical liability, there are no differences between contractual and non-contractual liability. The dichotomy does not exist

---

[32]   *Cf.* art. 10. 5º y 6º *Ley* 14 of 25 April 1986, repealed by *Ley* 41 of 2002 (now see arts. 2.2, 2.3 and 4–5 *Ley* 41, 2002).

[33]   STS (Civil Division) 25 April 1994, *Aranzadi Westlaw, RJ* 1994, 3073 and STS 27 June 1997, *Aranzadi Westlaw, RJ* 1997, 5758.

[34]   See below.

[35]   See STS (Civil Division) 12 January 2001, *Aranzadi Westlaw, RJ* 2001, 3: 'Informed consent constitutes a fundamental human right; it is precisely one of the latest contributions of the theory of human rights. It is a necessary consequence or explanation of the classic rights of life, physical integrity and freedom of conscience. It is a right of personal liberty to decide for oneself regarding the person himself and his own life and the consequences of self-determination concerning his own body.' See also STS 27 April 2001, *Aranzadi Westlaw, RJ* 2001, 6891, and 11 May 2001, *Aranzadi Westlaw, RJ* 2001, 6197.

under Public Law. However, civil courts have discussed whether to apply contractual liability when the defendant was a public medical system (STS (Civil Division) 29 October 1992).[36]

In the private system of medical liability, there is contractual liability if a contract between the defendant and the plaintiff has been agreed. In other cases, the liability incurred by a doctor as the result of harm caused to his or her patient is non-contractual. However, in practice, patients have a choice between either contract or tort. The courts choose either the contractual or non-contractual norms based on article 218.1 of the Civil Procedure Law (*Ley de Enjuiciamiento Civil*).[37] Some judgments suggest that choosing one or another regulation makes no difference; it is argued that the physician's duty of care is the same.[38]

8   Standard of care

The standard of care of health professionals is higher than the general standard of the 'reasonable person' established in article 1104 CC. As skilled professionals, their liability is measured in relation to the parameters of the so-called *lex artis ad hoc*, i.e. the standard of care that must be met by a skilled professional in medicine who acts in accordance with the state of the art of medical science.[39]

Concerning the standard of care, there are three issues that must be pointed out in Spanish law in addition to informed consent.[40] The first is the increasing level of required care. To this purpose, it is worth comparing judgments from the 1980s (*culpa incontestable y patente*) and from recent years (*agotamiento de la diligencia*).[41] The second is that some judgments show the influence of French doctrine with relation to *obligaciones de medios reforzadas*.[42] The third issue relates to the recognition of the so-called *medicina necesaria* vis-à-vis *medicina satisfactiva*.[43]

---

[36] *Aranzadi Westlaw, RJ* 1992, 8178.   [37] BOE 8 January 2000, p. 575.
[38] One of the first decisions in this sense was STS 7 February 1990, *Aranzadi Westlaw, RJ* 1990, 668.
[39] M. Martín Casals, J. Solé Feliu, J. C. Seuba Torreblanca, 'Compensation in the Spanish Health Care Sector', p. 340.
[40] B. Trigo García, *Contrato de servicios. Perspectiva jurídica actual* (Granada: Comares, 1999), pp. 240–66.
[41] STS (Civil Division) 26 May 1986, *Aranzadi Westlaw, RJ* 1986, 2824; STS (Civil Division) 28 July 1997, *Aranzadi Westlaw, RJ* 1997, 5954.
[42] STS (Civil Division) 25 April 1994, *Aranzadi Westlaw, RJ* 1994, 3073.
[43] STS (Civil Division) 2 December 1997, *Aranzadi Westlaw, RJ* 1997, 8964, STS (Civil Division) 28 June 1999, *Aranzadi Westlaw, RJ* 1999, 4894.

Authors and courts in Spain have accepted the figure of 'informed consent' and, consequently, the duty to warn has been recognised for a long time.[44] As discussed earlier, several state and regional statutes point out the duty to warn. The breach of the duty to inform the patient is grounds for a case of negligent malpractice. This legally established duty is part of the standard of diligence. As such, a doctor who breaches the duty to warn violates the so-called *lex artis ad hoc* and he or she is liable.[45] However, it is not obvious when a breach of the duty to warn exists. The physician has a duty to give fair, clear and appropriate information about the illness, the treatment, the risks and the consequences.

The concrete content of the information is a topic that affects an objective standard of diligence, e.g. professional diligence. According to this standard, the physician is not obliged to inform about an unknown risk. Some opinions and judicial decisions stated that the physician only had to inform his patient of the 'normally foreseeable risks' and did not have to tell him or her about the 'exceptional risks' (for instance, STS (Civil Division) 28 December 1998[46]). However, other judgments held that the patient must be informed about exceptional risks (STS (Civil Division) 23 July 2003[47]), about a one-out-of-a-hundred risk, whether risks are specific or generic (STS (Civil Division) 10 April 2003[48]), typical of the intervention, or related to the pathology of the individual patient or to his or her personal circumstances (STS (Civil Division) 2 July 2002[49]). The only risks that are excluded from the duty to warn are those risks that are unknown to medical science at the moment of the intervention (STS (Civil Division) of October 2005[50]).

The standard of diligence may be adapted to a concrete case in relation to the particular circumstances of the doctor and the patient. That is to say, if in a specific case the doctor is aware that a particular issue is especially important to a patient, although it is not so for the majority, he or she should provide this information as well (for example, the possibility of a blood transfusion, if it is known that the patient objects to this type of treatment).

---

[44] M. P. García Rubio, 'Incumplimiento del deber de información. Relación de causalidad y daño en la responsabilidad civil médica', in E. Llamas Pombo (ed.), *Libro Homenaje al Pr. Mariano Alonso*, vol. 1 (Madrid: Laley-Actoalidad, 2006), p. 801.

[45] According to STS (Civil Division) 21 December 2005, *Aranzadi Westlaw*, RJ 2005, 1014: 'Informed consent constitutes a principle and an essential element of the *lex artis*.'

[46] *Aranzadi Westlaw*, RJ 1998, 10164.   [47] *Aranzadi Westlaw*, RJ 2003, 5462.

[48] *Aranzadi Westlaw*, RJ 2003, 3702.   [49] *Aranzadi Westlaw*, RJ 2002, 5514.

[50] *Aranzadi Westlaw*, RJ 2005, 8547.

9   Proof and causation

Within the general framework of tort liability for fault established in article 1902 CC, Spanish courts reverse the burden of proof of fault so systematically that it can be assumed that the general rule in Spanish Tort Law for fault is the presumption of fault with the reversal of the burden of proof. However, medical liability is the only area where this general reversal does not take place and, since the plaintiff cannot avail himself or herself of a presumption of fault, he or she has to duly prove the fault of the physician or other health care personnel[51] (for instance, STS (Civil Division) 23 March 2001[52] and STS (Civil Division) 24 November 2005[53]).

This is the result of qualifying the obligation of the physician as an 'obligation of means' and not as an 'obligation of result'. This approach is used when the liability of the physician is in contract or in tort. In contract law, the proof of the breach of contract overlaps with the proof of fault, because proving the breach of contract involves proving that the debtor was at fault when performing the service. Fault of the physician also becomes apparent in a similar way when it is seen from the point of view of tort liability.

On the other hand, a few isolated judgments of the Supreme Court have presumed the fault of the physician and have reversed the burden of proof. The common ground for these decisions is that they deal with cases in which the damage is the result of the use of devices or techniques, such as anaesthesia, x-rays, or radiotherapy, which are especially dangerous. For instance, with regard to damage resulting from anaesthesia, STS (Civil Division) 4 February 2002[54] recognised that 'in spite of the fact that some isolated decisions have reversed the burden of proof against (him), as an indispensable condition of (his) obligation to compensate for the damage caused, the proof of (his) fault or negligence is always required'. However, not all judgments that deal with the application of this type of dangerous technique systematically reverse the burden of proof.

Furthermore, in some cases the Spanish courts consider that some specific types of medical intervention entail the obligation to obtain a result and, accordingly, that these obligations are governed by a strict liability regime. The judgments that seem to back up this position refer to plastic surgery,

---

[51] M. Martin Casals, J. Ribot and J. Solé Feliu, 'Medical Malpractice Liability in Spain: Cases, Trends and Developments' (2003) *European Journal of Health Law* 153–81.
[52] *Aranzadi Westlaw, RJ* 2001, 3984.   [53] *Aranzadi Westlaw, RJ* 2005, 7855.
[54] *Aranzadi Westlaw, RJ* 2002, 593.

to dental operations, and to vasectomies. Nevertheless, with regard to the liability of physicians, there is not really a strict liability regime. The only implication is that they will have to intensify their care. Therefore, it will neither be sufficient that they perform the operation according to the *lex artis ad hoc* or professional standard of care required for the specific operation, nor will it be sufficient that they inform the patient about the risks entailed; it will also be necessary for the physician to inform the patient about the possibility that the operation may not accomplish the intended result, as well as about further measures, activities and tests that are necessary in order to verify the success of the operation or to facilitate the intervention process.

On the other hand, there are two groups of cases in which the Spanish courts actually accept a true exception to the general rule of no presumption of fault which is specific to health care liability:

1. The first group of exceptions are those in which the gravity of the damage experienced by the patient is out of all proportion to the diagnosis that has been made or the operation that has been performed (doctrine of the so-called *daño desproporcionado* (disproportionate harm)). This doctrine appears for the first time in the Supreme Court judgment of 2 February 1999,[55] concerning the case of a woman who, after an apparently normal labour, suffered a haemorrhage which was so serious that several blood transfusions were required and the bleeding could only be fully stopped by a full removal of her uterus. The great quantity of blood she lost was the cause of a brain anoxia which gave rise to serious injuries. Here the Supreme Court states that, in the cases of medical liability, it is possible to presume the physician's negligence when his action produces an outcome that 'on account of its disproportion in comparison to what, according to the rules of experience and to common sense, is usual, presents signs that reveal the negligent shortage in the means employed, with regard to the state of science and the circumstances of time and place, or the oversight of its due and timely use'.

   Some judgments connect the doctrine of 'disproportionate damage' as a device that aims to ease the proof of fault on the plaintiff, to other devices, such as the common law doctrine of *res ipsa loquitur*, the German *Anscheinsbeweis* or the French *faute virtuelle* which, in other legal systems, fulfil a similar function.[56]

---

[55] *Aranzadi Westlaw, RJ* 1996, 8938.
[56] The link among the disproportionate damage doctrine and these other devices of comparative law is expressed, for instance, in STS (Civil Division) 31 January 2003, *Aranzadi Westlaw, RJ* 2003, 646.

2. The second group of exceptions is made up of those judgments that reverse the burden of proof of fault, arguing that the defendant, due to circumstances such as that he or she has an easier access to evidence, is in a better position to furnish proof. This is not a rule specific to health care liability but a general rule of procedure which, since enforcement of the new Civil Procedure Act, has its legal foundation in article 217.6 ('In order to apply what is provided in the prior parts of this article the court will have to take into account the availability and the facility of proof that corresponds to each of the parties in the proceeding'). According to this rule, it is not always the physician who has the burden of proof because there are circumstances that only the patient can know and prove. However, generally, the doctor is in a better position to furnish proof.[57]

Finally, it must be borne in mind that all these rules will not be applicable in those areas of health care liability governed by strict liability rules. This is the case, for instance, with the rules referring to tort liability of the Public Administration.

In the field of private health care, article 28 of the General Consumers Protection Act establishes that 'health care services' are governed by a strict liability regime. In spite of this, however, Spanish courts still apply the fault liability system established in articles 1902 and 1903 CC to private hospitals. Nevertheless, the exceptional application of article 28 of the General Consumers Protection Act can be found.[58]

The liability of the health professional or the hospital demands the negligence of the actor, the damage, and the causal link between the defendant's negligence and the plaintiff's loss. Since there are no specific rules for medical liability, the courts solve the problems of causation by applying the general rules of causation in tort liability.

The Spanish Supreme Court applies different terminology with reference to tort liability, including the field of medical liability, and may utilise either the label of *causa adecuada* or, with the same meaning, the expressions *causa eficiente* or *causa suficiente*.

It must be stressed that in Spanish medical liability, the requirement of causation is very strict, not only in the sense that it is an indispensable condition of liability, but also in the sense that it must be proven with

---

[57] The literature refers to this rule as 'dynamic distribution of the proof' (*distribución dinámica de la prueba*); see A. Domínguez Luelmo, *Derecho sanitario y responsabilidad médical* (Valladolid: Lex Nova, 2003), pp. 87–95.

[58] STS (Civil Division) 18 December 2002, *Aranzadi Westlaw, RJ* 2003, 47.

certainty, the burden of proof being upon the plaintiff, who would not be able to avail himself of any presumption.[59] However, in some cases, courts seem to admit the presumption of causation. So, in an implicit way, when the doctrine of 'disproportionate damage' is applied – presuming the negligence – courts are also presuming the causation between such negligent behaviour and the damage.

The problem of causation is very unclear in Spanish law, especially in cases of breaching the duty to warn.[60] The issue of 'when' the lack of warning is the 'cause' of the patient's damage is not clearly established in law.

It appears to be easier to detect the causal link in cases in which the injury was produced precisely by the fault or the omission of information, because the provision of the correct information would in all likelihood have prevented the damage. We can refer to cases of 'wrongful conception', which involve an intervention designed to eliminate reproductive capacity (e.g. a vasectomy) and in which the doctor does not inform the patient of the additional method or methods of prevention which should be taken during the post-surgery period. It is more difficult to determine a causal link in which the damage occurred during the medical intervention, but not due directly to a factor of lack of information. In these cases, the doctor is liable when, in addition to the lack of information, he or she performs the medical intervention in a negligent fashion. The physician is liable for his or her technical malpractice and he or she must compensate the damage caused.

At the same time, in other cases of medical malpractice the informed consent plays a negative role in the sense that although the patient was adequately informed, the doctor is responsible for his or her malpractice (STS (Administrative Division) 7 June 2001[61]).

The most difficult cases are those in which there is a lack of information, the technical *praxis* is correct, and, for unknown reasons, a risk factor occurs which causes personal injury to the patient. In Spain, as well as in other countries, there are numerous claims of the breach of the duty to warn by the doctor who has violated the informed consent of the patient. In these types of situations, the test of 'but for' or the test of *conditio sine qua non* seem to fail. Applying these rules, one may conclude that the patient would have suffered the same damage if the defendant had not

---

[59] M. Martín Casals, J. Ribot and J. Solé Felui, 'Medical Malpractice Liability in Spain: Cases, Trends and Developments' (2003) *European Journal of Health Law* 161.

[60] M. P. García Rubio, 'Incumplimiento del deber de información. Relación de causalidad y daño en la responsabilidad civil médica', p. 801.

[61] *Aranzadi Westlaw, RJ* 2001, 4198.

performed that action or omission; this action (or omission) cannot be considered to be the cause of the injury. With this line of reasoning, it is very important to determine if the appropriately informed patient would or would not have consented to the intervention in question.

Spanish Supreme Court judgments are not uniform regarding this topic. There are judgments that absolutely deny that in these cases causation exists (for example, STS (Civil Division) 16 December 1997[62]). A different position derives from the STS (Civil Division) 2 July 2002[63] which admits that the risk of complications about which information was not provided 'is important enough to consider the decision of rejecting surgery' and seems to suppose that if the patient had known of the risk, he or she would not have consented to surgery. The STS (Civil Division) 8 September 2003[64] is along the same line. But the most clear of all is the STS (Administrative Division) 4 April 2000.[65] The Supreme Court decided a claim of a person who suffered permanent injuries after surgery. Neither the patient (a minor) nor his parents had been informed of the possible risk. The judgment recognised the lack of warning about this infrequent risk, but considered that the absence of information was not the cause of the damage produced. However, as we will later see, the judgment did recognise the 'virtual causality' of the deficient information in relation to the production of 'other types of damage'. In sum, the tendency of the Spanish Supreme Court is to deny the causal link between the lack or absence of information and the personal injuries suffered by the patient.

Nevertheless, from another point of view, a sufficient causal relationship can be established if it can be proven that the patient would not have suffered the same injury if the doctor had provided correct and adequate information. There is no doubt that the patient would not have suffered injury if he or she had not consented to the intervention at that time and place. The damage must be assigned to the doctor for two reasons. One, the doctor did not give the patient the opportunity to decide in a conscious and free manner. Two, to breach the duty to inform must be punished by law.

10   Who then is liable?

The answer to the question of 'who is liable' in a case of medical malpractice in a hospital depends upon whether the institution is public or private. In

---

[62] *Aranzadi Westlaw, RJ* 1997, 8690.   [63] *Aranzadi Westlaw, RJ* 2002, 5514.
[64] *Aranzadi Westlaw, RJ* 2003, 6065.   [65] *Aranzadi Westlaw, RJ* 2000, 3258.

the first case, according to public law rules, the vicarious liability of the Public Administration[66] insulates its agents from personal liability. The liability of the public hospital is strict; there is no need for the victim to establish that the physician has behaved wrongfully. It must be emphasised that within the framework of this set of rules, article 145 LRJAP provides that the claim can only be brought against the Administration, and not against the specific civil servant or contracted member of the personnel who has caused the harm. Once compensation has been paid, however, the Administration can bring a claim for contribution against the tortfeasor who has caused the damage, but only in so as far as he or she has acted with intent or, at least, has been grossly negligent.

In the area of private health care, both in contract (articles 1101 ff. CC) and in tort (article 1902 CC), the victim can claim damages against the tortfeasor. Usually, however, the victim can also be compensated by the private hospital. When the patient who has suffered harm has made a contract with the hospital or health care centre in which the medical personnel, who have caused the harm, perform their activities, it must be considered that the centre is liable for the damage caused by them. When the patient and the private centre did not make a contract, an extra-contractual liability of the centre may exist. According to article 1903.4 CC which governs tortious liability of the principal for damage caused by its agents, the private hospital is liable only if the 'at fault' physician is its dependant. The question of when a doctor is a dependant of the hospital has long been disputed. In this case, article 1903.4 CC provides for liability for the acts of the employees on the grounds of *culpa in eligendo* or *in vigilando* of the employer. Fault of the employer is presumed (article 1903.6 CC), which can, of course, be rebutted. However, the courts recognise that the liability of the hospital is strict.

When both the physician and the hospital are responsible, Spanish courts consider that the two are obligated to indemnify the claimant in a joint, consolidated fashion.

11   Damages

In relation to the issue of which damages are recoverable, the Spanish general provisions on contract and tort liability do not make any distinction between pecuniary and non-pecuniary losses. Therefore, both legal

---

[66] M. Martín Casals, J. Solé Feliu and J. C. Seuba Torreblanca, 'Compensation in the Spanish Health Care Sector', p. 342.

literature and courts understand that both types of damages are recoverable. Since there are no specific rules about medical liability that provide otherwise, the same general rule applies in the area of health care liability. This means that both pecuniary and non-pecuniary losses resulting from personal injury are recoverable.[67]

The determination of the type of damage that can be compensated is also heavily argued in cases of lack of warning. What damages must be compensated by the liable doctor? There are several possible answers: all of the personal injuries, some of the personal injuries, or some other type of damage. The answers given in Spanish courts are also very varied. Some of them hold the doctor liable for all of the consequences relating to the occurrence of the risk, although the intervention was performed correctly; this is the judgment of STS (Civil Division) 13 April 1999.[68] But there is an inherent problem in this opinion: it does not appear logical that the doctor whose only error was to provide insufficient information about the risk should be liable in the same way as a doctor who did not provide adequate information and, moreover, did not perform the intervention correctly. For this reason there are more judgments that, in the case of accidental occurrence of a risk about which the patient had not been correctly informed, declare the responsibility of the doctor and establish a partial or moderate compensation of the personal injuries suffered by the patient.

One of the more common arguments is the reference to the so-called 'loss of a chance'. A clear example of this is the case cited above (STS (Civil Division) 8 September 2003[69]) in which, after a surgical intervention, the patient suffered a complication about which she had not been informed. The judgment stated that the doctor should have proven the existence of consent, which he did not do. It was considered that 'what should be evaluated in legal terms is the deprivation of the right of the patient to have clear information, previous to the consent and its consequences (the right to new consultations, the right to choose, the right to delay the intervention, etc)'. The Supreme Court added, 'the compensation [...] should only correspond to the deprivation of that right and the possibilities that, in another case, the patient had'. This moderate compensation for injuries is generally well accepted in the Spanish literature. Nevertheless, there is no clear mechanism by which the amounts of compensation can be measured, nor the criteria to reduce the compensation, although some

---

[67] Ibid., at p. 340.   [68] *Aranzadi Westlaw, RJ* 1999, 2583.
[69] *Aranzadi Westlaw, RJ* 2003, 6065.

parameters to keep in mind are recommended, such as the existence or non-existence of alternatives, the previous clinical status, the foreseeable evolution of the illness if intervention had not occurred, personal or professional circumstances, etc.

However, it can be said that the partial liability of the doctor in these types of cases is somewhat artificial. We must remember that 'informed consent' is designed to protect one right of the individual, the right of self-determination, and also that failure to provide any or sufficient information is a violation of this right. This right of the autonomy of the patient exists independently of the outcome of the treatment. Nevertheless, it is unthinkable that a patient who has experienced a successful medical treatment would claim damages from a doctor because the patient becomes aware that some risk existed about which he or she had not been informed and did not suffer. In this sense, there are abundant opinions of judges and authors that deny compensation in absence of injury.[70]

From the point of view of informed consent, the harm caused to the patient whose informed consent was not respected appears to be essentially against the personal dignity of said person and, as such, is of the nature of a non-pecuniary loss (*daño moral*). This type of argumentation was used in the previously cited STS (Administrative Division) 4 April 2000,[71] which stated that 'this unconscious situation provoked by the lack of information [...] supposes in itself a serious non-pecuniary loss different and apart from the bodily injuries derived from the intervention'. This judgment has been followed by other judgments.[72]

In some cases of wrongful birth, pecuniary as well as non-pecuniary losses have been recognised as damage derived from the lack of information concerning possible anomalies of the foetus during pregnancy. The previously cited STS (Civil Division) of 21 December 2005[73] considered 'the suffering occasioned by the birth and later development of a handicapped child who foreseeably will never be able to live independently' to be a non-pecuniary loss. This judgment also considered 'the cost of the diagnostic tests, of an unnecessary pregnancy and birth, and the adaptation of the parents to the new social, family, and economic situation and the special situation caused by an unforeseen and extraordinary fact

---

[70] Among the latest judgments, STS (Administrative Division) 20 April 2005, *Aranzadi Westlaw*, RJ 2005, 4312.

[71] *Aranzadi Westlaw*, RJ 2000, 3258.

[72] For instance, STS (Administrative Division) 9 May 2005, *Aranzadi Westlaw*, RJ 2005, 4902.

[73] *Aranzadi Westlaw*, RJ 2005, 10149.

for them, as is the birth of a child affected by Down's Syndrome' to be property damage.

12   Exemption clauses

As discussed earlier, usually, before any medical treatment, patients sign written forms, giving their consent to the treatment. Generally this written consent is not as valuable as an exemption clause.[74] However, the opposite idea appears in some singular cases.[75]

13   Liability insurance

In Spain there is not a Public Insurance Scheme which covers the harm that patients sustain in the course of health care assistance. However, in some special situations such as infections of AIDS or Hepatitis C, a system of public 'compensation funds' is provided (public assistance – *ayudas públicas*)[76] as long as the acquired infection results from a blood transfusion or treatment with blood products and is occasioned within the framework of public medical health care assistance. In these cases, the victim who decides to take advantage of this public assistance must waive the liability claims against the Public Administration, its hospitals, and/ or their staff.

According to article 46 of *Ley* 44/2003 (21 November) relating to the regulation of health professionals, a compulsory insurance of civil liability or a financial guarantee that covers the compensations that may be derived from an eventual harm, is demanded of health care practitioners in the private health system and the legal entities of this same private health system.

These insurance contracts are governed by rules established by the Insurance Contract Act (*Ley* 50/1980, of 8 October, *del Contrato de Seguro*),[77] within which the victim can act directly in order to claim

---

[74]   STS (Civil Division) 27 April 2001, *Aranzadi Westlaw, RJ* 2001, 6891.

[75]   STS (Administrative Division) 27 November 2000. *Cf.* also STS (Administrative Division) 26 November 2004, *Aranzadi Westlaw, RJ* 2005, 22.

[76]   *Real Decreto-Ley* 9, 1993, of 28 May, *sobre concesión de ayudas a los afectados por el Síndrome de Inmunodeficiencia Humana* (BOE 1 June 1993, p. 16420) and *Ley* 14, 2002, of 5 June, *por la que se establecen ayudas sociales a las personas con hemofilia u otras coagulopatías congénitas que hayan desarrollado la hepatitis C como consecuencia de haber recibido tratamiento de concentrados de factores de coagulación en el ámbito del sistema sanitario público* (BOE 6 June 2002, p. 20254).

[77]   BOE 17 October 1980, p. 23126.

damages from the insurance company. As a rule, physicians usually buy liability insurance from an insurance company that offers collective coverage to all physicians who are members of a specific medical association (*Colegios de Médicos*), with some basic conditions for all members. The possibility of increasing coverage when purchasing an individual policy is left open.[78]

14   Harmonisation at the European level

In our opinion, a recent development in this field, the Proposal for a Directive of the European Parliament and of the Council on services in the internal market,[79] which is called the 'Bolkestein Directive', must be mentioned. Although not directly related, the measure could affect medical liability. This may be the case with the following articles: 22 (information on providers and their services) and 23 (that tries to establish professional insurance and guarantees, in order to cover damages as a requirement).

15   Conclusion

In comparison with other systems within the Western European context, the apparition and development of civil liability for medical malpractice in Spain demonstrates a notable delay. It is surprising that the first judgment of the Spanish Supreme Court treating the question occurred in 1923 and that the second occurred in 1950. The liability of the physician was not recognised in either case, even though the facts of both cases appeared to demonstrate that the physician had acted with grave negligence. Actually, it was not until the 1980s that Spanish courts began to recognise the obligation of a physician to compensate (a patient) for damage caused in the exercise of his or her profession when he or she had not acted with required diligence.

The legal literature concerning medical malpractice was scarce until the end of the 1970s and it showed a significant influence of the French (and to a lesser degree, the Italian) experience(s). From the 1980s onward, the recognition of the issue of medical civil liability in the courts and in the literature evolved in parallel fashion and began to become abundant

---

[78] M. Martín Casals, J. Solé Feliu and J. C. Seuba Torreblanca, 'Compensation in the Spanish Health Care Sector', p. 357.

[79] Common Position (EC) No. 16, 2006 adopted by the Council on 24 July 2006, OJ 2006 C 270E, 7 November 2006.

in Spain. Today, it is one of the most frequent topics in the field of civil liability.

Looking at the last fifteen years, one can appreciate an increase in the importance of this material, particularly relating to the standard of care, informed consent, or the extent of damage. The influence of common law systems is especially interesting with respect to material aspects (informed consent) as well as to rules relating to the burden of proof in the judicial process (e.g. *res ipsa loquitur*).

In general, it is now understood in Spanish law that the physician must compensate for harm caused when the physician is at fault. There are very few cases which speak about the strict liability of the physician or the hospital.

Today there are three areas regarding the 'standard of care' practised by health professionals that must be pointed to in Spanish law. One is the increase in the level of required care from the 1980s to the present day. Second, some judgments show the influence of French doctrine concerning the so-called *obligaciones de medios reforzadas*.[80] The third area concerns the recognition of the difference between 'necessary medicine' (*medicina necesaria*) and 'satisfactory medicine' (*medicina satisfactiva*).[81] Moreover, writ and courts in Spain have accepted the figure of 'informed consent' and, consequently, a duty to warn has been recognised for a long time.

Relating to the burden of proof, medical liability is the only area of Spanish civil liability where the general reversal of the burden of proof does not take place. Consequently, since the plaintiff cannot avail himself or herself of a presumption of fault, he or she has to duly prove the fault of the physician or other health care personnel. Nevertheless, a few isolated judgments of the Supreme Court have presumed the fault of the physician and have reversed the burden of proof. Moreover, there are two groups of cases in which the Spanish courts actually accept a true exception to the general rule of no presumption of fault which is specific to health care liability. These are the judgments that apply the 'disproportionate damage' doctrine or the procedural rule of 'dynamic distribution of the proof'.

In order to determine the causal link, as there are no specific rules of medical liability, the courts solve problems of causation by applying the general rules of causation in tort liability. It must be stressed that, in Spanish medical liability, the requirement of causation is very strict, not

---

[80] STS (Civil Division) 25 April 1994, *Aranzadi Westlaw, RJ* 1994, 3073.
[81] STS (Civil Division) 2 December 1997, *Aranzadi Westlaw, RJ* 1997, 8964, and STS (Civil Division) 28 June 1999, *Aranzadi Westlaw, RJ* 1999, 4894.

only in the sense that it is an indispensable condition of liability, but also in the sense that it must be proven with certainty (the burden of proof being upon the plaintiff, who would not be able to avail himself or herself of any presumption). However, the problem of causation is very unclear in Spanish law, especially in cases of breaching the duty to warn. The issue of 'when' the lack of warning is the 'cause' of the patient's damage has not been firmly established.

The general provisions on contract and tort liability do not draw any distinction between pecuniary and non-pecuniary losses. Therefore, both legal literature and courts understand that all losses are recoverable. Since there are no specific rules about medical liability that provide otherwise, the same general rule applies in the area of health care liability.

In Spain there is not a public insurance scheme in the field of medical liability. However, in some special cases, as with infections of AIDS or Hepatitis C, a system of public 'compensation fund' provides public assistance (*ayudas públicas*) to the victims.

APPENDIX: CODE PROVISIONS

The texts provided in this Appendix provide the main texts of national codes dealing with both delict and with medical compensation.

1 Austrian Civil Code (1811)

§ 1293 'Damage' means any disadvantage which a person suffers in relation to his person, rights or property. This is to be distinguished from the loss of the profit which a person could have expected in the normal course of things.

§ 1294 Damage arises from the wrongful conduct or omission of another. Unlawful damage occurs either intentionally or unintentionally. Intentional damage is based either on malicious intention, when the damage is known and willed, or on foresight when it is caused by blameworthy ignorance or by lack of required intention or endeavour. Both are called fault.

§1295 (1) Anyone is justified in claiming compensation for the damage that has resulted from fault. Damage may be caused either through the breach of a contractual duty or without relationship to contract.

(2) A person is liable for causing intentional damage by infringing good morals, even if it occurred through the exercise of a right, where this exercise of a right had the clear purpose of harming the other.

§1296 In case of doubt, it is presumed that damage has arisen without the fault of another.

§1297 It is however presumed that anyone who has the use of reason is competent to show the degree of diligence and attention that would be exercised by a person with usual competences. A person is guilty of fault where his failure to exercise this skill and attention leads to the violation of the rights of another.

§1298 Whoever admits that he was prevented without his fault from fulfilling his contractual or legal obligation has the burden of proving this. Insofar as he is only bound by contract for gross negligence, he must also prove that this standard does not apply.

§1299 Whoever openly claims an office or skill in relation to a trade or handicraft, or whoever voluntarily and without necessity takes over a task whose completion requires his own knowledge of art or unusual skill thereby accepts that he vouches for the necessary industry and the required but unusual knowledge. Where the person who entrusts the task to him knew of his inexperience or could have known this through usual attention, then he is also responsible together with that person.

§1300 A professional is responsible when he deliberately gives advice for reward in matters within his skill or knowledge. Apart from this case, the advice giver is only liable for the damage that he knowingly causes to another through the giving of advice.

§1306 In general, a person is not liable for damage that he causes without fault or through involuntary conduct.

§1306a When someone causes damage in order to avoid an immediate threat of danger to himself or to another, the judge shall assess whether the person harmed omitted to take measures out of consideration for the danger threatening another, as well as the relationship between the size of the damage to this danger or eventually to the property of the person creating the harm and that of the person harmed, and whether and to what extent the damage is to be replaced.

§1311 A mere accident occurs to someone where his property or person is affected. Where, however, someone causes an accident through fault, or where he has infringed a statute which seeks to avoid that accidental damage, or where he has involved himself in the affairs of another without necessity, he is liable for any damage which would not otherwise have occurred.

§1312 Where a person provides a service to another in case of necessity, then the damage which he failed to prevent is not attributed to him. It is different where that person has through fault prevented another who would have offered a greater service. But even in this latter case, he is entitled to bring the useful things he has clearly achieved into account with the damage caused.

§1313 As a rule, a person is not liable for external and unlawful conduct in which he did not take part. Even where statute provides otherwise, he is entitled to have recourse against the person causing the damage.

§1313a Where a person is obliged to perform something, he is liable for the fault of his legal representative as well as for the people whom he uses to achieve it.

§1314 Where one person takes on a servant without references or knowingly takes into his service or residence a person who is dangerous in body or character, he is liable to the householder or the occupants of a household to compensate for the damage caused by the dangerous constitution of that person.

§1315 Above all a person who incompetently or knowingly uses a dangerous person to conduct his affairs is liable for the damage which this person causes in this business to a third party.

§1323 To compensate for damage caused, everything must be put back into its original position or, where this is not possible, then its value must be paid. Where the compensation concerns only the damage caused, then this is a harmless approach. Insofar as it involves a gain forgone or the removal of suffering caused, full compensation is required.

§1325 Where somebody suffers bodily injury, he may recover the costs of treatment or where the person harmed is unable to earn, he may recover the loss of future earnings. In addition, he may be paid where claimed a sum for pain and suffering appropriate to the circumstances.

§1326 Where the person harmed is disfigured through ill-treatment, if she is of the female sex, and insofar as these circumstances can be taken into account, she must be compensated for her best future which is hindered thereby.

§1327 If death follows from bodily injury then not only any expenses must be compensated that have resulted, but also any persons left behind for whom the deceased had a legal obligation of care.

2　France

A　Civil Code (1804)

Art. 1382 Any human act whatever which causes damage to another obliges him by whose fault it occurred to make reparation.

Art. 1383 Each one is liable for the damage which he causes not only by his own act but also by his negligence or imprudence.

Art. 1384 [para.1] He is liable not only for the damage which he caused by his own act, but also for that which is caused by the act of persons for whom he is responsible, or by things which he has in his keeping.

[para.2][1] However, he who possesses by whatever right all or part of a building or of personal property in which a fire occurs is liable vis-à-vis third persons for damage caused by such fire only if it is proved that it should be attributed to his fault or to the fault of persons for whom he is responsible.

[para.3][2] This provision does not apply to relations between owners and tenants which remain regulated by Articles 1733 and 1734 of the Civil Code.

[para.4][3] The father and mother, to the extent that they exercise the right of custody, are jointly liable for damage caused by their minor children living with them.

[para.5] Masters and principals (are liable) for damage caused by their domestics and employees in the functions for which they have been employed.

---

[1] Text resulting from the law of 7 November 1922.　　[2] Ibid.

[3] Text resulting from law n° 70–459 of 4 January 1970.

[para.6] Teachers and artisans (are liable) for damage caused by their pupils and apprentices during the time when they are under their surveillance.

[para.7][4] The above liability arises unless the father and mother and the artisans prove that they could not prevent the act which gave rise to such liability.

[para.8] As to teachers, the faults, imprudence or negligence alleged against them as having caused the damaging act must be proven according to ordinary law by the plaintiff in the suit.

Art. 1385 The owner of an animal or he who avails himself of it while it is being put to his use is liable for the damage which the animal causes, whether the animal was in his keeping or whether it had strayed or escaped.

Art. 1386 The owner of a building is liable for damage caused by its ruin, when this occurred through want of maintenance or by a construction defect.

B   Code de la santé publique (2002)[5]

Art. L1142-1

I. Except in the case where liability is incurred because of a defect in a health product, the professionals mentioned in the fourth part of this code, as well as any establishment, service or body in which acts of prevention, diagnosis or care are carried out are only liable for the damage resulting from such acts of prevention, diagnosis or care in the case of fault.

The establishments, services or bodies mentioned above are liable for damage caused by nosocomial infections, unless they can demonstrate some external cause.

Where there is no liability on the part of a professional, establishment, service or body mentioned in I above nor of a producer of products, a medical accident, an iatrogenic disease or a nosocomial infection gives rise to a right to compensation for the patient or, in the case of death, for his heirs on the basis of social solidarity, when these are directly imputable to the acts of prevention, diagnosis or care and they have had abnormal consequences for the patient taking account of the state of his health as well as its likely development and that they had a seriousness of a level established by decree, assessed in relation to the loss of functional capacity and measurable consequences for his private and professional life taking particular account of the level of permanent incapacity or the temporary inability to work.

There is a right to compensation for such damage on the basis of social solidarity which exceed a percentage of a specific scale fixed by decree; this percentage, at least equal to 25%, shall be determined by the said decree.

---

[4] Text resulting from the law of 5 April 1937.
[5] Provisions resulting from the law of 4 March 2002, as amended.

Art. L1142-1-1

... The right to compensation based on national solidarity:

(1) Damage resulting from nosocomial infections in the establishments, services or bodies mentioned in paragraph I of art. L1142-1 amounting to a permanent incapacity greater than 25% measured by the scale mentioned in paragraph II of the same article, as well as death resulting from these nosocomial infections.

(2) Damage resulting from the intervention in exceptional circumstances of a professional person in an establishment, service or body outside his activity of prevention, diagnosis or care.

Art. L1142-2 [Requires medical professionals as well as establishments, services and bodies mentioned in art. 1142-1 to be insured.]

Art. L1142-3 [Excludes biomedical research from these provisions, since there are special provisions in art. L1121-10.]

Art. L1142-4 Any person who is or considers himself to be the victim of damage attributable to activities of prevention, diagnosis or care, or his heirs, if he is dead, or, in appropriate cases, his legal representative shall be informed by the professional, or by the health establishment, service or body concerned of the circumstances and causes of that damage.

This information shall be given to him at the latest within a fortnight following the discovery of the damage or his express request in the course of an interview during which the person may be accompanied by a doctor or another person of his choice.

Art. L1142-5 In every region, a regional commission for conciliation and compensation shall be tasked with the settlement of litigation relating to medical accidents, iatrogenic diseases or nosocomial infections, as well as of litigation between the users and health professionals, health establishments, services or bodies or producers of health products mentioned in articles L1142-1 and 1142-2.

Art. L1142-6 Regional commissions for conciliation and compensation for medical accidents, iatrogenic diseases or nosocomial infections shall be chaired by an administrative judge or a civil judge, in post or retired. They shall be composed of representatives of patients and users of the health system, health professionals and managers of health establishments, services or bodies, representatives of the office mentioned in art. L1142-22, and of insurance companies.

Art. L1142-7 Any person who considers himself to be the victim of damage attributable to activities of prevention, diagnosis or care, or his heirs, if he is dead, or, in appropriate cases, his legal representative may refer the matter to the regional commission ...

Any such reference suspends a prescription period or litigation until the end of the procedure described in this chapter.

Art. L1142-8 When the damages suffered have the serious character described in paragraph II of article L1142-1, the commission shall issue an opinion on the circumstances, causes, nature and extent of the damages, as well as on the compensation regime applicable.

The opinion of the commission shall be issued within six months from the making of the reference. It is sent to the person making the reference, to any person involved in the litigation, and to the office mentioned in art. 1142-22.

This opinion may only be challenged during a compensation action brought by the victim before a competent court or in subrogation actions brought under articles L1142-14, L1142-15 and L1142-17.

Art. L1142-14

When the regional commission for conciliation and compensation for medical accidents, iatrogenic diseases or nosocomial infections considers that damage falling within the first paragraph of article L1142-8 gives rise to liability on the part of a health professional, health establishment, service or body mentioned in articles L1142-1 or a producer of health products mentioned in article 1142-2, the insurer underwriting the civil or administrative liability of the person considered liable by the commission shall send to the victim or his heirs within four months of receipt of the opinion a compensation offer concerning the full compensation of all damage suffered within the scope of the ceilings set by the insurance policy.

[The insurer shall have a subrogation action against the person responsible for the harm.]

… If the competent judge in an action brought by the victim who has refused an offer considers that the offer was manifestly insufficient, he shall order the insurer to pay the office [mentioned in art. L1142-22] a sum at most equal to 15% of the compensation granted, over and above any damages paid to the victim.

Art. L1142-15 Where the insurer is silent or expressly refuses to make an offer, or where the person responsible is not insured or his insurance cover… is exhausted, the office created under article L1142-22 is substituted for the insurer…

Art. L1142-17 When the regional commission considers that the damage is compensable under paragraph II of article L1142-1 or under article L1142-1-1, the office shall send to the victim or his heirs within four months of the receipt of the opinion an offer of full compensation for the damage suffered…

Art. L1142-17-1 Where the regional commission considers that the aggravation of harm suffered as a result of a nosocomial infection involves the level of permanent incapacity exceeding the percentage mentioned in article L1142-1-1 or his death, the office shall send to the victim or his heirs an offer of compensation in the terms set out in article 1142-17 and shall reimburse the insurer for the compensation initially paid to the victim.

Art. L1142-21 Where in a compensation action arising from the harmful consequences of acts of prevention, diagnosis or care are carried out in a health establishment the competent court considers that the damages suffered are compensable within paragraph II of article L1142-1 or under article L1142-1-1, the office shall be joined as if it had been an initial party to the litigation. It becomes a defendant in the proceedings.

[Where an order is made against the office, it has a subrogation action against the person responsible or his insurer.]

Art. L1142-22

The National Office for the Compensation of Medical Accidents, Iatrogenic Diseases or Nosocomial Infections is a public, administrative body of the State under the supervision of the Minister of Health. It is tasked with the compensation on the basis of national solidarity of damage caused by a medical accident, an iatrogenic disease or a nosocomial infection on the grounds set out in paragraph II of article L1142-1, article L1142-1-1 and article L1142-17, as well as the compensation imposed on it by articles L1142-15 and L1142-18.

The office is also responsible for the compensation for damage directly resulting from a compulsory vaccination under article L3111-9, of compensation for the victims of harm resulting from the Human Immune-deficiency Virus under article L3122-1 and the compensation for damage directly imputable to an activity of prevention, diagnosis or care resulting from measures taken in accordance with article L3131-1 and L3131-4...

Art. L1142-28 Actions brought concerning the liability of health professionals or of public or private health establishments in relation to acts of prevention, diagnosis or care shall be time barred after ten years from the materialisation of the damage...

These actions are not governed by the prescription period in article 2232 of the Civil Code.

3   Netherlands

A   Civil Code (Ordinary delict provisions)

Art. 6:74 Any failure to perform an undertaking obliges the debtor to compensate the damage suffered by the creditor, unless the failure cannot be attributed to the debtor.

Art. 6:99 Where the damage may have resulted from two or more events for each of which a different person is liable, and where it has been determined that the damage has arisen from at least one of these events, the obligation to repair the damage rests upon each of these persons, unless he proves that the damage is not the result of the event for which he himself is liable.

Art. 6:101 When the damage is partly caused by an occurrence that can be imputed to the injured party, the obligation to pay compensation is reduced by apportioning the damage between the injured party and the liable party in proportion to the degree in which the occurrences that can be imputed to the parties have contributed to the damage, provided that account is taken of the disparity in the seriousness of the respective faults, or other circumstances of the case, to decide whether fairness demands that an alternative apportionment or full recovery takes place or that the obligation to pay lapses.

Art. 6:106 (1) For damage which is not property damage, the victim has the right to compensation fixed according to fairness:

a. where the person responsible had the objective of bringing about such damage;
b. where the victim has suffered physical injury, his honour or good name is harmed or he is affected in any other way in his person; or
c. where the damage relates to the memory of a deceased person and the claim is brought by a spouse who is not separated, a registered partner, or a blood relative to the second degree, that person may take the place of the deceased if, were he still alive, the deceased would have had a right to compensation for injury to his honour or good name.

(2) The right to compensation set out in the previous paragraph is not capable of being transmitted by way of seizure unless an agreement is established or a claim is made in law. The transfer is complete under the general title when the person has informed the other party responsible for making compensation.

Art 6:162 A person who commits an unlawful act towards another, which can be imputed to him, must repair the damage, which the other person suffers as a consequence thereof.

Except where there is a ground of justification, the following acts are deemed to be unlawful: the violation of a right, an act or omission violating a statutory duty or a rule of unwritten law pertaining to proper social conduct.

An unlawful act can be imputed to its author if it results from his fault or from a cause for which he is answerable according to law or common opinion.

Art. 6:163 No duty to compensate arises whenever the violated norm does not protect against the damage that the victim has suffered.

Art. 6:168 (1) The judge may reject a claim to forbid unlawful conduct on the ground that it should be tolerated by reason of pressing social interests. The victim retains his right to compensation under the relevant title [of this Code]…

(3) Where an order for compensation or for conserving a situation is not complied with, then the judge may, if necessary, forbid the conduct.

Art. 6:169 A person who exercises parental authority or guardianship over a child of under fourteen years of age is liable for damage done to another by such conduct of that child *which must be considered as an act*, where this act, but for the child's age, could be imputed to him as an unlawful act.

B   Civil Code: The contract for medical services (1994)[6]

(1) **Art. 7:446** (1) The contract concerning medical services – in this subchapter hereinafter to be referred to as the contract for medical services – is the contract whereby a natural person or a legal person, the health care provider, in pursuance of his professional or business health care activities in respect of another party, the principal, undertakes to provide medical services directly relating to the person of the principal or of a specific third party. The party to whose person the medical services directly relate shall hereinafter be referred to as the patient.

(2) The provision of medical services shall be understood to mean:
   a. all activities – including examination and giving advice – which directly concern a person and which are intended to cure that person of a disease, to prevent that person from contracting a disease or to assess the condition of that person's health, or which constitute obstetrical assistance;
   b. activities other than those referred to under a. which directly concern a person and which are carried out by a physician or dentist in a professional capacity.

(3) The activities, referred to in paragraph one, shall include nursing and care of the patient related thereto as well as the direct provision for the patient of the material framework within which such activities may be carried out.

(4) There shall be no contract for medical services if the activities are carried out to assess the condition of a person's health or to provide medical care to a person under the authority of another person with regard to the settlement of claims or duties, the acceptance by an insurance or care facility, or the assessment of one's aptitude for an education, a labour relation or the exercise of certain work.

---

[6] Act of 17 November 1994, *Staatsblad* 837 to amend the Civil Code and other legislation in connection with the incorporation of provisions concerning the contract to provide medical services, as renumbered by Decree of the Minister of Justice of 15 December 1994, *Staatsblad* 837.

Art. 7:447 Minors

(1) A minor who has reached the age of sixteen years shall be competent to conclude a contract for medical services for himself, and to carry out legal acts directly connected with the contract.

(2) The minor shall be liable for the fulfilment of any obligations resulting from the contract, without prejudice to his parents' obligation to bear the costs of care and upbringing.

(3) With respect to matters bearing on the contract for medical services the minor shall be competent to act both before a court and outside a court.

Art. 7:448 Informed consent

(1) The health care provider shall inform the patient clearly and, if requested, in writing, about the proposed examination and treatment and about the developments concerning the examination, the treatment and the condition of the patient's health. The health care provider shall inform a patient who has not reached the age of twelve years yet in such a way as fits his comprehension.

(2) In the pursuance of the obligations under paragraph one the health care provider shall be guided by that which the patient reasonably needs to know about:
   a. the nature and the purpose of the examination or treatment which he considers necessary and of the activities which are to be carried out;
   b. the likely consequences for and risks to the patient's health;
   c. other possible types of examination or treatment;
   d. the prospect for the latter's health from the point of view of the field to which the examination or treatment relates.

(3) The health care provider shall only be entitled to withhold information as referred to above where the provision of such would clearly be to the serious disadvantage of the patient. If the patient's interests so require, the health care provider should impart the said information to a party other than the patient. Such information shall still be communicated to the patient as soon as there is no further danger of the said disadvantage arising. The health care provider shall not use the competence referred to in the first sentence than after consulting another health care provider about it.

Art. 7:449 Right not to know

If the patient has stated that he does not wish to receive any information, it shall not be provided, except where the patient's interests in not receiving information are outweighed by the detrimental effects which failure to provide information might have on him or others.

Art. 7:450 Consent

(1) The patient's consent shall always be required for activities in pursuance of a contract for medical services.

(2) If the patient is a minor who is at least twelve years of age, but who is not yet sixteen years of age, the consent of the parents who exercise the parental control over him, or his guardian shall also be required. An activity may, however, be carried out without the consent of the parents or the guardian if it is clearly necessary in order to prevent serious damage to the patient, and if the patient, even after consent has been refused, adheres to a well-considered desire that the activity be carried out.

(3) In case a patient over sixteen years of age cannot be considered capable of a reasonable valuation of his interests concerned, the health care provider and the person referred to in paragraphs two or three of article 7:465, shall follow the patient's clear views laid down in writing when he still was capable of such reasonable valuation and containing a refusal of consent as referred to in paragraph (1). The health care provider may depart herefrom in case he considers legitimate reasons therefore are present.

Art. 7:451 Record of consent

At the patient's request the health care provider shall in every case record in writing those activities of a major nature for which consent has been given.

Art. 7:452 Cooperation by the patient

The patient shall to the best of his ability provide the health care provider with the information and cooperation reasonably required by the latter for the performance of the contract.

Art. 7:453 Level of care

In the exercise of his activities a health care provider shall exercise the level of care expected from a conscientious health care provider and he shall act in accordance with the responsibility following from the professional standard for health care providers.

Art. 7:454 Records

(1) The health care provider shall open a file on the patient's treatment. In this file he shall keep notes of data concerning the patient's health and the activities carried out in relation to the patient and he shall place therein such other documents containing such data, as are necessary for a conscientious provision of health care for the patient.

(2) If requested, the health care provider shall add a declaration by the patient concerning the documents contained in the file.

(3) Without prejudice to the provisions of article 7:455, the health care provider shall keep the documents referred to in the previous paragraphs for a period of ten years, effective from the date on which they were drawn up, or as much longer as may reasonably be expected from a conscientious health care provider.

Art. 7:455 Destruction of records

(1) The health care provider shall destroy the documents referred to in article 7:454 which are kept by him, within three months after the patient has made a request to that effect.
(2) Paragraph one shall not apply insofar as the request relates to documents which, if kept, may reasonably be thought to be of considerable importance to a party other than the patient, as well insofar as the destruction of documents is prohibited by virtue of or pursuant to statutory provisions.

Art. 7:456 Access to records

If requested the health care provider shall provide the patient as soon as possible with access to and copies of the documents referred to in article 7:454. The provision will not take place insofar as this is necessary for the protection of another party's privacy. The health care provider may charge a reasonable fee for the provision of copies.

Art. 7:457 Provision of information

(1) Without prejudice to the provisions of the second sentence of article 7:448 paragraph three, the health care provider shall not provide persons other than the patient with information about the patient or give them access to or copies of the documents referred to in article 7:454 without the patient's consent. If provision takes place, this will only occur insofar as it does not harm another party's privacy. The provision may occur without the restrictions referred to in the previous sentences if this is compulsory by virtue of or pursuant to statutory provisions.
(2) Persons other than the patient shall not include those who are directly involved in the performance of the contract for medical services and the person who is acting as substitute to the health care provider, insofar as provision is necessary for the activities in that regard.
(3) Nor shall this category include persons whose consent is required in connection with the performance of the contract for medical services pursuant to articles 7:450 and 7:465. However, if the health care provider by supplying information concerning the patient or by giving access to or copies of the patient's documents cannot be considered to comply with the level of care expected from a conscientious health care provider, he shall not take such a course of action.

Art. 7:458 Scientific research

(1) Contrary to the provisions of article 7:457 paragraph one, information about the patient or access to documents referred to in article 7:454 may, without the consent of the patient, be provided to another party if this information is needed for the purpose of statistical or other scientific research relating to public health, if:
   a. it is in all reasonableness impossible to ask for consent and concerning the performance of the research such guarantees are provided, that the privacy of the patient won't be disproportionately harmed, or;
   b. it is in all reasonableness impossible to ask for consent regarding the nature and purpose of the research, and the health care provider has taken care that the data shall be provided in such a way that conversion to individual natural persons reasonably shall be prevented.

(2) Provision according to paragraph one shall only be possible if the following conditions have been met:
   a. the research serves the public interest;
   b. the research cannot be carried out without the relevant data; and
   c. insofar the patient concerned did not expressly object to its provision.

(3) In case of a provision in accordance with paragraph one, a note of this shall be kept in the file.

Art. 7:459 Observers

(1) The health care provider shall perform the activities relating to the contract for medical services without being observed by persons other than the patient, unless the patient has consented to the presence of outside observers during the said activities.

(2) Persons other than the patient shall not include persons whose professional assistance is required in the performance of an activity.

(3) Nor shall this category include those whose consent is required concerning activities carried out pursuant to articles 7:450 and 7:465. However, if allowing observers to be present may not be considered compatible with the level of care expected from a conscientious health care provider, the latter shall not take such a course of action.

Art. 7:460 Right to terminate

Unless there are important reasons for doing so, a health care provider may not terminate the contract for medical services.

Art. 7:461 Fees

The principal owes the health care provider payment, except insofar as the latter receives payment for his work by virtue of or pursuant to statutory provisions or on some other basis as provided for in the contract.

Art. 7:462 Hospital liability

(1) If activities in pursuance of the contract for medical services are carried out in a hospital which is no party to the contract, the hospital shall be jointly liable in the event of any deficiency, as if it were itself a party to the contract.

(2) The term 'hospital' as referred to in the paragraph 1 shall be understood to mean any institution or part of an institution recognised under the Health Insurance Act or the Exceptional Medical Expenses (Compensation) Act as a hospital, nursing home or mental institution, as well as teaching hospitals, abortion clinics within the meaning of the Termination of Pregnancy Act and dental clinics within the meaning of the Dental Clinics Act of 1986.

Art. 7:463 Exemption clauses

The liability of the health care provider or, in the case referred to in article 7:462, of the hospital, cannot be limited or excluded.

Art. 7:464

(1) If in the pursuance of a medical profession or business medical services are provided, otherwise than according to a contract for medical services, this subchapter as well as the articles 7:404, 7:405 paragraph two and 7:406 of subchapter one of this title shall be of equal applicability, insofar as the nature of the legal relation is not incompatible with the application.

(2) If activities as referred to in article 7:446 paragraph five are concerned:

    a. the documents referred to in article 7:454 shall only be kept as long as it is necessary for the purpose of research, unless provisions by virtue of or pursuant to statutory law prohibit destruction;

    b. the person whom the examination concerns shall be given the opportunity to announce if he wants to be informed about the results and the consequences of the examination and, if desired, if he wants to take note at first in order to be able to decide if others shall be informed thereof.

Art. 7:465 Legal representatives

(1) Any obligations resulting from this subchapter on the part of the health care provider shall, in case the patient has not yet reached the age of twelve years, be fulfilled by the health care provider towards the parents exercising parental control over the patient or towards the patient's guardian.

(2) The same shall apply if a patient has reached the age of twelve years, but cannot be considered capable of a reasonable valuation of his interests concerned, unless the patient in question has reached the age of majority and

is under guardianship or if for the benefit of the patient a *mentorschap*[7] has been established, in which cases obligations shall be fulfilled towards the guardian or *mentor*.

(3) If an adult patient cannot be considered capable of a reasonable valuation of his interests concerned and he has neither been placed under guardianship nor a *mentorschap* has been established for his benefit, any obligations towards the patient arising on the part of the health care provider from this section shall be fulfilled towards the person authorised in writing by the patient to act on his behalf. In the absence of such person, or in the event of such person failing to take the necessary steps, obligations shall be fulfilled towards the patient's spouse or partner, unless that person refuses, or, in the absence of the latter, towards a parent or child of the patient, unless that person refuses.

(4) The health care provider shall fulfil his obligations towards the legal representatives of the patient as referred to in paragraph one and two and the persons referred to in paragraph three, unless the fulfilment is not compatible with the level of care expected from a conscientious health care provider.

(5) The person towards whom the health care provider under paragraph two or three is obliged to fulfil the obligations that result from this subchapter shall act in accordance with the level of care expected from a conscientious representative. This person is obliged to involve the patient as much as is possible in the fulfilment of his task.

(6) If the patient resists against an activity of a major nature for which a person as referred to in paragraph two or three has consented, the activity will only be carried out if this is clearly necessary to avoid serious harm for the patient.

Art. 7:466 Emergencies

(1) If the consent required pursuant to article 7:465 for the performance of an activity need only be obtained from a person within the meaning of that article instead of from the patient, the activity may be carried out without such consent if there is insufficient time to obtain such consent on the grounds that immediate performance of the activity is clearly necessary in order to prevent serious harm to the patient.

(2) Consent as required by articles 7:450 and 7:465 may be considered to have been given if the activity in question is not of a major nature.

---

[7] The *mentor* is a natural person, appointed by a judge, who represents the person who has reached the age of majority but cannot be considered capable to valuate his non-material interests because of a mental or physical deficiency.

Art. 7:467 Human tissue

(1) Anonymous human tissues and organs separated from the body may be used for medical statistical or other medical research insofar as the patient whom the tissue or organ originates from does not object to such research and the research is conducted with due care.
(2) Research with anonymous human tissues and organs separated from the body is research whereby it is guaranteed that the human tissue to be used in the research and the data based thereupon is not convertible to a person.

Art. 7:468 Mandatory law

Parties may not derogate to the detriment of the patient from the provisions of this subchapter nor from articles 7:404, 7:405 paragraph two and 7:406 of subchapter one of this title.

4 Spanish Civil Code (1889)

Art. 1902 The person who by action or omission causes damage to another by fault or negligence is obliged to repair the damage caused.

Art. 1903 The obligation imposed in the preceding article applies not only for a person's own acts or omissions, but also for those persons for whom a person is responsible.

The father and the mother are responsible for the harm caused by their minor children who are living with them.

Tutors are liable for the harm caused by minors or incapacitated persons under their authority and living with them.

Employers or directors of an establishment or firm are liable for the harm caused by their employees in the performance of tasks that are entrusted to them or of their functions.

The State is liable under this head for the acts of its special agents, but not when the harm has been caused by a civil servant entrusted with practical administration, for which case the preceding paragraph applies.

Masters and directors of arts and trades are liable in respect of the harm caused by their pupils or apprentices, as long as they remain under their control.

The liability under this article ceases when the persons mentioned prove that they have shown the diligence of the good father of the family to avoid the harm.

Art. 1905 The possessor of an animal or a person who makes use of one is liable for the harm that it causes, even where it had strayed or escaped. This liability only ceases when he proves that the harm resulted from a fortuitous event or from the fault of the person who suffered the harm.

Art. 1906 The owner of a building is liable for the harm caused to neighbouring property when he has not taken the necessary steps to prevent them increasing ...

Art. 1908 The owner of objects causing harm is also liable:

1. By the explosion of machines that had not been kept with due care and by the burning of explosive substances that were not stored in safe and suitable place.
2. By excessive smoke, that is injurious to the people or the property.
3. By the falling of trees located on thoroughfares, when this is not caused by force majeure.
4. By emanations of sewers or deposits of infected matter, built without the precautions appropriate to the place in which they were located.

INDEX

abortion and wrongful life/wrongful
birth, 147, 154, 155
Ackner, Lord, 154
Action for Victims of Medical
Accidents (AVMA), UK, 56
Acute Care Trusts in Scotland, 55
ADEPA (Association for the Defence of
the Patient), Spain, 169
administrative law
in France, 72, 80–2, 89–92
in Spain, 160, 164, 169, 181
aléa thérapeutique cases in France,
90–1, 95, 99
Alonso Pérez, Mariano, 167
alternative dispute resolution
arbitration, in the Netherlands, 149
conciliation
in Austria, 115, 131
in France, 73, 76, 88, 95, 97, 98
grievance committees in the
Netherlands, 140
mediation
in England and Wales, 51
in Scotland, 57
ombudsman arrangements in
Austria, 115, 131
America. *See* United States
arbitration, in the Netherlands, 149
Association for the Defence
of the Patient (ADEPA),
Spain, 169
Ataz López, Joaquín, 167
Australia
Cottanach v. Melchior, 39
informed consent in, 48
legislative proposals to manage
medical liability in, 9

Austria, 108–9
causation in, 123–6
Civil Code
on damages, 128
on fault, 121–3
on tortious and contractual
liability, 113
on vicarious liability, 127, 128
codes of conduct and disciplinary
bodies, 110, 114
compensation funds, 116–17
conciliation panels, 115, 131
contract law in, 112, 113
criminal liability in, 118
damages in, 126, 128
documentation, importance of, 124
exemption clauses in, 129
fault liability in, 121–3, 128
German influence on, 108
historical background to medical
liability in, 8, 108–9
hospitals and clinics in, 109, 112,
116–17
increased number of claims in,
111, 129
informed consent in, 118–21, 125
medical liability insurance in, 111
Nordic patient insurance scheme,
interest in, 21
ombudsman arrangements, 115, 131
ordinary courts, public and private
health care dealt with by, 5
patients' rights in, 114–16, 129
personal liability in, 126–7
predisposition or precondition in
patient, 126
private health insurance in, 111

Austria (*cont.*)
  proof of medical liability in, 123–6
  public and private health systems in,
    4, 109–13
  reasons for development of medical
    liability in, 109, 130–1
  responsible parties in, 126–8
  splitting liability in, 125–6
  tort law in, 113
  vicarious liability in, 113, 126–8
  wrongfulness in, 117–18
Austrian Medical Chamber, 110,
  111–12
Austrian statute law
  1806 decree excluding tort law
    actions against civil servants
    performing duties of their
    office, 112
  Ärztegesetz (ÄrzteG), 114, 124, 128
  Krankenanstaltengesetz (KAG), 114
  Reichssanitätsgesetz, 110
  Versicherungsvertragsgesetz
    (VersVG), 111
autonomy, 40, 50, 104, 183
AVMA (Action for Victims of Medical
  Accidents), UK, 56

Belgian interest in Nordic patient
  insurance scheme, 21
Benzo Cano, Eduardo, 165
Bingham, Lord, 48
Bolam principle, 12, 42–6, 61, 64, 102,
  143
Bolkestein directive on services, 22, 185
breach of contract. *See* contract law
breach of duty. *See* duty of care/breach
  of duty; standard of care
Bridge of Harwich, Lord, 11, 14, 44, 49
Britain. *See* England and Wales;
  Scotland
Brooke LJ, 40
Brougham, Lord, 59
Browne-Wilkinson, Lord, 44
burden of proof. *See* proof of medical
  liability
'but for' test (*conditio sine qua non*), 15,
  47, 179
Bydlinski, Franz, 125

Care Trusts in UK, 30–1, 55
causation, 15
  in Austria, 123–6
  'but for' test (*conditio sine qua non*),
    15, 47, 179
  in England and Wales, 47–50, 53
  in France, 83, 84, 104
  in the Netherlands, 154
  in Scotland, 65
  in Spain, 164, 178–80, 186
Clyde, Lord President, 60
codes of conduct and disciplinary
    bodies, 7
  in Austria, 110, 114
  in England and Wales, 31–4
  in France, 7, 75–6
  licensing of physicians, 33
  in the Netherlands, 136, 140
  in Scotland, 56–7
  in Spain, 171
comparative law
  on damages for wrongful life/
    wrongful birth, 16–18
  on standard of care, 13, 144
compensation funds. *See* no-fault
    compensation schemes
conciliation
  in Austria, 115, 131
  in France, 73, 76, 88, 95, 97, 98
conditio sine qua non ('but for' test),
    15, 47, 179
conduct codes. *See* codes of conduct
    and disciplinary bodies
confidentiality, patient right of
  in the Netherlands, 140
  in Spain, 173
constitutional law, role of, 5, 87–8
contract law, 6–7
  in Austria, 112, 113
  in England and Wales, 6, 7, 35
  in France, 6, 71, 73, 80
  in the Netherlands, 6, 25, 134–6,
    137–8, 146–56
  in Scotland, 6, 58
  in Spain, 162, 170, 173–4, 176, 181,
    187
  tort law versus, 6–7, 51
  in United States, 51

corrective justice, 50
Council of Europe, 21, 158
criminal liability, 5
    in Austria, 117–18
    England and Wales, negligent
        manslaughter in, 36
    in France, 5, 11, 73–5, 79
    in the Netherlands, 149
    in Spain, 5, 11, 161, 163, 167, 170
    standard of care, 11

damages, 16–18
    in Austria, 126, 128
    in England and Wales, 18, 66–9
    in France, 17
    legislative proposals to manage, 9
    in the Netherlands, 16–17, 146
    in Scotland, 17, 66–9
    in Spain, 181–4
    wrongful life/wrongful birth, 16–18,
        146–56
Denmark
    Act on Patient Safety, 10
    claim rate, 3
    patient insurance in (See Nordic
        patient insurance scheme)
    reporting requirements, 10
Denning, Lord, 15, 27, 38, 46, 47
DES (diethylstilbestrol) cases,
    148–53
Dickson, Robert, 66
diethylstilbestrol (DES) cases,
    148–53
dignity, human, 154–6
disabled persons, wrongful life/birth
    cases involving. See wrongful
    life/wrongful birth
disciplinary bodies. See codes of
    conduct and disciplinary
    bodies
discovery in United States, 14
disproportionate harm, doctrine of, in
    Spain, 177, 179, 186
distributive justice, 40
documentation, importance of
    in Austria, 124
    in the Netherlands, 140
    in Spain, 173

Dutch Association of Surgeons, 143
Dutch law. See Netherlands
duty of care/breach of duty. See also
        standard of care
    in England and Wales, 12, 37–47
    in Scotland, 63
duty to warn. See informed consent
dynamic distribution of the proof,
        Spanish doctrine of, 178, 186

ECHR (European Convention on
        Human Rights), 21
economic change and medical liability,
        24
ELD (European Legal Development)
        Project, 1, 2, 23, 146
Ellenborough, Lord, 36
England and Wales, 27–9
    Bolam principle, 12, 42–6, 61, 64,
        102, 143
    causation, 47–50, 53
    claim rate, 3
    codes of conduct and disciplinary
        bodies, 31–4
    contract law in, 6, 7, 35
    costs/number of claims compared to
        Scotland, 66–9
    criminal manslaughter charges, 36
    damages, measure of, 18, 66–9
    duty of care/breach of duty in, 12,
        37–47
    expert witnesses in, 11, 37, 43, 45–6,
        47
    fault liability in, 37, 38
    France compared, 101–2
    future of medical liability in,
        50–3
    historical background to medical
        liability in, 8
    informed consent in, 44, 48–9, 50,
        138
    legislative proposals to manage
        medical liability in, 9
    Making Amends (Chief Medical
        Officer report, UK), 51–3
    negligence, 6, 36–7
    NHSLO (National Health Service
        Litigation Office), 3

England and Wales (*cont.*)
  no-fault compensation scheme
    proposals, 51–3
  Nordic patient insurance scheme,
    interest in, 21
  patients' rights in, 10, 11, 31–4
  private health care in, 31
  proof of medical liability in, 14
  public health system (NHS or
    National Health Service) in, 4,
    30–1
  public policy issues in, 39, 50
  reporting requirements, 10
  res ipsa loquitur (prima facie
    negligence), 14, 47
  responsible parties in, 16
  rise in medical liability claims in,
    27–9
  Scotland and, cross-border
    assimilation between, 61–2,
    63–4
  standard of care in, 11, 34–47
  tort law in, 6, 7, 37
  vicarious liability in, 37–8
  wrongful life/wrongful birth, 18,
    38–42
English and Welsh case law
  *Allen v. Bloomsbury Health
    Authority,* 39
  *Allied Marples Group Ltd v.
    Simmons & Simmons,* 49
  Anns v. Merton LBC, 50
  Arthur JS Hall & Co. v. Simons, 29
  *Barnett v. Chelsea and Kensington
    Hospital Management
    Committee,* 47
  Benarr v. Kettering Health Authority,
    39
  Blyth v. Birmingham Waterworks, 42
  *Bolam v. Friern Hospital
    Management Committee,* 12,
    42–6, 61, 64, 102, 143
  *Bolitho v. City and Hackney Health
    Authority,* 42, 43, 44–5, 61, 63,
    102
  Bonham's Case, 33
  Bull v. Devon Area Health Authority,
    38

Caparo Industries Plc v. Dickman, 50
Cassidy v. Ministry of Health, 38, 47,
  64, 65
Chappel v. Hart, 48
Chester v. Afshar, 2, 48–9, 50
*Collins v. Hertfordshire County
  Council,* 38
*D v. South Tyneside Health Care
  NHS Trust,* 45
Donoghue v. Stevenson, 137
Doughty v. General Dental Council,
  34
*Edward Wong Finance Co. Ltd v.
  Johnson, Stokes and Masters,* 43
*Emeh v. Kensington and Chelsea
  and Westminster Area Health
  Authority,* 39
Evans v. Liverpool Corporation, 38
Eyre v. Measday, 35
*Fairchild v. Glenhaven Funeral
  Services Ltd,* 47, 48, 49, 65
Fish v. Wilcox, 39
Freitas v. O'Brien, 44
Goevelt v. Burnell, 33
Gold v. Essex County Council, 38
Gold v. Haringey Health Authority,
  39, 43
*Goodwill v. British Pregnancy
  Advisory Service,* 39
*Greaves & Co. (Contractors) Ltd v.
  Baynham Meikle & Partners,* 35
Greenfield v. Irwin, 35, 40
Gregg v. Scott, 37, 50, 64
Grenville v. College of Physicians, 33
Hardman v. Amin, 41
Harnett v. Fisher, 8
Hatcher v. Black, 27
*Heath v. West Berkshire Health
  Authority,* 143
Hills v. Potter, 44
*Hillyer v. The Governors of St
  Bartholomew's Hospital,* 38, 64
*Hotson v. East Berkshire Health
  Authority,* 35, 49
Hucks v. Cole, 43
Hunt v. NHS Litigation Authority, 45
*Jones v. Berkshire Area Health
  Authority,* 39

Jones v. Randall, 39
Knight v. West Kent Health
    Authority, 45
Lanphier v. Phipos, 37
Lee v. Taunton and Somerset NHS
    Trust, 41
Lloyds Bank v. Savory & Co, 43
Luxmoore-May v. Messenger May
    Baverstock, 43
M v. Blackpool Victoria Hospital
    NHS Trust, 45
MacDonald v. Glasgow Western
    Hospital Board of Management
    and Another, 38
Marriott v. West Midlands Health
    Authority, 45
Marshall v. Lindsey County Council,
    38, 43
Maynard v. West Midlands Regional
    Health Authority, 44, 62
McFarlane v. Tayside Health Board
    (Scottish case applied in
    English law), 17, 35, 39–41, 64
McKay v. Essex Area Health
    Authority, 18, 154
Morris v. West Hartlepool Steam
    Navigation Co., 62
Nettleship v. Weston, 42
Newell and Newell v. Goldberg, 43
Parkinson v. St James and Seacroft
    Hospital NHS Trust, 40, 41
Pearce v. United Bristol Healthcare
    NHS Trust, 45
Pepper v. Hart, 150
Pittman Estate v. Bain, 35
R v. Adomako, 36
Rand v. East Dorset Health
    Authority, 41
Ratcliffe v. Plymouth and Torbay
    Health Authority, 47
Rees v. Darlington Memorial NHS
    Trust, 35, 40, 41
Reynolds v. Health First Medical
    Group, 35
Reynolds v. North Tyneside Health
    Authority, 45
Rich v. Pierpont, 37
Richardson v. Mellish, 39

Riebl v. Hughes, 63
Robertson v. Nottingham Health
    Authority, 38
Robinson v. Salford Health
    Authority, 39
Roe v. Minister of Health, 16, 38, 64
Rogers v. Whittaker, 63
Rondel v. Worsley, 29
Roylance v. GMC, 34
Ruscillo v. Council for Regulation of
    Health Care Professionals, 34
Salih v. Enfield Health Authority, 39
Searle v. Prentice, 36
Shakoor v. Situ, 45
Sidaway v. Board of Governors of
    the Royal Bethlem Hospital, 11,
    44, 63
Skyrne v. Butolf, 36
Smith v. Martin and the Corporation
    of Kingston-upon-Hull, 38
Strangeways-Lesmere v. Clayton, 38
Stratton v. Swanlord, 36
Thake v. Maurice, 35, 36, 39
Townsend v. Worcester District
    Health Authority, 46
Udale v. Bloomsbury Area Health
    Authority, 39
Walkin v. South Manchester Health
    Authority, 39
Watson v. British Boxing Board of
    Control, 37
White v. Chief Constable of South
    Yorkshire, 40
Whitehouse v. Jordan, 34–47
Wilsher v. Essex Health Authority,
    14, 42, 47, 49, 65
X v. Bedfordshire County Council, 38
English and Welsh statute law
    Chiropractors Act 1994, 33
    Congenital Disabilities (Civil
        Liability) Act 1976, 18
    Dentists Act 1984, 33
    Human Rights Act 1998, 33
    Medical Act 1858 and 1983, 33
    Nurses, Midwives and Health
        Visitors Act 1997, 33
    Nursing and Midwifery Order 2001,
        33

English and Welsh statute law (*cont.*)
  Opticians Act 1989, 33
  Osteopaths Act 1993, 33
  Pharmacy Act 1954, 33
  Unfair Contract Terms Act 1977, 35
Erle CJ, 37, 42
error versus fault, in France, 101
ethical codes. *See* codes of conduct and
    disciplinary bodies
European Convention on Human
    Rights (ECHR), 21
European Court of Justice, 23
European Legal Development (ELD)
    Project, 1, 2, 23, 146
European Social Agenda, 2005 to 2010,
    23
European Union (EU)
  harmonisation of medical liability
    law across, 21–3, 25–6, 158, 185
  informed consent in, 11
  Nordic patient insurance scheme,
    EU interest in, 21, 157
  proof of medical liability in, 14
  services liability in, 14, 22
euthanasia in the Netherlands, 139
evidence of medical liability. *See* proof
    of medical liability
exemption/exclusion clauses, 18–19
  in Austria, 18–19
  in Germany, 132, 134, 138, 157
  in the Netherlands, 18, 156–7
  in Spain, 184
expert witnesses, 7, 24
  in England and Wales, 11, 37, 43,
    45–6, 47
  in France, 102
  in Scotland, 62–3

Farwell LJ, 38
fault liability
  in Austria, 121–3, 128
  in England and Wales, 37, 38
  error versus fault, in France, 101
  in France (*See under* France)
  gross fault (*faute lourde*) versus
    ordinary fault, 5, 11, 24
  proof of fault generally required for
    finding of liability, 14

in Spain, 162, 164, 170, 176–8, 186
standard of care, 11
Faure, Michael, 2
Ferguson, Quintana, 165
Fernández Costales, Javier, 167
Fernández Hierro, José Manuel, 167
Finland, 1
  claim rate, 3
  patient insurance in, 19–20.
    (*See also* Nordic patient
    insurance scheme)
  patients' rights in, 158
France, 70
  administrative law in, 72, 80–2,
    89–92
  aléa thérapeutique cases, 90–1, 95,
    99
  American litigation culture, critique
    of, 92
  bacterial infections contracted
    on medical premises, strict
    liability for, 93–4, 99
  causation, 83, 84, 104
  Civil Code
    on contract law, 71
    on informed consent, 103
    on liability limitations, 71
    on negligence, 78
    on product liability, 100
    strict liability for damage by
      objects or things in, 84
    on tort law, 71, 78, 79
  claim rate, 3
  codes of conduct and disciplinary
    bodies in, 7, 75–6
  conciliation service, 73, 76, 88, 95,
    97, 98
  contract law in, 6, 71, 73, 80
  criminal versus civil liability in, 5,
    11, 73–5, 79
  damages, measure of, 17
  England and Wales compared, 101–2
  error versus fault, 101
  expert witnesses in, 102
  fault liability in, 70
    administrative law, 80–2
    criminal cases, 74
    current role of, 98–101

error versus fault, 101
historical development of, 78, 106-7
public versus private health systems, 71
reasons for evolution of, 84-9
shift towards strict liability, 82
significant developments in 1990s, 89-92
statutory compensation scheme and, 73, 93, 95, 98-101
wrongful life/wrongful birth, 106
historical background to medical liability in, 8, 77-98
immunity claims in, 77
increase in number of claims in, 86, 92
industrial accident liability compared to medical liability in, 84
informed consent in, 79, 100, 102
limitations periods, 71, 96
loss of chance doctrine, 83, 103-4
medical liability insurance
availability of, 85
bacterial infections, strict liability for, 94
private practitioners required to have, 94, 95
public hospitals required to obtain, 81
statutory insurance scheme, responsibilities under, 95, 96
negligence, 77-80, 83, 101-2
Netherlands influenced by, 132, 134
ONIAM (Office National d'indemnisation des accidents médicaux, des affections iathrogènes et des infections nosocomiaux), 3
patients' rights in, 5, 87-8, 158
personal liability in, 72-3
product liability in, 94, 99-100
public versus private health systems in, 4, 70-2
res ipsa loquitur (prima facie negligence), 101

responsible parties in, 16, 72-3
Spain, influence on, 174
standard of care in, 11, 13
statutory compensation scheme, 73, 93-101
availability of insurance and development of, 85
claims made under, 96-7
effect on compensation of victims, 97-8
fault liability and, 73, 93, 95, 98-101
insurers' responsibilities under, 95, 96
legislation establishing, 93
procedure for obtaining compensation under, 95-6
serious medical accidents, guarantee of compensation for, 93-5
strict liability
bacterial infections contracted on medical premises, 93-4, 99
reasons for evolution towards, 84-9
shift towards, 82
significant developments in 1990s, 89-92
statutory compensation scheme, effect of, 99
tort law in, 6, 71, 73, 78, 79
vicarious liability in, 72-3
wrongful life/wrongful birth, 17, 21, 104
Fraser, Lord, 35
French case law
Bailly case, 90
Bianchi case, 91
Cohen case, 90
Mercier case, 6, 8, 71, 80
Perruche case, 17, 25, 92, 105-6, 148, 154
French statute law
Law of 9 April 1898, 84
Law of 5 April 1928, 86
Law of 13 July 1930, 85
Law of 21 December 1941, 86
Law of 31 December 1970, 88

French statute law (*cont.*)
  French Product Liability Act 1988,
    94
  Law of 19 May 1998, 94
  Law of 10 July 2000, 74
  Law of 4 March 2002, 2, 25, 70, 71,
    73, 75, 88, 93, 103, 104, 105
  Law of 30 December 2002, 73, 94
  Law of 13 August 2004, 76

Gaius, 58
García Rubio, María Paz, 160
General Medical Council (GMC), UK,
  33, 57
General Medical Service (GMS)
  agreements in UK, 31
Germany
  claim rate, 3
  criminal versus civil liability, 5, 11
  damages for wrongful life/wrongful
    birth, 17
  exemption/exclusion clauses, 19,
    132, 134, 138, 157
  informed consent in, 138
  Netherlands influenced by, 132, 134,
    138, 157
  Nordic patient insurance scheme,
    interest in, 21
  personality rights in constitutional
    law, 5
  standard of care in, 11, 13
Glegg, A. T., 59
global harmonisation of medical
  liability, 23
GMC (General Medical Council), UK,
  33, 57
GMS (General Medical Service)
  agreements in UK, 31
González Morán, Luis, 167, 168
Great Britain. *See* England and Wales;
  Scotland
grievance committees in the
  Netherlands, 140
gross negligence. *See* negligence
Guthrie, Lord, 60

Hale, Baroness, 49
Hale LJ, 40

harmonisation of medical liability law
  across Europe, 21–3, 25–6, 158,
  185
Hartkamp, Dutch Advocate-General,
  149
Harvard Medical Practice Study, 2
Haute Autorité de Santé, France, 76
historical background to medical
  liability, 8–10
Hoffmann, Lord, 48
Holland. *See* Netherlands
Hondius, Ewoud, 1, 132, 161
Hope, Lord, 41, 49
hospitals
  in Austria, 109, 112, 116–17
  France, fault in administrative law
    in, 80–2
  in the Netherlands, 138, 144, 146
  in Spain, 4, 164, 168, 181
  standard of care, institutional, 13,
    144
  vicarious liability of (*See* vicarious
    liability)
human dignity, 154–6

ICAS (Independent Complaints and
  Advocacy Service), UK, 32, 56
immunity claims, in France, 77
Independent Complaints and
  Advocacy Service (ICAS), UK,
  32, 56
Independent Healthcare Association,
  UK, 57
informed consent, 11–12
  in Austria, 118–21, 125
  in England and Wales, 44, 48–9, 50,
    138
  in France, 79, 100, 102
  in the Netherlands, 138–9, 143, 147
  in Spain, 163, 166, 167, 175, 177,
    179–80, 182–3, 186
insurance
  institutional standard of care for,
    144
  medical liability insurance
    in Austria, 111
    in France (*See under* France)
    in Spain, 184–5

Nordic scheme (*See* Nordic patient insurance scheme)
private health insurance
   in Austria, 111
   in England and Wales, 31
   Netherlands, compulsory private insurance in, 4, 133
   in Scotland, 55, 57
Izquierdo Tolsada, Mariano, 167

Japan's interest in Nordic patient insurance scheme, 157
joint liability
   in the Netherlands, 146
   in Spain, 181
jurisdictional conflicts. *See* administrative law; criminal liability; public versus private health systems and legal coverage
Justinian, Institutes, 58

Koch, Bernhard A., 2, 108
Koninklijke Nederlandse Maatschappij voor de Geneeskunst, 141, 142
Koziol, Helmut, 2

Landelijke Patinten/Consumenten Platform, Netherlands, 142
Leenen, Hank, 11, 25, 137
lex artis ad hoc, 174, 175, 177
licensing of physicians, 33
limitations periods, in France, 71, 96
living wills in the Netherlands, 139
Llamas Pombo, Eugenio, 167
loss of chance doctrine
   in France, 83, 103–4
   in the Netherlands, 158
   in Spain, 182
Luxembourg Declaration on Patient Safety, 22

Making Amends (Chief Medical Officer report, UK), 51–3
manslaughter in England and Wales, 36
Marañón, Gregorio, 165
market share liability, concept of, 149
Mas Oliver, Dr, 162

McCall Smith, A., 46
McNair J, 42–4, 61
MDDUS (Medical and Dental Defence Union of Scotland), 55, 66
measure of damages. *See* damages
mediation
   in England and Wales, 51
   in Scotland, 57
Medical and Dental Defence Union of Scotland (MDDUS), 55, 66
medical devices left in patients' bodies after surgery, 15, 82, 145
medical liability, 1–3
   causation (*See* causation)
   claims data and rates, 3
   codes of conduct and disciplinary bodies, 7
   constitutional law, role of, 5
   contract law on (*See* contract law)
   countries selected for study of, 1
      See also (Austria; England and Wales; France; Netherlands; Scotland; Spain)
   criminal versus civil liability, 5
   damages for (*See* damages)
   EU, across (*See* European Union)
   evidence of (*See* proof of medical liability)
   exclusion of/exemption from (*See* exemption/exclusion clauses)
   global harmonisation of, 23
   historical background, 8–10
   insurance against (*See under* insurance)
   legislative proposals to manage, 9
   patient insurance for (*See* Nordic patient insurance scheme)
   patients' rights (*See* patients' rights)
   proof of (*See* proof of medical liability)
   public versus private (*See* public versus private health systems and legal coverage)
   purpose or aim of, controversy regarding, 10
   reasons for changes and developments in, 23–5
   reporting requirements, 10

medical liability (*cont.*)
  responsible parties, 15–16
  scope of present study, 2
  standard of care (*See* standard of
    care)
  tort law on (*See* tort law)
medical recordkeeping, importance of
  in Austria, 124
  in Netherlands, 140
  in Spain, 173
Merry, A., 46
Millett, Lord, 39, 41
misconduct, sanctioning. *See* codes
    of conduct and disciplinary
    bodies
Montaner, Dr, 162
Montel, A., 166

Nathan, Lord, 28
National Health Service (NHS),
    England and Wales, 4, 30–1
National Health Service in Scotland
    (NHSiS), 4, 54–6
National Health Service Litigation
    Office (NHSLO), England, 3
National Institute for Health and
    Clinical Excellence (NICE),
    UK, 32, 56
negligence
  Austria, concept of wrongfulness in,
    117–18
  in England and Wales, 6, 36–7
  in France, 77–80, 83, 101–2
  prima facie (*See res ipsa loquitur*)
  in Scotland, 6, 57–62
  in Spain, 161, 164
Netherlands, 132–3
  arbitration in, 149
  causation in, 154
  Civil Code
    of 1838, 132, 134
    of 1992, 132, 135–6
    exclusion clauses, invalidity of, 18
    on exemption/exclusion clauses,
    156
    French influence on, 132, 134
    German influence on, 132, 134,
    157

informed consent in, 143
joint liability in, 146
patients' rights in, 158
responsible parties under, 16
standard of care in, 12, 143
wrongful life/wrongful birth, 148,
    149, 152, 155
codes of conduct and disciplinary
    bodies in, 136, 140
contract law in, 6, 25, 134–6, 137–8,
    146–56
criminal liability in, 149
damages, measure of, 16–17, 146
documentation, importance of, 140
euthanasia in, 139
exemption/exclusion clauses, 18,
    156–7
French influence on, 132, 134
German influence on, 132, 134, 138,
    157
grievance committees, 140
historical background to medical
    liability in, 8, 136
hospitals in, 138, 144, 146
informed consent in, 138–9, 143, 147
joint liability in, 146
living wills in, 139
loss of chance doctrine, 158
Nordic patient insurance scheme,
    interest in, 21
ordinary courts, public and private
    health care dealt with by, 5
patients' rights in, 11, 25, 133,
    137–41
personality rights in constitutional
    law, 5
privacy/confidentiality, patient right
    of, 140
private health insurance in, 4, 133
product liability in, 152
proof of medical liability in, 15, 145
public policy issues in, 152
responsible parties in, 16, 145, 151
standard of care in, 12, 13, 141–5
tort law in, 6, 25, 134–6, 137
wrongful life/wrongful birth, 16–17,
    22, 146–56
Netherlands case law

DES case, 148–53
*Flierman v. Stichting Katholieke
    Universiteit*, 147
Kelly case *(Leids Universitair
    Medisch Centrum v. Kelly
    Molenaar)*, 17, 22, 133, 147–8,
    153–6
Lindenbaum v. Cohen, 132, 137
Missing IUD case, 148
Nuboer case *(Aarts v. Nuboer)*, 145
Schepers v. De Bruijn, 145
Speeckaert v. Gradener, 141
Timmer v. Deutman, 145
Netherlands statute law
    Act on Medical Services,
        137–41, 146
NHS (National Health Service),
        England and Wales, 4, 30–1
NHS Quality Improvement Scotland
        (NHS QIS), 56
NHSiS (National Health Service in
        Scotland), 4, 54–6
NHSLO (National Health Service
        Litigation Office), England, 3
NICE (National Institute for Health
        and Clinical Excellence), UK,
        32, 56
Nichols, Lord, 49
no-fault compensation schemes
    Austria
        compensation funds, 116–17
        splitting liability in, 125–6
    England and Wales, proposals in,
        51–3
    France, statutory compensation
        scheme in *(See under* France)
    Scotland, proposals in, 69
    Spanish compensation fund, 184–5,
        187
Nordic patient insurance scheme,
        19–21
    claim rate, 3
    European interest in, 21, 157
    as major shift in practice, 2, 24
    use of references to, 1
Norway
    damages in wrongful life/wrongful
        birth, 17

patient insurance in (*See* Nordic
        patient insurance scheme)

*Office National d'indemnisation
        des accidents médicaux,
        des affections iathrogènes et
        des infections nosocomiaux*
        (ONIAM), France, 3, 96, 97, 98
ombudsman arrangements in Austria,
        115, 131
ONIAM (*Office National
        d'indemnisation des accidents
        médicaux, des affections
        iathrogènes et des infections
        nosocomiaux*), France, 3, 96,
        97, 98
Ordre des médecins, France, 7, 75
Oviedo Convention on Human Rights
        and Biomedicine, 21, 154–6,
        158, 172

Patient Advocacy Liaison Services
        (PALS), UK, 32
patient insurance. *See* Nordic patient
        insurance scheme
patient ombudsman arrangements in
        Austria, 115, 131
Patients' Association, UK, 10, 32, 56
patients' rights, 10–1
    in Austria, 114–16, 129
    in England and Wales, 10, 11, 31–4
    in France, 5, 87–8, 158
    in the Netherlands, 11, 25, 133,
        137–41
    personality rights in constitutional
        law, 5, 87–8
    in Scotland, 10
    in Spain, 172–3
PCTs (Primary Care Trusts) in UK,
        30–1, 32, 55
Pearson Committee, 51
Penneau, J., 82, 84, 85
Pennsylvania Project on Medical
        Liability, 2
personal liability
    in Austria, 126–7
    in France, 72–3
    in Spain, 181

Personal Medical Services (PMS)
    agreements in UK, 31
personality rights, 5, 87–8
PMS (Personal Medical Services)
    agreements in UK, 31
predisposition or precondition in
    patient, in Austria, 126
prima facie negligence. *See res ipsa
    loquitur*
Primary Care Trusts (PCTs) in UK,
    30–1, 32, 55
privacy, patient right of
    in the Netherlands, 140
    in Spain, 173
private systems. *See* public versus
    private health systems and
    legal coverage, and under
    insurance
Proculus, 58
product liability
    in France, 94, 99–100
    in the Netherlands, 152
professional bodies. *See* codes of
    conduct and disciplinary
    bodies
Project on Medical Liability,
    Pennsylvania, 2
proof of medical liability, 14
    in Austria, 123–6
    in England and Wales, 14
    fault (*See* fault liability)
    negligence (*See* negligence)
    in the Netherlands, 15, 145
    res ipsa loquitur (prima facie
        negligence) (*See res ipsa
        loquitur*)
    reversal of burden of, 14–15, 64–5,
        145, 176–8, 186
    in Scotland, 64–5
    in Spain, 14, 176–8, 186
public policy issues
    in England and Wales, 39, 50
    in the Netherlands, 152
    wrongful life/wrongful birth, 39
public versus private health systems
    and legal coverage, 1–3. *See
    also* subhead 'private health
    insurance', under insurance

in Austria, 4, 109–13
in England and Wales, 4, 30–1
in France, 4, 70–2
Netherlands, compulsory private
    insurance in, 4, 133
in Scotland, 4, 54–6
in Spain, 4, 5, 160, 164, 168, 169–70

Rang, Jaap, 11, 25, 137
record-keeping, importance of
    in Austria, 124
    in the Netherlands, 140
    in Spain, 173
Regional Conciliation and
    Compensation Commissions,
    France, 95–6
regulation of medical profession.
    See codes of conduct and
    disciplinary bodies
Reid, Lord, 47
reporting requirements, 10
res ipsa loquitur (prima facie
    negligence), 14, 15
    in England and Wales, 14, 47
    in France, 101
    in Scotland, 65
    Spain influenced by, 186
responsible parties, 15–16. *See also*
    joint liability; personal liability;
    vicarious liability
    in Austria, 126–8
    in England and Wales, 16
    in France, 16, 72–3
    in the Netherlands, 16, 145, 151
    in Spain, 180–1
reversal of burden of proof, 14–15,
    64–5, 145, 176–8, 186
risks, duty to inform patient of.
    See informed consent
Roca Juan, J., 166
Roman law, 58
Ross Report, Scotland, 66, 67, 68, 69

Saleilles, R., 84
Savatier, R., 87
Scarman, Lord, 12, 44
Scotland, 54–6
    causation in, 65

codes of conduct and disciplinary
    bodies in, 56–7
contract law in, 6, 58
costs/number of claims compared to
    England and Wales, 66–9
damages, measure of, 17, 66–9
duty of care/breach of duty, 63
England and Wales, cross-border
    assimilation with, 61–2, 63–4
expert witnesses in, 62–3
future of medical liability in, 69
historical background to medical
    liability in, 57–61
increase in number of claims, 66–7
mediation in, 57
negligence, 6, 57–62
no-fault compensation scheme
    proposals, 69
Nordic patient insurance scheme,
    interest in, 21
patients' rights in, 10
private health care in, 55, 57
proof of medical liability, 64–5
public health system (NHSiS or
    National Health Service in
    Scotland) in, 4, 54–6
res ipsa loquitur (prima facie
    negligence), 65
Ross Report, 66, 67, 68, 69
standard of care in, 12, 61–3
tort law in, 57–62
vicarious liability of hospitals, 64
wrongful life/wrongful birth, 17, 64
Scottish case law
    Aird v. Ramsay, 65
    Beasley v. Fife Health Board, 63
    Castell v. De Greef, 63
    Clark v. McLennan, 65
    Craig v. Glasgow Victoria and
        Leverndale Hospitals Board of
        Management, 65
    Crawford v. Campbell, 59
    Devaney v. Glasgow Health Board,
        65
    Devlin v. Ghosh, 64
    Dickson v. Hygienic Institute, 59, 63
    Dougan v. Lanarkshire Acute
        Hospitals NHS Trust, 61, 63

Duffy v. Lanarkshire Health Board,
    63
Edgar v. Lamont, 59
Fallone v. Lanarkshire Acute
    Hospitals NHS Trust, 64
Farquhar v. Murray, 59
Foote v. Greenock Hospital, 64
Fox v. Glasgow South Western
    Hospitals Board, 64
Gardner v. Ferguson, 58
Gerrard v. Royal Infirmary of
    Edinburgh NHS Trust, 60, 62,
    63
Gillespie v. Grampian Health Board,
    65
Goorkani v. Tayside Health Board, 62
Gordon v. Wilson, 63
Hayward v. Edinburgh Royal
    Infirmary Board of
    Management, 64
Honisz v. Lothian Health Board, 62,
    63
Hunter v. Hanley, 12, 42, 60–2, 64,
    66, 143
Kay's Tutor v. Ayrshire and Arran
    Health Board, 64
Kelly v. Sir Frank Mears and
    Partners, 65
Kenyon v. Bell, 60, 64
Lavelle v. Glasgow Royal Infirmary,
    38, 64
Littlejohn v. Ayrshire and Arran
    Health Board, 65
Macdonald v. Glasgow Western
    Hospitals Board of
    Management, 64
McFarlane v. Tayside Health Board
    (Scottish case applied in
    English law), 17, 35, 39–41, 64
McGhee v. National Coal Board, 47,
    48, 64, 65
Morris v. Caithness Hospitals, 64
Moyes v. Lothian Health Board, 61,
    62
Muir v. Grampian Health Board,
    61, 62
Murray v. Lanarkshire Acute
    Hospitals NHS Trust, 64

Scottish case law (*cont.*)
   Phillips v. Grampian Health Board,
      62
   Purves v. Landell, 59
   Reidford v. Magistrates of Aberdeen,
      38
   Simpson v. Allan, 59
   Toner v. McLeod, 64
   Urquhart v. Grigor, 59
   Wardlaw v. Bonnington Castings
      Ltd, 64
Scottish statute law
   National Health Service (Scotland)
      Act 1947, 54
   National Health Service (Scotland)
      Act 1978, 54
   Scotland Act 1998, 54
self-regulation of medical profession.
   See codes of conduct and
   disciplinary bodies
services liability in EU, 14, 22
Shifts in Compensation project, 2–3
Sieburgh, C. H., 154–6
social security regimes
   in Austria, 110–11
   England and Wales, NHS (National
      Health Service) in, 4, 30–1
   Scotland, NHSiS (National Health
      Service in Scotland) in, 4,
      54–6
Sorn, Lord, 59
Spain, 160–1
   administrative law in, 160, 164, 169,
      181
   causation in, 164, 178–80, 186
   Civil Code
      private health system cases
         governed by contract law of,
         170
         responsible parties in, 181
         vicarious liability in, 164
   codes of conduct and disciplinary
      bodies in, 171
   contract law in, 162, 170, 173–4, 176,
      181, 187
   criminal liability in, 5, 11, 161, 163,
      167, 170
   damages in, 181–4

disproportionate harm, doctrine of,
   177, 179, 186
documentation, importance of, 173
dynamic distribution of the proof,
   doctrine of, 178, 186
exemption/exclusion clauses in,
   184
fault liability in, 162, 164, 170, 176–8,
   186
French influence in, 174
historical background to medical
   liability in, 8, 161–8
   case law, 161–5, 185
   legal literature, 165–8, 185
hospitals in, 4, 164, 168, 181
increase in medical liability claims
   in, 160, 164, 169, 186
informed consent in, 163, 166, 167,
   175, 177, 179–80, 182–3, 186
joint liability in, 181
loss of chance doctrine in, 182
medical liability insurance in,
   184–5
negligence in, 161, 164
no-fault compensation fund in,
   184–5, 187
patients' rights in, 172–3
personal liability in, 181
privacy/confidentiality, patient right
   of, 173
proof of medical liability in, 14,
   176–8, 186
public versus private health systems
   and legal coverage in, 4, 5, 160,
   164, 168, 169–70
res ipsa loquitur (prima facie
   negligence), influence of, 186
responsible parties in, 180–1
standard of care in, 11, 174–5, 186
statistical information regarding,
   168–9
strict liability in, 170, 176, 178, 181,
   186
tort law in, 161, 170, 173–4, 176, 178,
   181, 187
vicarious liability in, 164, 169, 181
wrongful life/wrongful birth, 169,
   179, 183

Spanish statute law
  Ley 50/1980 (Insurance Contract
    Act), 184
  Ley 14/1986 (General Law of
    Health), 171, 172
  Ley 30/1992 (Administrative Law),
    165, 169, 181
  Ley 9/1993, 184
  Ley 29/1998, 170
  Ley 4/1999, 169
  Ley 41/2002, 172–3
  Ley 44/2003 (Regulation of Health
    Professionals), 171, 184
  Civil Procedure Law, 174, 178
  General Consumers Protection Act,
    170, 178
Spier, Jaap, 9
splitting liability in Austria, 125–6
standard of care, 11–14
  comparative law on, 13, 144
  in England and Wales, 11, 34–47
  evolution of, 25
  in France, 11, 13
  institutional, 13, 37–8
  in Netherlands, 12, 13, 141–5
  in Scotland, 12, 61–3
  small jurisdictions and, 12–13,
    143–4
  in Spain, 11, 174–5, 186
Starck, B., 85
Steyn, Lord, 40, 41
Strategic Health Authorities in UK,
    30–1, 32
strict liability
  in France (*See under* France)
  in Spain, 170, 176, 178, 181, 186
Swain, Warren, 27
Sweden
  claim rate, 3
  patient insurance in (*See* Nordic
    patient insurance scheme)
Switzerland, institutional standard of
    care in, 14, 145

Taylor, Simon, 70
technological change and medical
    liability, 23
Tindal CJ, 37

tort law, 6–7
  in Austria, 113
  in England and Wales, 6, 7, 37
  in France, 6, 71, 73, 78, 79
  in Netherlands, 6, 25, 134–6, 137
  in Scotland, 57–62
  in Spain, 161, 170, 173–4, 176, 178,
    181, 187
Trigo García, Belén, 160

Ulpian, 58
United Kingdom. *See* England and
    Wales; Scotland
United States
  contract versus tort law, 51
  discovery in, 14
  early development of medical
    negligence law in, 1, 8
  English rise in medical liability
    claims compared to, 28
  French critique of litigation culture
    of, 92
  informed consent, American origins
    of, 138
  legislative proposals to manage
    medical liability in, 9
  licensing of physicians in, 33
  market share liability, concept of,
    149
  Netherlands not influenced by,
    136
  Patient Safety and Quality
    Improvement Act of 2004, 10
  reporting requirements in, 10
  Sindell v. Abbott Laboratories,
    149
Universal Declaration of Human
    Rights 1948, 87

Van Gerven, Walter, 17, 148
vicarious liability
  in Austria, 113, 126–8
  in England and Wales, 37–8
  in France, 72–3
  in Scotland, 64
  in Spain, 164, 169, 181
Viney, Geneviève, 6, 85
virtual fault, 82

Whitty, Niall R., 54
WHO (World Health Organization),
    23
Willcock, John, 37
Winiger, B., 2
Wissink, M. H., 154
Woolf, Lord, 28, 29, 45
World Health Organization (WHO), 23
wrongful life/wrongful birth
    abortion and, 147, 154, 155
    changes wrought to medical liability
        concepts by, 25
    damages in, 16–18, 146–56
    DES (diethylstilbestrol) cases,
        148–53

in England and Wales, 18, 38–42
EU harmonisation, feasibility of,
    21–2
in France, 17, 21, 104
in the Netherlands, 16–17, 22,
    146–56
Oviedo Convention on Human
    Rights and Biomedicine, 154–6
public policy issues, 39
in Scotland, 64
in Spain, 169, 179, 183
wrongfulness as medical liability
    concept in Austria, 117–18

Zimmermann, R., 2